CONTINUITIES IN THE STUDY OF
SOCIAL CONFLICT

LEWIS A. COSER

Continuities

IN THE STUDY OF

Social Conflict

 THE FREE PRESS, New York
COLLIER-MACMILLAN LIMITED, London

First Free Press Paperback Edition 1970
Library of Congress Catalog Card Number: 67–25330.

Printing number
1 2 3 4 5 6 7 8 9 10

For Rose, again

Acknowledgments

I would like to acknowledge the kindness of the editors and publishers of the following publications in permitting me the use of articles and papers that originally appeared, sometimes in a different form, in their pages:

Routledge, Kegan Paul Ltd., London, for "Social Conflict and the Theory of Social Change" from *The British Journal of Sociology*, VIII, 3 (Sept. 1953); the editors of *The Journal of Conflict Resolution*, for "The Termination of Conflict" in Vol. V, 4 (Dec. 1961) of that journal; Grune & Stratton, Inc., for "Violence and the Social Structure" from *Science and Psychoanalysis*, Vol. VI, edited by Jules Masserman, published by Grune & Stratton, New York, 1963, reprinted by permission; The American Academy of Political and Social Science, for "Some Social Functions of Violence" from *The Annals*, Vol. 364, March 1966; The University of Chicago Press, for "Some Functions of Deviant Behavior and Normative Flexibility," reprinted from *The American Journal of Sociology*, LXVIII, 2 (Sept. 1962), copyright © 1962 by The University of Chicago; "Durkheim's Conservatism and Its Implications for His Sociological Theory" is reprinted by permission from *Emile Durkheim, 1858–1917: A Collection of Essays, with Translations and a*

Bibliography, edited by Kurt H. Wolff, copyright © 1960 by the Ohio State University Press; The Society for the Study of Social Problems gave permission to reprint "The Dysfunctions of Military Secrecy" from *Social Problems,* XI, 1 (Summer 1963); the editors of *Dissent* gave permission for the reprinting of "Prospects for the New Nations," *Dissent,* X, 1 (Winter 1963), "The Breakup of the Soviet Camp," *Dissent,* XII, 2 (Spring 1965), "The Myth of Peasant Revolt," *Dissent,* XIII, 3 (May–June 1966).

"Karl Marx and Contemporary Sociology" was first presented as a contribution to a Presidential Session on Karl Marx at the Chicago meeting of the American Sociological Association in August, 1965. "Internal Violence as a Conflict Resolution Mechanism" was presented to the Sixth World Congress of Sociology at Evian, France, in September, 1966.

CONTENTS

ix

PART   III

CONFLICT THEORY AND CURRENT POLITICS   181

CONTINUITIES IN THE STUDY OF
SOCIAL CONFLICT

Introduction

WHEN THE FUNCTIONS OF SOCIAL CONFLICT[1] WAS PUB-
lished a little over a decade ago, I expressed the hope that it
would contribute to a revival of the then much neglected study
of social conflict, and that, more specifically, it would help revitalize the study of its functions, as distinct from its dysfunctions. The study attempted to codify and consolidate conceptual
schemes pertinent to data of social conflict and, by taking stock
of past contributions, to advance the formulation of future inquiries. Given the then prevalent emphasis on harmony and
equilibrium models of the social structure, it attempted to right
the balance of analysis by focusing attention on conflicting types
of interaction and by stressing the determinate functions of
social conflict in groups and interpersonal relations.

It is most pleasant to be able to record that in the mean-
time other sociologists have made significant contributions to
the study of social conflict that point in the same general
direction as my own work. This is not the place to list such

1. Lewis A. Coser, *The Functions of Social Conflict,* New York, The
Free Press, 1954.

works in detail, but at least a few major contributors to the development of theories of social conflict ought to be mentioned here.

While I was putting the finishing touches on my own book, Professor Max Gluckman of the University of Manchester gave a series of six lectures[2] in the spring of 1965 that were subsequently published under the title of *Custom and Conflict in Africa*.[3] When I read this book, while my own was in press, I was struck by the startling similarity in our respective approaches. It was especially gratifying to note that a social scientist, working in the main with anthropological materials from Africa, had come to theoretical conclusions very similar to my own. Using his own extensive fieldwork as a point of departure, Gluckman also built on the work of such leading British anthropologists as E. E. Evans-Pritchard, Elizabeth Colson, Meyer Fortes, and I. Schapera. The central thesis of the book involved an account of "how men quarrel in terms of certain of their customary allegiances, but are restrained from violence through other conflicting allegiances which are also enjoined on them by custom. The result is that conflicts in one set of relationship . . . . lead to re-establishment of social cohesion."[4]

This overall view was then illustrated by a series of brilliant analyses of African political systems, of conflicting kinship loyalties, of witchcraft, and of the ritual enactment of societal tensions. Gluckman further elaborated this approach in subsequent works, among which *Politics, Law, and Ritual in Tribal Society*[5] is especially noteworthy. In this book the

2. On the Third Program of the British Broadcasting Corporation.

3. Max Gluckman, *Custom and Conflict in Africa*, New York, The Free Press, 1956.

4. *Ibid.*, p. 2

5. Max Gluckman, *Politics, Law and Ritual in Tribal Society*, Chicago, Aldine Company, 1965.

perennial discussion as to the relative weight of societal change and societal equilibrium is handled in a very sensitive way. Gluckman refuses to consider these terms as polar opposites and argues instead that "as we see equilibrium in social systems . . . we deal with constant disturbance and change . . . . Disturbance and change of parts is inherent in these systems"[6]

Among specifically sociological contributions to the theory of social conflict, the work of the German sociologist Ralf Dahrendorf seems the most fertile and important. His *Soziale Klassen und Klassenkonflikt in der industriellen Gesellschaft,* first published in 1957 and translated, revised, and expanded in *Class and Class Conflict in Industrial Society*[7] is his most important contribution. Part Two, "Toward a Sociological Theory of Conflict in Industrial Society," although building on past theoretical works, contains a number of new leads. Here I can mention only one of these, the important distinction between two dimensions of social conflict, intensity, and violence. "Intensity refers to the energy expenditure and degree of involvement of conflicting parties . . . . By contrast . . . , the violence of conflict relates rather to its manifestations than to its causes; it is a matter of the weapons that are chosen . . . ."[8] The two, Dahrendorf stresses, may vary independently and are therefore distinct aspects of any conflict situation. Dahrendorf discusses specific situations in which either intensity or violence or both are minimized or increased. For example, organized conflict groups tend to use less violent means of combat than those that lack organization. These and other highly valuable analytical distinctions will no doubt have to be incorporated into any future codification of a general theory of social conflict.

6. *Ibid.,* p. 280.
7. Ralf Dahrendorf, *Class and Class Conflict in Industrial Society,* Stanford, Calif., Stanford University Press, 1959.
8. *Ibid.,* pp. 211–212.

After publishing the German version of his *Class and Class Conflict*, Dahrendorf continued his concern for the development of a theory of social conflict by publishing a series of papers among which, "Out of Utopia: Toward a Reorientation of Sociological Analysis"[9] and "Toward a Theory of Social Conflict"[10] are noteworthy. These and other pertinent papers were later collected in his book *Gesellschaft und Freiheit*.[11] Although I feel these papers are must reading for anyone concerned with the analysis of social conflict, I fear that Dahrendorf's polemical stances against Parsonian theorizing and what he considers functional theory has often led him to formulations that are unlikely to stand up well under analysis.

In particular, there has been a shift in the relative status of conflict theory in Dahrendorf's earlier and later work. He argued in his first book that we do not as yet have a sociological theory that can successfully integrate conceptions of social conflict and social consensus, hence sociologists must at present operate with separate theories of integration and conflict. Later, however, he stated that, "All social life is conflict, because it is change."[12] This smacks of pan-conflict imperialism, it seems a misguided effort to neglect relatively enduring structures and their analysis under the pretext that "everything is change." One is reminded of Heinrich Rickert's cool neo-Kantian reply to Georg Simmel's vitalistic philosophy: "Movement is a relational concept and presupposes an unmoved in relation to which something is moving."[13] To see all social life

9. *American Journal of Sociology,* LXIV, 2 (1958) pp. 115–127.
10. *The Journal of Conflict Resolution,* II, 2 (1958).
11. Ralf Dahrendorf, *Gesellschaft und Freiheit,* Munich, R. Piper and Co., 1961.
12. *Ibid.,* p. 235.
13. Quoted in Lewis A. Coser, ed., *Georg Simmel,* Englewood Cliffs, N. J., Prentice-Hall Inc. 1965, p. 23.

as change without paying attention to its source and outcome will turn out to be a stumbling block not only in the analysis of social structures but in the further development of the theory of conflict. Nor is it fruitful, as I will show later, to assert with Dahrendorf in his later work that coercion rather than consensus is the foundation of all social order.

Dahrendorf has criticized me for my alleged exclusive focus on the integrative functions of social conflict and my alleged neglect of those types of social conflict that disrupt social systems and lead to fundamental social change. I believe that this criticism is hardly justified, as a number of studies in this volume will testify. It is, however, amusing to note, in this context, that a British sociologist, John Rex, in his *Key Problems of Sociological Theory*,[14] criticizes Dahrendorf along with Gluckman and me for neglecting or underemphasizing large-scale disruptive conflicts. Further discussion of these important issues will have to be reserved for the next section of this Introduction.

Pierre van den Berghe in his "Dialectic and Functionalism: Toward a Theoretical Synthesis"[15] presents a valuable lead on how sterile oppositions as between conflict and stability, equilibrium and disequilibrium might profitably be overcome. He argues that both functionalism and the Hegelian-Marxian dialectic present one-sided but complementary and reconciliable views of society. He sees his effort as a prolegomenon to a theory of society "that achieves an adequate balance between stability and the various sources of endogenous and exogenous change, between consensus and conflict, and between equilibrium and disequilibrium."

14. John Rex, *Key Problems of Sociological Theory*, London, Routledge and Kegan Paul, 1961.

15. *American Sociological Review*, XXVIII, 5 (Oct. 1963) pp. 695–705.

Johan Galtung, of the University of Oslo, with whom I had the privilege of working during a six-month stay in Norway in 1961, for a number of years has concerned himself with a series of problems in the sociology of conflict. Most of his recent papers have been published in *The Journal of Peace Research* (Oslo) which he edits. Among these papers, his "A Structural Theory of Aggression"[16] seems of special relevance. There he presents the thesis that aggression between individuals, groups, and nations is most likely to arise when their respective social positions are in "rank-disequilibrium," that is, when individuals or groups have dissimilar ranks in different status dimensions so that they are "topdogs" in one dimension and yet "underdogs" in another. This conceptualization is applied to a variety of areas from the relations between nations to revolutions and deviant behavior. The paper is most stimulating and deserves to be better known among American sociologists.

Special mention must be made of a paper by Raymond W. Mack and Richard C. Snyder, "The Analysis of Social Conflict—Toward an Over-view and Synthesis."[17] This seems to me the best codification of theoretical and empirical work in the area of social conflict. Although a good deal has been written since it appeared, it remains indispensable to any student in this field of inquiry.

I shall not comment here on a variety of studies that attempt to advance the theory of conflict through game theory or other mathematical models. I have profited from reading

16. *The Journal of Peace Research,* I, 2 (1964) pp. 95–115. Cf. also Johan Galtung, "Rank and Social Integration" in Joseph Berger *et al,* ed., *Sociological Theories in Progress,* Boston, Houghton Mifflin Co. 1966.

17. *The Journal of Conflict Resolution,* I, 2 (June 1957) pp. 212–248.

such books as Kenneth Boulding's *Conflict and Defense*,[18] Thomas Schelling's *The Strategy of Conflict*[19] and Anatol Rapoport's *Fight, Games, and Debates*.[20] I have had occasion to quote some of these works in the pages that follow, but I am not yet convinced that these approaches have been particularly fruitful in the development of a *sociological* theory of social conflict.

Raymond Mack has recently argued that "Coser's *The Functions of Social Conflict* runs the risk of being accorded that peculiar form of academic obeisance in which a work is cited by everyone and heeded by no one."[21] Mack especially deplored the lack of empirical work informed by conflict theory. His strictures appear to me a bit too severe. There have been significant empirical as well as theoretical developments since my book was written. James Coleman's unpretentious study *Community Conflict*,[22] for example, represents a valuable attempt to test a set of general theoretical propositions in empirical analysis. He studied a series of conflicts over fluoridation in a variety of communities in order to "lay bare the processes underlying community controversy." His analysis contributes significantly to an understanding of the conditions under which controversies may escalate and move from initially limited and peripheral issues to fundamental conflicts attacking the basis of community consensus.

Although I believe that some progress has been made, I

18. Kenneth Boulding, *Conflict and Defense,* New York, Harper and Row, 1962.

19. Thomas Schelling, *The Strategy of Conflict,* Cambridge, Harvard University Press, 1960.

20. Anatol Rapoport, *Fights, Games, and Debates,* Ann Arbor, The University of Michigan Press, 1960.

21. Raymond W. Mack, "The Components of Social Conflict," *Social Problems* XXII, 4 (Spring 1965) pp. 388–397.

22. James Coleman, *Community Conflict,* New York, The Free Press, 1957.

do to some extent share some of Raymond Mack's disappointment when I note that my own work as well as that of the others discussed above has not yet led to the initiation of more empirical studies. There have been a few attempts to follow these leads in small-group research and a few anthropological studies have been specifically guided by hypotheses advanced by conflict theorists.[23] Students of race relations have, for fairly obvious reasons, felt the need to pay more attention to social conflict theory.[24] But the empirical testing of this theory in sustained inquiries seems to me yet rather neglected.

II

Before proceeding to comment on the essays that form the bulk of this book, I should like to raise a general issue already adumbrated in the preceding brief review of current literature. There has recently been the tendency among a number of writers to advance the thesis that sociological theory should be reconstructed by replacing a consensus theory of society, which they feel currently dominant, by a coercion or conflict theory.[25] In the words of one of them, they contend that "Coercion, conflict, and change do seem, on balance, to be more basic societal attributes than consensus and equilib-

23. See for example, Robert F. Murphy, "Intergroup Hostility and Social Cohesion" *American Anthropologist*, 59, 6 (December 1957), pp. 1018–1033, and Chandra Jayawardena, *Conflict and Solidarity in a Guianese Plantation*, London, The Athlone Press, 1963.

24. Cf., for example, Lewis Killian and Charles Grigg, *Racial Crisis in America*, Englewood Cliffs, N.J., Prentice-Hall Inc., 1964, and Joseph S. Hines, "The Functions of Racial Conflict," *Social Forces, 45,* 1 (September 1966) pp. 1–10.

25. See in particular, John Horton, "Order and Conflict Theories of Social Problems as Competing Ideologies" and Bert N. Adams, "Coercion and Consensus Theories: Some Unresolved Issues" in *American Journal of Sociology,* LXXI, 6 (May 1966) pp. 701–713 and pp. 714–717.

rium."[26] I fear that such an approach is profoundly misleading. I do not think that it can be shown that factors that make for societal conflict are more "fundamental" elements of historical and social processes than those creating an underlying harmony, nor are events and behavior that contribute to harmony more "essential" elements of social life. In fact, the very way the question is formulated seems to me metaphysical rather than scientific. One should have thought that sociologists had long abandoned the illusory quest for the "real" and "basic" and "fundamental" essence of the social, and for first and final causes, in favor of the more mundane but more rewarding task of establishing social uniformities and accounting for the operation of social structures and processes. I fully agree with Robin Williams who recently wrote in a spirited rebuttal of such views, that, "Actual societies are held together by consensus, by interdependence, by sociability, and by coercion. . . . The real job is to show how actual social structures and processes operating in these ways can be predicted and explained."[27]

When one refers to conflict theory or integration theory one does not, or should not, consider them rival explanatory systems like, say, Ptolemaic astronomy versus Copernican. They are partial theories sensitizing the students to one or another set of data relevant to a full theoretical explanation. In the last analysis there can be only one overall sociological theory even though it consists of sets of partial theories of the middle range considered important for the illumination of this or that particular social dimension. Just as sophisticated political theory has long abandoned the fruitless discussion as to whether consent or coercion is the "real basis" of government; just as psychology

26. *Ibid.* p. 717.
27. Robin Williams, Jr., "Some Further Comments on Chronic Controversies" *American Journal of Sociology,* LXXI, 6 (May 1966) pp. 717–721.

has long abandoned the vain quest of deciding whether nature or nurture is the main determinant of personality; so sociology should be mature enough to leave aside such fruitless lines of inquiry. A mature political theory is aware that consent *and* coercion are at the basis of the political order; a mature psychology is aware of the indissoluble and intricate interplay of nature *and* nurture in the determination of psychological phenomena. It would be a regressive step indeed were sociology to revert at this stage to such primitive and fruitless dichotomizing. It seems high time finally to realize that whenever we deal with temporary equilibria it behooves us to investigate the peculiar conflicting forces that led to their establishment in the first place. Conversely, we must be sensitized to the fact that wherever there is conflict or disruption there will be social forces that press toward the establishment of some new kind of equilibrium.

In the pages that follow, reference is sometimes made to the analytical shortcomings of certain harmony or consensus models now widely prevalent in the social sciences. Let it be clearly understood that such criticism is not meant to imply that these should be superseded and supplanted by conflict models. I only wish to warn students of the one-sidedness of such models, not of their disutility. As I argue in the paper on Karl Marx, "Concentration on one set of variables, although it may be exceedingly valuable and productive of insights, always carries with it the inherent danger of wittingly or unwittingly slighting the importance of others." There lurks the danger that social theorists mistake their logically closed system of theory for an empirically closed system.[28] This is why it seems necessary to attempt to determine the way in which preponderant emphasis on one or the other set of variables may hinder the full under-

28. Talcott Parsons, *The Structure of Social Action*, New York, The Free Press, 1949, p. 476.

standing of the operation of a social system even as it may illuminate some of its aspects. Conflict theory, as I understand it, aims at the explanation of certain variables neglected in other theorizing. It is not meant to supplant the analysis of other social processes.

III

The papers collected in this volume were not originally written as part of a systematic plan to publish a book in the field of social conflict. They emerged out of a variety of theoretical or practical considerations and responed to specific preoccupations at different moments in time. Yet I flatter myself in believing that they exhibit a certain unity of outlook and conception and that this book can be read now as a relatively unified whole. Papers previously published have been changed but slightly for inclusion in these pages. All the essays collected here grew out of the attempt to develop more fully one or the other aspect or facet of ideas first adumbrated in *The Functions of Social Conflict*. Some papers, as "Social Conflict and Social Change" and "Some Functions of Deviant Behavior and Normative Flexibility," attempt further theoretical elaboration; whereas others such as the three interrelated papers on violence and the papers on current politics illustrate the uses of conflict theory in the explanation of concrete events on the social scene. I have attempted in all the essays printed here to bring the earlier theory up to date by the incorporation of new findings and ideas.

The essays presented in this book have been grouped in three parts: (1) The Functions of Social Conflict Revisited, (2) Social Theory and Social Conflict, and (3) Conflict Theory and Current Politics. The first part presents material intended to supplement and to extend theoretical findings and analyses first published in my earlier book. Thus the paper "Social Conflict and Social Change," which was actually written at the same time as the book, is intended to supplement the analysis of changes *within* social systems, with which the book was mainly concerned, to the analysis of changes *of* social systems. Its analytical focus is upon instances in which social systems are unable to contain social conflicts within their boundaries so that these conflicts eventually burst these boundaries and lead to the establishment of new social systems. The paper "The Termination of Conflict," as its title implies, is more particularly concerned with those institutionalized and normative factors that help to bring a conflict to an end. It is focused on the structural conditions that foster or impede the transformation of potentially infinite processes of conflict into finite and regulated contentions whose end-points can be specified and recognized by the contenders.

The three interrelated papers on violence attempt to apply a number of earlier general conceptualizations to the type of conflicts that is marked by violence. "Violence and the Social Structure" deals more particularly with the social determinants of homicidal and other criminal violence; whereas "Some Social Functions of Violence" and the companion paper "Internal Violence as a Mechanism for Conflict Resolution" discuss certain functions of mass violence in crowd behavior such as riots, revolutions, and the like. The last paper in this part, "Some Functions of Deviant Behavior and Normative Flexibility," aims at building some bridges between current theorizing in deviance and a theory of social conflict. It is meant to counteract the popular view that deviance is necessarily dysfunctional for the social structures in which it occurs and stresses the latent functional contributions of the deviant role. It distinguishes criminal deviance from nonconformist deviant behavior and assesses the functional impact on various group structures of conflicts between conforming and nonconforming individuals or groups.

The second part of the book, "Social Theory and Social Conflict," consists of a critical examination of two seminal sociological thinkers, Emile Durkheim and Karl Marx, from the point of view of conflict theory. The Durkheim paper specifies how his disregard of the notion of conflict led him to neglect significant areas of social structures so as to impair his overall vision of the nature of the social. The chapter on Karl Marx has an obverse purpose in so far as it means to indicate how modern sociology is impoverished by not paying sufficient attention to Marx's self-conscious focus on social conflict.

The third part of this volume, "Conflict Theory and Current politics," consists of a variety of essays all of which attempt to utilize previously developed theoretical perspectives in the elucidation of a series of current political problems. "Prospects for the New Nations" represents an assessment of the chances of these nations to build relatively stable democratic systems, if not in the immediate future, then at least in the long run. The focus here is on the degree to which power is centralized or decentralized in these polities. It stresses the functional importance of conflicts between a variety of subgroups for creating democratic structures, and assesses the chances of criss-crossing allegiances eventually breaking through the crust of centralized authoritarian control. The related essay, "Frantz Fanon's Myth of the Peasant Revolution," is a critical examination of the work of perhaps the most original thinker that the anti-colonial movement in the new nations has so far produced. The paper is especially concerned with Fanon's thesis that the world's peasantry rather than the proletariat now constitute the major revolutionary potential in the former colonial territories and discusses Fanon's myth of the regenerative virtues of violence. "The Breakup of the Soviet Camp" deals with the present confrontation between the Soviet Union and China and suggests reasons why monolithic Communist power has been fragmented into a variety of contending and conflicting polycentric communist nations. The final chapter, "The Dysfunctions of Military Secrecy," discusses the current super-power confrontation on the international scene and raises questions as to the part played by military secrecy in the escalation of these conflicts. It suggests that an elimination of secrecy between these powers and a "politics of disclosure" may be one promising avenue for decreasing tensions and one of the ways by which conflicts between them may be de-escalated.

I

THE FUNCTIONS OF
SOCIAL CONFLICT REVISITED

1

Social Conflict and the Theory of Social Change

This paper was written at the same time as and was meant to supplement, *The Functions of Social Conflict.* Whereas problems of social change were only touched in a peripheral way in that book, they are at the center of attention in the present essay.

This chapter attempts to move beyond the trite and theoretically unrewarding assertion that social life always involves change. I am making an attempt to distinguish between the perpetual slow movement of change that marks the course of even the most static types of societies and profound and deep-going changes that give birth to new social systems after the breakup and dissolution of an old social order.

Parsons' distinction between change *within* and change *of* systems proved helpful in this respect and points to an analogy with linguistic changes. Though linguistic structures are highly formalized and standardized, a language never stands still since it must deal with an ever-changing environment. "A language full of archaisms of content and structure would not only give an over-simple and distorted conception of the world as it is; it would also lead to functional strains and tensions. There needs to be 'linguistic spontaneity,' 'plasticity,' 'flexibility'."* For language

* Joyce D. Hertzler, *A Sociology of Language*, New York, Random House, 1966, p. 141.

17

to remain an effective tool, it must not be frozen. Yet linguistic changes will often encounter resistance, be it from grammarians, lexicographers, or others with vested interests in proper usage and established rules. These must be overcome in the process of linguistic adaptation, but they are likely to be overcome at uneven rates and with an uneven tempo in different elements of linguistic structure. Changes in speech habits come fairly fast, but are only slowly incorporated into the standardized linguistic system. Changes in vocabulary are frequent, but the phonetic system and the morphological structure may change only at a glacial speed.* Too abrupt and rapid changes of language would disorient and dislocate the very thought styles of a community and interfere with its customary ways of structuring the world of experience. Too slow changes, on the other hand, would petrify thought and render it functionally inadequate to deal with new experience.

Although the analogy with language structure holds for changes *within* the social systems, it is more difficult to apply it to changes *of* social systems, be it only because "linguistic revolution" is a much rarer phenomenon than social revolution. Yet even here one can think of the relatively rapid way in which various romance languages evolved from common Latin roots into separate linguistic systems. In these cases, it may be impossible to tell at which precise moment the language moved from a variation of Latin to the emergence of a new language; yet there is a point at which there is no doubt that we are dealing with French or Spanish rather than with a variety of Latin. As in languages, so too in social systems. Even though it may be difficult to pinpoint the exact time at which one social system has been transformed into another, we can talk of changes *of* social systems when all major structural relations, basic institutions, and prevailing value systems have been transformed.

In this chapter, an attempt is made to specify the structural conditions under which social conflicts lead to inner adjustments of social systems or to the breakup of existing social orders and the emergence of a new set of social relations within a new social structure.

* *Ibid.*, p. 142ff.

THIS CHAPTER ATTEMPTS TO EXAMINE SOME OF THE functions of social conflict in the process of social change. I shall first deal with some functions of conflict *within* social systems, more specifically with its relation to institutional rigidities, technical progress, and productivity, and will then concern myself with the relation between social conflict and the changes *of* social systems.

A central observation of George Sorel in his *Reflections on Violence* which has not as yet been accorded sufficient attention by sociologists may serve as a convenient springboard. Sorel wrote:

> We are today faced with a new and unforeseen fact—a middle class which seeks to weaken its own strength. The race of bold captains who made the greatness of modern industry disappears to make way for an ultracivilized aristocracy which asks to be allowed to live in peace.
>
> The threatening decadence may be avoided if the proletariat hold on with obstinacy to revolutionary ideas. *The antagonistic classes influence each other in a partly indirect but decisive manner.* Everything may be saved if the proletariat, by their use of violence, restore to the middle class something of its former energy.[1]

Sorel's specific doctrine of class struggle is not of immediate concern here. What is important for us is the idea that conflict (which Sorel calls violence, using the word in a very special sense) prevents the ossification of the social system by exerting pressure for innovation and creativity. Though Sorel's call to action was addressed to the working class and its interests, he conceived it to be of general importance for the total social system; to his mind the gradual disappearance of class conflict might well lead to the decadence of European culture. A social

1. George Sorel, *Reflections on Violence*, ch. 2, par. 11.

system, he felt, was in need of conflict if only to renew its energies and revitalize its creative forces.

This conception seems to be more generally applicable than to class struggle alone. Conflict within and between groups in a society can prevent accommodations and habitual relations from progressively impoverishing creativity. The clash of values and interests, the tension between what is and what some groups feel ought to be, the conflict between vested interests and new strata and groups demanding their share of power, wealth, and status, have been productive of vitality; note for example the contrast between the "frozen world" of the Middle Ages and the burst of creativity that accompanied the thaw that set in with Renaissance civilization.

This is, in effect, the application of John Dewey's theory of consciousness and thought as arising in the wake of obstacles to the interaction of groups. "Conflict is the gadfly of thought. It stirs us to observation and memory. It instigates to invention. It shocks us out of sheep-like passivity, and sets us at noting and contriving. . . . Conflict is a *sine qua non* of reflection and ingenuity"[2]

Conflict not only generates new norms, new institutions, as I have pointed out elsewhere,[3] it may be said to be stimulating directly in the economic and technological realm. Economic historians often have pointed out that much technological improvement has resulted from the conflict activity of trade unions through the raising of wage levels. A rise in wages usually has led to a substitution of capital investment for labor and hence to an increase in the volume of investment. Thus the extreme mechanization of coal-mining in the United States has been

2. John Dewey, *Human Nature and Conduct,* New York, The Modern Library, 1930, p. 300.
3. Lewis A. Coser, *The Functions of Social Conflict,* New York, The Free Press, 1956.

partly explained by the existence of militant unionism in the American coalfields.[4] A recent investigation by Sidney C. Sufrin[5] points to the effects of union pressure, "goading management into technical improvement and increased capital investment." Very much the same point was made recently by the conservative British *Economist* which reproached British unions for their "moderation" which it declared in part responsible for the stagnation and low productivity of British capitalism; it compared their policy unfavorably with the more aggressive policies of American unions whose constant pressure for higher wages has kept the American economy dynamic.[6]

This point raises the question of the adequacy and relevancy of the "human relations" approach in industrial research and management practice. The "human relations" approach stresses the "collective purpose of the total organization" of the factory, and either denies or attempts to reduce conflicts of interests in industry.[7] But a successful reduction of industrial conflict may have unanticipated dysfunctional consequences for it may destroy an important stimulus for technological innovation.

It often has been observed that the effects of technological change have weighed most heavily upon the worker.[8] Both in-

4. Cf. McAlister Coleman, *Men and Coal,* New York, Farrar and Rinehart, 1943.

5. *Union Wages and Labor's Earnings,* Syracuse, Syracuse University Press, 1951.

6. Quoted by Will Herberg, "When Social Scientists View Labor," *Commentary,* Dec. 1951, XII, 6, pp. 590–6. See also Seymour Melman, *Dynamic Factors in Industrial Productivity,* Oxford, Blackwell, 1956, on the effects of rising wage levels on productivity.

7. See the criticism of the Mayo approach by Daniel Bell, "Adjusting Men to Machines," *Commentary,* Jan. 1947, pp. 79–88; C. Wright Mills, "The Contribution of Sociology to the Study of Industrial Relations," *Proceedings of the Industrial Relations Research Association,* 1948, pp. 199–222.

8. See, e.g., R. K. Merton, "The Machine, The Workers and The Engineer," *Social Theory and Social Structure,* New York, The Free Press,

formal and formal organization of workers represent in part an attempt to mitigate the insecurities attendant upon the impact of unpredictable introduction of change in the factory.[9] But by organizing in unions workers gain a feeling of security through the effective conduct of institutionalized conflict with management and thus exert pressure on management to increase their returns by the invention of further cost-reducing devices. The search for mutual adjustment, understanding, and "unity" between groups who find themselves in different life situations and have different life chances calls forth the danger that Sorel warns of, namely that the further development of technology would be seriously impaired.

The emergence of invention and of technological change in modern Western society, with its institutionalization of science as an instrument for making and remaking the world, was made possible with the gradual emergence of a pluralistic and hence conflict-charged structure of human relations. In the unitary order of the medieval guild system, "no one was permitted to harm others by methods that enabled him to produce more quickly and more cheaply than they. Technical progress took on the appearance of disloyalty. The ideal was stable conditions in a stable industry."[10]

In the modern Western world, just as in the medieval world, vested interests exert pressure for the maintenance of

---

1949, pp. 317–28; Georges Friedmann, *Industrial Society*, New York, 1956.

9. For informal organization and change, see Roethlisberger and Dickson, *Management and the Worker*, Cambridge, 1939, especially pp. 567–8; for formal organization, see Selig Perlman, *The Theory of the Labor Movement;* on general relations between technology and labor, see Elliot D. Smith and Richard C. Nyman, *Technology and Labor,* New Haven, Yale University Press, 1939.

10. Henri Pirenne, *Economic and Social History of Medieval Europe,* London, Routledge and Kegan Paul, 1949, p. 186.

established routines; yet the modern Western institutional structure allows room for freedom of conflict. The structure no longer being unitary, vested interests find it difficult to resist the continuous stream of change-producing inventions. Invention, as well as its application and utilization, is furthered through the ever-renewed challenge to vested interests, as well as by the conflicts between the vested interests themselves.[11]

Once old forms of traditional and unitary integration broke down, the clash of conflicting interests and values, now no longer constrained by the rigidity of the medieval structure, pressed for new forms of unification and integration. Thus deliberate control and rationalized regulation of "spontaneous" processes was required in military and political, as well as in economic institutions. Bureaucratic forms of organization with their emphasis on calculable, methodical, and disciplined behavior[12] arose at roughly the same period in which the unitary medieval structure broke down. But with the rise of bureaucratic types of organization peculiar new resistances to change made their appearance. The need for reliance on predictability exercises pressure towards the rejection of innovation which is perceived as interference with routine. Conflicts involving a "trial through battle" are unpredictable in their outcome, and therefore unwelcome to the bureaucracy that must strive towards an ever-widening extension of the area of predictability and calculability of results. But social arrangements that have become habitual and totally patterned are subject to the blight of ritualism. If attention is focused exclusively on the habitual

11. See W. F. Ogburn, *Social Change,* New York, B. W. Huebsch, 1923, for the theory of "cultural lag" due to "vested interests."

12. Cf. Max Weber, "Bureaucracy," *From Max Weber,* Gerth and Mills, ed., pp. 196–244. For the pathology of bureaucracy, see R. K. Merton, "Bureaucratic Structure and Personality," *Social Theory and Social Structure,* op. cit., pp. 151–60.

clues, "people may be unfitted by being fit in an unfit fitness,"[13] so that their habitual training becomes an incapacity to adjust to new conditions. To quote Dewey again: "The customary is taken for granted; it operates subconsciously. Breach of wont and use is focal; it forms 'consciousness'."[14] A group or a system that no longer is challenged is no longer capable of a creative response. It may subsist, wedded to the eternal yesterday of precedent and tradition, but it is no longer capable of renewal.[15]

"Only a hitch in the working of habit occasions emotion and provokes thought."[16] Conflict within and between bureaucratic structures provides means for avoiding the ossification and ritualism that threaten their form of organization.[17] Conflict, though apparently dysfunctional for highly rationalized systems, may actually have important latent functional consequences. By attacking and overcoming the resistance to innovation and change that seems to be an "occupational psychosis" always threatening the bureaucratic office holder, it can help to insure that the system does not stifle in the deadening routine of habituation and that in the planning activity itself creativity and invention can be applied.

We have so far discussed change within systems, but changes of systems are of perhaps even more crucial importance for sociological inquiry. Here the sociology of Karl Marx serves us well. Writes Marx in a polemic against Proudhon:

13. Kenneth Burke, *Permanence and Change,* New York, New Republic, 1936, p. 18.
14. John Dewey, *The Public and Its Problems,* Chicago, Gateway Books, 1946, p. 100.
15. This is, of course, a central thesis of Arnold Toynbee's monumental *A Study of History,* O.U.P.
16. John Dewey, *Human Nature and Conduct,* op. cit., p. 178.
17. See, e.g., Melville Dalton, "Conflicts Between Staff and Line Managerial Officers," *Am. Soc. R.,* XV (1950), pp. 342–51. The author seems to be unaware of the positive functions of this conflict, yet his data clearly indicate the "innovating potential" of conflict between staff and line.

Feudal production also had two antagonistic elements, which were equally designated by the names of *good side* and *bad side* of feudalism, without regard being had to the fact that it is always the evil side which finishes by overcoming the good side. It is the bad side that produces the movement which makes history, by constituting the struggle. If at the epoch of the reign of feudalism the economists, enthusiastic over the virtues of chivalry, the delightful harmony between rights and duties, the patriarchal life of the towns, the prosperous state of domestic industry in the country, of the development of industry organized in corporations, guilds and fellowships, in fine of all which constitutes the beautiful side of feudalism, had proposed to themselves the problem of eliminating all which cast a shadow upon this lovely picture —serfdom, privilege, anarchy—what would have been the result? All the elements which constituted the struggle would have been annihilated, and the development of the bourgeoisie would have been stifled in the germ. They would have set themselves the absurd problem of eliminating history.[18]

According to Marx, conflict leads not only to ever-changing relations within the existing social structure, but the total social system undergoes transformation through conflict.

During the feudal period, the relations between serf and lord or between burgher and nobility underwent many changes both in law and in fact. Yet conflict finally led to a breakdown of all feudal relations and hence to the rise of a new social system governed by different patterns of social relations.

It is Marx's contention that the negative element, the opposition, conditions the change when conflict between the subgroups of a system becomes so sharpened that at a certain point this system breaks down. Each social system contains elements of strain and of potential conflict; if in the analysis of

18. Karl Marx, *The Poverty of Philosophy*, Chicago, Charles H. Kerr & Co., 1910, p. 132.

the social structure of a system these elements are ignored, if the adjustment of patterned relations is the only focus of attention, then it is not possible to anticipate basic social change. Exclusive attention to wont and use, to the customary and habitual bars access to an understanding of possible latent elements of strain that under certain conditions eventuate in overt conflict and possibly in a basic change of the social structure. This attention should be focused, in Marx's view, on what evades and resists the patterned normative structure and on the elements pointing to new and alternative patterns emerging from the existing structure. What is diagnosed as disease from the point of view of the institutionalized pattern may, in fact, says Marx, be the first birth pang of a new one to come; not wont and use but the break of wont and use is focal. The "matters-of-fact" of a "given state of affairs" when viewed in the light of Marx's approach, become limited, transitory; they are regarded as containing the germs of a process that leads beyond them.[19]

Yet, not all social systems contain the same degree of conflict and strain. The sources and incidence of conflicting behavior in each particular system vary according to the type of structure, the patterns of social mobility, of ascribing and achieving status and of allocating scarce power and wealth, as well as the degree to which a specific form of distribution of power, resources, and status is accepted by the component

19. For an understanding of Marx's methodology and its relation to Hegelian philosophy, see Herbert Marcuse, *Reason and Revolution*, N.Y., O.U.P., 1941.

Note the similarity with John Dewey's thought: "Where there is change, there is of necessity numerical plurality, multiplicity, and from variety comes opposition, strife. Change is alteration, or othering and this means diversity. Diversity means division, and division means two sides and their conflict." *Reconstruction in Philosophy*, N.Y., Mentor Books, 1950, p. 97. See also the able discussion of the deficiencies of Talcott Parsons' sociological theories by David Lockwood, *B.J.S.*, June, 1956.

actors within the different subsystems. But if, within any social structure, there exists an excess of claimants over opportunities for adequate reward, there arises strain and conflict.

The distinction between changes *of* systems and changes *within* systems is, of course, a relative one. There is always some sort of continuity between a past and a present, or a present and a future social system; societies do not die the way biological organisms do, for it is difficult to assign precise points of birth or death to societies as we do with biological organisms. One may claim that all that can be observed is a change of the organization of social relations; but from one perspective such change may be considered reestablishment of equilibrium whereas from another it may be seen as the formation of a new system.

A natural scientist, describing the function of earthquakes, recently stated admirably what could be considered the function of conflict. "There is nothing abnormal about an earthquake. An unshakeable earth would be a dead earth. A quake is the earth's way of maintaining its equilibrium, a form of adjustment that enables the crust to yield to stresses that tend to reorganize and redistribute the material of which it is composed. . . . The larger the shift, the more violent the quake, and the more frequent the shifts, the more frequent are the shocks."[20]

Whether the quake is violent or not, it has served to maintain or reestablish the equilibrium of the earth. Yet the shifts may be small changes of geological formations, or they may be changes in the structural relations between land and water, for example.

At what point the shift is large enough to warrant the conclusion that a change *of* the system has taken place, is hard to determine. Only if one deals with extreme instances are

20. Waldemar Kaemfert, "Science in Review," *New York Times.* July 27, 1952.

ideal types—such as feudalism, capitalism, and so on—easily applied. A system based on serfdom, for example, may undergo considerable change within—*vide* the effects of the Black Death on the social structure of medieval society; and even an abolition of serfdom may not necessarily be said to mark the end of an old and the emergence of a new system, *vide* nineteenth-century Russia.

If "it is necessary to distinguish clearly between the processes *within* the system and processes of change *of* the system," as Professor Parsons has pointed out,[21] an attempt should be made to establish a heuristic criterion for this distinction. We propose to talk of a change *of* system when all major structural relations, its basic institutions, and its prevailing value system have been drastically altered. (In cases where such a change takes place abruptly, as, for example, the Russian Revolution, there should be no difficulty. It is well to remember, however, that transformations of social systems do not always consist in an abrupt and simultaneous change of all basic institutions. Institutions may change gradually, by mutual adjustment, and it is only over a period of time that the observer will be able to claim that the social system has undergone a basic transformation in its structural relations.) In concrete historical reality, no clear-cut distinctions exist. Change *of* system may be the result (or the sum total) of previous changes *within* the system. This does not, however, detract from the usefulness of the theoretical distinction.

It is precisely Marx's contention that the change from feudalism to a different type of social system can be understood only through an investigation of the stresses and strains *within*

21. Talcott Parsons, *The Social System,* New York, The Free Press, 1951, p. 481.

I owe much to Prof. Parsons' treatment of this distinction despite a number of major disagreements with his theory of social change.

the feudal system. Whether given forms of conflict will lead to changes in the social system or to breakdown and to formation of a now system will depend on the rigidity and resistance to change, or inversely on the elasticity of the control mechanisms of the system.

It is apparent, however, that the rigidity of the system and the intensity of conflict within it are not independent of each other. Rigid systems which suppress the incidence of conflict exert pressure towards the emergence of radical cleavages and violent forms of conflict. More elastic systems, which allow the open and direct expression of conflict within them and which adjust to the shifting balance of power that these conflicts both indicate and bring about, are less likely to be menaced by basic and explosive alignments within their midst.

In what follows, the distinction between strains, conflicts, and disturbances within a system that lead to a reestablishment of equilibrium, and conflicts that lead to the establishment of new systems and new types of equilibria, will be examined.[22]

22. The concept of *equilibrium* is of great value in social science provided it is used, as by Schumpeter, as a point of reference permitting measurement of departures from it. "The concept of a state of equilibrium, although no such state may ever be realized, is useful and indeed indispensable for purpose of analyses and diagnosis, as a point of reference" (Joseph A. Schumpeter, *Business Cycle,* N.Y., McGraw Hill, 1939, p. 69). But certain types of sociological functionalism tend to move from this methodological use of the concept to one that has some clearly ideological features. The ideal type of equilibrium, in this illegitimate use, becomes a normative instead of a methodological concept. Attention is focused on the maintenance of a system that is somehow identified with the ethically desirable (see Merton's discussion of this ideological misuse of functionalism in *Social Theory and Social Structure,* op. cit., pp. 38 ff. and 116–17; see also my review of Parsons' Essays, *American Journal of Sociology,* 55, March 1950, pp. 502–4). Such theorizing tends to look at all behavior caused by strains and conflict as "deviancy" from the legitimate pattern, thereby creating the perhaps unintended impression that such behavior is somehow "abnormal" in an ethical sense, and obscuring

Such an examination will be most profitably begun by considering what Thorstein Veblen[23] has called "Vested Interests."[24]

Any social system implies an allocation of power, as well as wealth and status positions among individual actors and component subgroups. As has been pointed out, there is never complete concordance between what individuals and groups within a system consider their just due and the system of allocation. Conflict ensues in the effort of various frustrated groups and individuals to increase their share of gratification. Their demands will encounter the resistance of those who previously had established a "vested interest" in a given form of distribution of honor, wealth, and power.

To the vested interests, an attack against their position necessarily appears as an attack upon the social order.[25] Those who derive privileges from a given system of allocation of

---

the fact that some "deviant" behavior actually serves the creation of new patterns rather than a simple rejection of the old.

23. See especially *The Vested Interests and the State of the Industrial Arts,* New York, 1919.

24. Max Lerner ("Vested Interests," *Encyclopaedia of the Social Sciences,* XV, p. 240) gives the following definition: "When an activity has been pursued so long that the individuals concerned in it have a prescriptive claim to its exercise and its profit, they are considered to have a vested interest in it."

25. Veblen has described this aptly: "The code of proprieties, conventionalities, and usages in vogue at any given time and among any given people has more or less of the character of an organic whole; so that any appreciable change in one point of the scheme involves something of a change or readjustment of other points also, if not a reorganization all along the line. . . . When an attempted reform involves the suppression or thoroughgoing remodeling of an institution of first-rate importance in the conventional scheme, it is immediately felt that a serious derangement of the entire scheme would result. . . . Any of these innovations would, we are told, 'shake the social structure to its base,' 'reduce society to chaos,' . . . etc. The aversion to change is in large part an aversion to the bother of making the readjustment which any given change will necessitate" (*The Theory of the Leisure Class,* New York, The Modern Library, pp. 201–3)

status, wealth, and power will perceive an attack upon these prerogatives as an attack against the system itself.

However, mere "frustration" will not lead to a questioning of the legitimacy of the position of the vested interests, and hence to conflict. Levels of aspiration as well as feelings of deprivation are relative to institutionalized expectations and are established through comparison.[26] When social systems have institutionalized goals and values to govern the conduct of component actors, but limit access to these goals for certain members of the society, "departures from institutional requirements" are to be expected.[27] Similarly, if certain groups within a social system compare their share in power, wealth, and status honor with that of other groups *and* question the legitimacy of this distribution, discontent is likely to ensue. If there exist no institutionalized provisions for the expression of such discontents, departures from what is required by the norms of the social system may occur. These may be limited to "innovation" or they may consist in the rejection of the institutionalized goals. Such rebellion "involves a genuine transvaluation, where the direct or vicarious experience of frustration leads to full denunciation of previously prized values."[28] Thus it will be well to distinguish between those departures from the norms of a society that consist in mere "deviation" and those that involve the formation of distinctive patterns and new value systems.

What factors lead groups and individuals to question at a certain point the legitimacy of the system of distribution of

26. See Robert K. Merton and Alice S. Kitt, "Contribution to the Theory of Reference Group Behaviour" for a development of the concept of "relative deprivation" (originally suggested by Stouffer *et al.* in *The American Soldier*) and its incorporation into the framework of a theory of reference groups.

27. This whole process is exhaustively discussed by Merton in his paper on "Social Structure and Anomie," *Social Theory,* op. cit.

28. *Ibid.,* p. 145.

rewards lies largely outside the scope of the present inquiry. The intervening factors can be sought in the ideological, technological, economic, or any other realm. It is obvious, moreover, that conflict may be a result just as much as a source of change. A new invention, the introduction of a new cultural trait through diffusion, the development of new methods of production or distribution, and such, will have a differential impact within a social system. Some strata will feel it to be detrimental to their material or ideal interests, whereas others will feel their position strengthened through its introduction. Such disturbances in the equilibrium of the system lead to conditions in which groups or individual actors no longer do willingly what they have to do and do willingly what they are not supposed to do. Change, no matter what its source, breeds strain and conflict.

Yet, it may be well to repeat that mere "frustration" and the ensuing strains and tensions do not necessarily lead to group conflict. Individuals under stress may relieve their tension through "acting out" in special safety-valve institutions in as far as they are provided for in the social system; or they may "act out" in a deviant manner that may have serious dysfunctional consequences for the system and bring about change in this way. This, however, does not reduce the frustration from which escape has been sought since it does not attack their source.

If, on the other hand the strain leads to the emergence of specific new patterns of behavior of whole groups of individuals who pursue "the optimization of gratification"[29] by choosing what they consider appropriate means for the maximization of rewards, social change that reduces the sources of their frustration may come about. This may happen in two ways: if the social system is flexible enough to adjust to conflict situations we will deal with change *within* the system. If, on the other

29. T. Parsons, *The Social System,* op. cit., p. 498.

hand, the social system is not able to readjust itself and allows the accumulation of conflict, the "aggressive" groups, imbued with a new system of values that threatens to split the general consensus of the society and imbued with an ideology that "objectifies" their claims, may become powerful enough to overcome the resistance of vested interests and bring about the breakdown of the system and the emergence of a new distribution of social values.[30]

In his *Poverty of Philosophy*, Marx was led to consider the conditions under which economic classes constitute themselves:

> Economic conditions have first transformed the mass of the population into workers. The domination of capital created for this mass a common situation and common interest. This mass was thus already a class as against capital, but not for itself. It is in the struggle . . . that the mass gathers together and constitutes itself as a class for itself. The interests which it defends become class interests.[31]

With this remarkable distinction between class *in itself* and class *for itself* (which unfortunately he didn't elaborate upon in later writings though it informs all of them—if not the writings of most latter-day "marxists"), Marx illuminates a most important aspect of group formation: group belongingness is established by an objective conflict situation—in this case a conflict of interests;[32] but only by experiencing this

30. R. K. Merton, *Social Theory and Social Structure*, op. cit., pp. 42–3 and 116–17.

31. Karl Marx, *The Poverty of Philosophy*, op. cit., pp. 188–9.

32. This makes it necessary to distinguish between realistic and non-realistic conflict: social conflicts that arise from frustration of specific demands and from estimates of gains of the participants, and that are directed at the presumed frustrating object, may be called realistic conflicts. Non-realistic conflicts, on the other hand, are not occasioned by the rival ends of the antagonists, but by the need for tension release of one or both of them. Some groups may be formed with the mere purpose of releasing

antagonism, that is, by becoming aware of it and by acting it out, does the group (or class) establish its identity.

When changes in the equilibrium of a society lead to the formation of new groupings or to the strengthening of existing groupings that set themselves the goal of overcoming resistance of vested interests through conflict, changes in structural relations, as distinct from simple "maladjustment," can be expected.

What Robert Park said about the rise of nationalist and racial movements is more generally applicable:

> They strike me as natural and wholesome disturbances of the social routine, the effect of which is to arouse in those involved a lively sense of common purpose and to give those who feel themselves oppressed the inspiration of a common cause. . . . The effect of this struggle is to increase the solidarity and improve the morale of the "oppressed" minority.[33]

It is this sense of common purpose arising in and through conflict that is peculiar to the behavior of individuals who meet the challenge of new conditions by a group-forming and value-forming response. Strains that result in no such formations of new conflict groups or strengthening of old ones may contribute to bringing about change, but a type of change that fails to reduce the sources of strain since by definition tension-release behavior does not involve purposive action. Conflict through group action, on the other hand, is likely to result in a

tension. Such groups "collectivize" their tensions, so to speak. They can, by definition, only be disruptive rather than creative since they are built on negative rather than positive cathexes. But groups of this kind will remain marginal; their actions cannot bring about social change unless they accompany and strengthen realistic conflict groups. In such cases we deal with an admixture of non-realistic and realistic elements mutually reinforcing each other within the same social movements. Members who join for the mere purpose of tension release are often used for the "dirty work" by the realistic conflict groups.

33. Robert E. Park, "Personality and Cultural Conflict," *Publications of the Am. Soc. Soc.*, 25, 1931, pp. 95–110. See p. 107.

"deviancy" that may be the prelude of new patterns and reward systems apt to reduce the sources of frustration.

If the tensions that need outlets are continually reproduced within the structure, abreaction through tension-release mechanisms may preserve the system but at the risk of ever-renewed futher accumulation of tension. Such accumulation eventuates easily in the eruption of destructive unrealistic conflict. If feelings of dissatisfaction, instead of being suppressed or diverted, are allowed expression against "vested interests," and in this way to lead to the formation of new groupings within the society, the emergence of genuine transvaluations is likely to occur. Sumner saw this very well when he said: "We want to develop symptoms, we don't want to suppress them."[34]

Whether the emergence of such new groupings or the strengthening of old ones with the attendant increase in self-confidence and self-esteem on the part of the participants will lead to a change *of* or *within* the system will depend on the degree of cohesion that the system itself has attained. A well-integrated society will tolerate and even welcome group conflict; only a weakly integrated one must fear it. The great English liberal John Morley said it very well:

> If [the men who are most attached to the reigning order of things] had a larger faith in the stability for which they profess so great an anxiety, they would be more free alike in understanding and temper to deal generously, honestly and effectively with those whom they count imprudent innovators.[35]

34. Wm. G. Sumner, *War and Other Essays,* p. 241.
35. John Morley, *On Compromise,* London, Macmillan & Co., 1917, p. 263.

2

The Termination of Conflict

In the state of nature, to use Hobbesian terminology, conflict, whether it be waged for gain, for safety, or for glory, "ceaseth only in death." Hobbes' philosophical vision can be translated into modern sociological terminology when we note that social conflicts tend to continue or to escalate, and to end with the total destruction of at least one of the antagonists, when unchecked by societal regulation and by deliberate actions of the contenders. Social structures always contain or create mechanisms that help control and channel conflicts through normative regulation. Yet the degree to which conflicts are so regulated varies considerably. There are highly institutionalized conflicts, as duels or court procedures, that exhibit game-like features with built-in conventional termination points; at the other end of the scale, certain international conflicts, such as absolute wars, lack any specifiable form of normative control and approach a Hobbesian state of nature.

Analytical focus on the processes leading to the termination of conflicts has strategic value insofar as the very mode of ending a conflict serves to explain the distinctive type of the contention. When contenders share common attitudes as to the determination of the outcome of a conflict, they share some understanding of each other's conduct and hence tend to agree on some common rules and norms allowing them to assess their respective strength and will to action. If they cannot arrive at a way of ending their contention before one or both of them is totally annihilated, this indicates that such shared universe of discourse is absent so that they live in totally distinct moral and perceptual worlds.

If the participants in a conflict share a system of symbols indicating points in their contentions that may be taken to symbolize victory or defeat, or if they at least understand the key symbols of the other side, they have means of ending the conflict. If, in a war, to use a convenient example, it is agreed that the taking of a specific fortress or piece of territory may be taken to symbolize the defeat of one of the parties, then the agreement sets limits to the conflict. When, on the contrary, no common standards as to points of termination can be arrived at, then only total annihilation or total surrender will terminate the conflict. Hence, agreed upon symbolizations of this kind limit the extent of involvement, reduce costs, and maximize the predictability of outcomes. Such agreed upon termination points are hence likely to increase chances for conflict resolutions based on rational calculation. This means that mutually understood symbols and indices indicating the relative standing of contenders in their combat may maximize the chances of cutting the conflict short rather than pursuing the mirage of full victory.*

The chapter that follows deals with wars and other major conflicts in their totality. An alternative analytical strategy, as Edward Gross has pointed out,† is to deal with the smaller units that make up the overall process. When conflicts continue over time they may be analyzed in terms of battles, skirmishes,

* Johan Galtung's, "Institutionalized Conflict Resolution," *Journal of Peace Research*, No. 4, 1965, contains a number of valuable ideas concerning the institutionalization of conflict-resolution mechanisms. For a series of suggestive leads as to what points in a time, space, or value continuum may be especially favorable as unambiguous symbols leading to the termination of conflict, see Thomas Schelling, *The Strategy of Conflict*, Cambridge, Harvard University Press, 1960, esp. chapters II and III.
† In a private communication dated March 26, 1965.

sorties, major encounters, and the like. Each one of these can then be treated as a conflict in its own right and lends itself to the same kind of analysis that is here proposed for the total conflictual engagement. Such detailed sequential analyses might prove fruitful not only in the case of war but also in regard to a variety of conflicts, from lovers' quarrels to union-management contentions. In all such cases it would seem analytically profitable to record in detail how the total conflict moves through a number of patterned phases, each involving specific termination points.

CERTAIN SOCIAL PROCESSES ARE FINITE, I.E., THEY ARE defined by their transitory character and the manner of their termination is institutionally prescribed. Courtship ends when union with the beloved has been attained in marriage; formal education ends when the educational goal has been reached and examinations or commencement exercises mark completion of the process. Other social processes, however, such as friendship or love, have no precise termination point. They follow a law of social inertia insofar as they continue to operate if no explicit provision for stopping their course is made by the participants. Social conflict is such a process. Whereas in a game, for example, the rules for the process include rules for its ending, in social conflict explicit provisions for its termination must be made by the contenders. If no mutual agreements are made at some time during the struggle, it "ceaseth only in death" or in total destruction of at least one of the antagonists. The termination of conflict hence presents problems that do not arise in finite processes.

Various types of conflicts can be classified according to the degree of their normative regulation. Fully institutionalized conflicts, such as duels, may be said to constitute one extreme of a continuum whereas absolute conflicts, in which the goal is the total destruction of the enemy rather than a mutually agreed-upon settlement fall at the other extreme. In the second type, agreement is reduced to a minimum; the struggle ceases only upon the extermination of one or both of the contenders. As Hans Speier has said, "peace terminating an absolute war is established *without* the enemy."[1]

It stands to reason that conflicts of this kind—at least between contenders with a rough equality of strength—are exceedingly costly and exhausting. If the contenders wish to prevent

1. Hans Speier, *Social Order and the Risks of War*. New York, George W. Stewart, 1952, p. 223.

their struggle from becoming a zero-sum game in which the outcome can only be total defeat or total victory, they have a common interest in establishing mechanisms that can lead to an agreed-upon termination of the struggle. The fact is that most conflicts do indeed end long before the defeated has been totally crushed. "Resistance to the last man" is almost always a phrase. As long as one belligerent survives in one's camp further resistance is always possible; yet combat usually ceases long before this point is reached. This is so because both parties agree upon norms for the termination of the conflict.

Although absolute conflicts allow practically no agreements as to their termination, certain types of highly institutionalized conflicts have built-in termination points. Trials by ordeal, duels, and other agonistic struggles are centered upon symbolic endings that give them game-like features and determine the outcome automatically. A score is kept, a goal line established, maximum injury is conventionally fixed. When the score adds up to a certain number, when a certain type of injury has been established, or the goal line has been crossed, the conflict is over and the loser as well as the winner can easily perceive the outcome of the contention.

In conflicts not fully institutionalized, assessment of relative strength is not an easy matter so that the loser may not in fact concede that he has lost, nor may he even be aware of it. Therefore, it is to the interest of both contenders that the point at which victory is attained or the point beyond which no more gains can be anticipated, be marked as clearly as possible so as to avoid unnecessary exertions on both sides. Termination of conflict becomes a problem to be solved by both parties.

The termination of conflict is a social process dependent upon, but not directly deducible from its pursuits. It is, as Georg Simmel has noted, "a specific enterprise. It belongs neither to war nor to peace, just as a bridge is different from either bank it connects."[2] To be sure, the outcome of a conflict is related to the goals of the antagonists and to the means by which it is fought; its duration and intensity will depend on objectives and available resources plus the time and effort required to achieve a decision. But the termination of the conflict, that is, agreement as to what constitutes a true decision, highlights some factors that are not deducible from its pursuit and must hence be studied separately.

For all except absolute conflict, termination involves a reciprocal activity and cannot be understood simply as an unilateral imposition of the will of the stronger on the weaker. Therefore, contrary to what common sense might suggest, not only the potential victor but also the potential vanquished makes crucial contributions to the termination. As a military commentator has pointed out, "war is pressed by the victor, but peace is made by the vanquished. Therefore, to determine the causes of peace, it is always necessary to take the vanquished's point of view. Until the vanquished quits, the war goes on."[3] Victory, in other words, involves the yielding of the vanquished. By the very act of declaring himself beaten, he achieves a last assertion of power. With this act, as Georg Simmel has said, "he actually makes a gift to the victor."[4] The capacity of making gifts is a measure of autonomy.

If both victor and vanquished are to make a contribution to the termination of their conflict they must arrive at some agreement. Thomas Schelling has recently argued persuasively that "limited war requires limits . . . but limits require agreement or

2. Georg Simmel, *Conflict*. Trans. Kurt H. Wolff. New York, The Free Press, 1955, p. 110.
3. H. A. Calahan, *What Makes a War End*. New York, Vanguard Press, 1944, p. 18.
4. Simmel, *op. cit.*, p. 114.

at least some kind of mutual recognition and acquiescence."[5] This applies not only to the conduct but also to the termination of conflicts. In order to end a conflict the parties must agree upon rules and norms allowing them to assess their respective power position in the struggle. Their common interest leads them to accept rules that enhance their mutual dependence in the very pursuit of their antagonistic goals. Such agreements make their conflict, so to speak, self-liquidating. To the degree that such rules are provided, the conflict is partly institutionalized and acquires some of the features of the agonistic struggle alluded to earlier.

Agreements as to goals and determination of outcome shorten the conflict. Once a goal has been reached by one of the parties and this is accepted as a clue to the acceptance of defeat by the other, the conflict is ended. The more restricted the object of contention and the more visible for both parties the clues to victory, the higher the chances that the conflict be limited in time and extension. Emile Durkheim's dictum concerning human needs, "The more one has, the more one wants, since satisfaction received only stimulates instead of filling needs" is applicable in this connection. Agreed-upon limits upon the "appetites" of the contenders place normative restrictions upon a process that does not inherently contain self-limiting properties. The history of trade unionism provides interesting examples.

Struggles engaged in by business unionism, given its limited goals, provide for the contending parties an opportunity for settlement and furnish them at the same time with recognizable signals as to the opportune moment for ending a conflict. Revolutionary syndicalism, on the other hand, has always been plagued by the problem of ending strike action. Since its goal

5. Thomas C. Schelling, *The Strategy of Conflict.* Cambridge, Mass., Harvard University Press, 1960, p. 53.

is the overthrow of the capitalist order rather than improvements within it, it cannot accept as the end of the conflict outcomes which would constitute victories from the point of view of business unionism. Revolutionary syndicalism is faced with the dilemma that no outcome of a strike, short of the overthrow of capitalism, can be considered an acceptable form of conflict resolution so that its strategy is foredoomed to failure. Not sensitized to clues that would allow them to conclude that a victory has been reached, unable to recognize peace overtures or concessions from the adversary, revolutionary syndicalists are not in a position to take advantage of partial gains. Paradoxically, in this case, those who are under ordinary conditions the *weaker* party demand "unconditional surrender" of the stronger so that they make it inevitable that the struggle can cease only upon total exhaustion.

The above examples illustrate how closely specific outcomes are related to the aims of the contenders. The smaller the sacrifice a party demands from the opponent, the more limited the aims, the higher the chances that the potential loser will be ready to give up battle. The loser must be led to decide that peace is more attractive than the continuation of the conflict; such a decision will be powerfully enhanced if the demands made upon him are not exorbitant.[6] When the war aims of the winning side are limited as, say, in the Spanish-American war or the Russo-Japanese conflict of 1905, the making of peace is relatively easy. Once the Japanese war aims—the stopping of Russian penetration into the Far East—had been reached, Japan could afford to make the first move for peace by appealing to Theodore Roosevelt to act as a mediator. Once Cuba was liberated and the Spanish fleet defeated, American war aims were attained and the United States had no interest in continuing the war through an attack upon the Spanish mainland.

6. Calahan, *op. cit.,* p. 253 *et passim.*

It remains, however, that no matter how the activities of the potential winner have facilitated an early termination of the conflict, the final decision to end the war remains with the potential loser. How, then, is the loser moved to decide that he has, in fact, lost? Not only the objective situation but the perception of the situation is crucially important since only the latter will bring forth the requisite admission of defeat. "If an opponent," writes Clausewitz, "is to be made to comply with our will, we must place him in a situation which is more oppressive to him than the sacrifice we demand."[7] This elegantly phrased dictum is, however, meaningless unless the criteria be specified that determine how the antagonist will in fact assess the situation. Different contenders might arrive at variant estimates as to the degree of oppressiveness of a situation and of the value of the sacrifice demanded. Since such assessments are difficult to make and do not depend on rational calculations alone, they are greatly facilitated by the availability of symbolic signposts.

Whenever wars have been strictly limited, as in eighteenth-century warfare, some visible event, such as the taking of a particular fortress, the reaching of some natural barrier, and the like, symbolized to both parties that the desired objective has been reached by one of them and that the conflict could now be considered solved through the subsequent acquiescence of the loser. When such mutually acceptable symbolic clues are not available, the resolution of the conflict will be more difficult.

The nature of such symbolic clues may vary considerably[8] and it is hence important that the potential winner ascertain

7. Karl von Clausewitz, *On War*, London, Routledge and Kegan Paul, 1956, vol. I, p. 5.

8. One must further distinguish between purely symbolic events, such as the capture of a flag, and events which, as in the examples that follow, have realistic as well as symbolic significance.

which clues will be accepted by the potential loser as symbols of defeat. If in the common consciousness of the citizens, the capital symbolizes the very existence of the nation, then its fall will be perceived as defeat and will lead to the acceptance of the terms of the victor. The Fall of Paris in 1871 and 1940 symbolized to the bulk of Frenchmen the end of the war despite the fact that Gambetta had rallied significant numbers of undefeated troops in the provinces, and that de Gaulle appealed for the continuation of the war from London. Only a relatively small number of Frenchmen refused to accept the Fall of Paris as a symbol of defeat. In less centralized nations, however, where the capital has no such symbolic significance, its fall is not perceived as a decisive event. Pretoria and Bloemfontein fell to the British in 1900, yet Boer resistance, rather to the surprise of the British, continued for two more years. The British failed to understand that, to the rural Boers, the vast countryside rather than the cities symbolized the nation; to them the war ended only when want of forage, capture, and overwork decimated the Boer horses. In a country in which men were bred in the saddle, the decimation of horses symbolized defeat.[9] Similarly, the sacking of Washington in 1812 did not signal defeat to Americans for whom the open spaces of the country rather than the federal capital symbolized national independence. In other situations the capture of charismatic warlords rather than any taking of a locality will symbolize defeat.

The structure of the opposing camp furnishes clues as to meaningful symbols of defeat and victory. It is hence of the utmost importance for both sides to have as much knowledge as possible about the characteristic features of their respective structure and symbols. When ignorant armies clash at night, their pluralistic ignorance militates against their ability to come to terms short of mutual exhaustion.

9. Calahan, *op. cit.*, p. 114.

The contenders' ability to make use of one another's symbols of defeat and victory does not only depend on their awareness of the structure of the opposing camp, but also on the dynamics within each camp. Internal struggles may be waged over what set of events may be considered a decisive symbol of defeat. A minority may consider that resistance can be continued even though the majority has accepted defeat. Subgroups may consider that the decision-makers have betrayed the cause by agreeing to end the conflict. Peace terms provide ample material for internal conflict within each of the contending camps. These terms are, morover, likely to be defined and redefined in the course of the conflict in tune with the fortunes of battle. Different parties may disagree violently on whether a given event is to be considered decisive or of only incidental significance. Such contentions are likely to be the more deep-going the less integrated the social structure. In integrated structures, internal contentions may vitalize and strengthen the groups' energies, but if divergencies as to appropriate action affect the basic layers of common belief, symbolizations of victory and defeat are also likely to be basically divergent.[10] In highly polarized social systems where a number of internal conflicts of different sorts are superimposed upon one another, there exists hardly any common definition of the situation binding all members of the society to commonly held perceptions.[11] To the extent that a society or group is rent into rival camps so that there is no community of ends between the parties, if one party is not willing to accept the definition of the situation that the other propounds, the making of peace becomes an almost impossible enterprise. In such situations a

10. Lewis A. Coser, *The Functions of Social Conflict.* New York, The Free Press, 1956, pp. 72–80.

11. *Ibid.*, p. 76ff. See also Ralf Dahrendorf, *Class and Class Conflict in Industrial Society.* Stanford, Calif., Stanford University Press, 1959, pp. 213ff.

prior settlement of scores within, an unambiguous definition or redefinition of the balance of power between contending groups, may be the precondition for concluding peace without. The Russian provisional government after the March 1917 revolution being continuously goaded and challenged by the growing Bolshevik Party, was unable either to wage war effectively or to conclude peace; once the Bolsheviks had seized power their definition of the situation prevailed and peace could be concluded at Brest Litowsk.

Even when such deep-going fissures are not present in a social structure, the ever-present divergencies between the perspectives of the leaders and the led, between those in authority and those submitted to it,[12] require considerable effort on the part of the leaders to make the led accept their definition of the situation. Just as at the beginning of the struggle the leaders must convince the led that the sacrifice demanded of them will redound to their benefit and that the conflict concerns wide interests of all rather than the narrow interests of the top stratum, so the leaders must also be able to convince the led that the acceptance of defeat is warranted and even desirable from the point of view of the total system rather than in terms of special leadership interests. To make defeat palatable may require as much effort as to make war desirable.

Leaders will typically differ from the led not only in terms of social perspectives but also in regard to their cognitive horizon so that leaders may be able to assess consequences and relative advantages more rationally than the led. A leader foreseeing a defeat that is not as yet visible to his followers must adjust his strategy to the need of convincing the followers. In such an effort it might be advantageous to him to construe partial defeat in such a way as to make it appear as at least a partial victory. Often the led, like the mark in a con game,

12. Dahrendorf, op. cit., ch. 5.

might have to be cooled out by being told that what they experience as a loss is "really" a partial victory.[13]

Contentions within enemy camps as to the proper definition of the situation once again highlight the importance of symbolization. The leader will have to rely on his ability to manipulate the symbolic system by which the led define the situations if he is to soften the blow that defeat implies. In labor-management conflicts, for example, events that may appear to an outsider as having only peripheral importance may in fact have highly charged emotional significance to the participants. The return to work of a few strikers or, alternatively, the success of a demonstration or the support of public officials or the reactions of an organ of public opinion, may be invested by the rank and file with high symbolic significance and trigger off a return to work or a revival of the will to victory. This is why it is important for the leaders to manage the symbols that structure the perception of the led. The strike leader must know how to end a strike at the opportune moment, but his knowledge would serve him but little if he did not also have the ability to communicate his knowledge to the led. This may often involve the highlighting for the rank and file of a partially attained victory in order to divert attention from a partially suffered defeat.

This is the stuff of which compromises are made. Often seen by the rank and file as a "betrayal" by the leaders, they actually derive from the structural circumstance that the leader's position allows them a view of the total situation that is denied to the led. Moreover, leadership roles require to so manage intragroup tensions as to keep the group united in adversity even though this might entail certain sacrifices insofar as the attainment of the group's goals are concerned. "System

13. Erving Goffman, "On Cooling the Mark Out," *Psychiatry*, 15 (November, 1952), pp. 451–63.

maintenance," to use Parsons' terminology, may sometimes require lowered task performance.

Indeed, most conflicts end in compromises in which it is often quite hard to specify which side has gained relative advantage. Hence, one must distinguish between the will to make peace and the will to accept defeat. Quite often the former may be present although the later is not. The parties to the conflict may be willing to cease the battle when they recognize that their aims cannot be attained or that they can be attained only at a price that they are not willing to pay, or, more generally, when they conclude that continuation of the conflict is less attractive than the making of peace. In neither of these cases would they be willing to accept defeat although they are willing to stop short of victory. In such situations they may be impelled to explore the chances for a compromise. The willingness to negotiate a compromise, that is to stop chasing the mirage of victory, will, of course, depend on correct assessment of the situation and such assessment, just as in the cases discussed earlier, will be facilitated by the availability of indices of relative standing in the battle. It is one of the key functions of the mediator to make such indices readily available to both parties. To the extent that the contenders share a common system of symbols allowing them to arrive at a common assessment, to that extent they will be able to negotiate. Symbols of defeat and victory thus turn out to be of relevance in order to stop short of either.

Relative appraisal of power is difficult before the contenders have measured their respective strength in conflict. But accommodation may be reached once such an assessment has been achieved. Such redefinitions in the course of a struggle often bring to the fore elements that remained hidden during its onset. Accommodation is facilitated if criteria are available that allow the contenders to gauge the situation. The chance of attaining peace without victory depends on the possibility of achieving consensus as to relative strength and on the ability to make this new definition "stick" within each camp. When the United States chose the neck of Korea as their symbolic standing place in the Korean war, they succeeded in conveying to the other side as well as to the American people their determination to hold it. When enough blood had been let and it became clear to both sides that the other could be beaten only at a cost that neither was willing to incur, negotiations got down to a compromise that took into account the real balance of political and military power and proved acceptable at home. "Peace through stalemate," writes B. H. Liddell-Hart, "based on a coincident recognition by each side of the opponent's strength, is at least preferable to peace through common exhaustion."[14]

Although it is true that in many cases an assessment of the relative strength of the opponents is possible only in conflict, it is also true that their travail may be shortened if clear symbolizations of outcome and relative strength are readily available. When recourse to such measures of success or failure has been highly institutionalized, the duration of the conflict can be shortend and its intensity limited. In this sense, research directed toward an understanding of those symbols that move men to accept compromise or even defeat might be as valuable as research to uncover symbols which incite to war.

14. B. H. Liddell-Hart, *Strategy, the Indirect Approach*. London, Faber and Faber, 1955, p. 370.

3

Violence and the Social Structure

The analysis of social statics, to use August Comte's terms, has been almost completely divorced from that of social dynamics. Whereas the former has been in the forefront of concern in sociological writing, the latter has been neglected. As a result, recent American sociological investigations in such fields as juvenile delinquency and crime have brought a rich harvest of results, but the analysis of collective behavior or of revolutionary events has remained fairly barren. In "social statics" increasingly sophisticated theoretical work has been combined with advanced empirical method; in contrast, in "social dynamics" *ad hoc* explanations of a fairly low level of sophistication have tended to predominate.*

Moreover, where periods of social breakdown and upheaval have been dealt with, there has been a tendency to offer different explanations for such periods of change than for social phenomena occurring in periods of relative social stability. In this chapter an effort is made to forge some links between the investigation of social statics and social dynamics by pointing out that the same theoretical formulations can be applied to both areas.

* But cf. James C. Davies, "Toward a Theory of Revolution," *Am. Soc. Review* XXVII, 1 (February 1962), pp. 5–19, for an attempt at linking the study of revolution more closely to the mainstream of contemporary sociological inquiry.

In the first chapter I attempted to demonstrate that, though the problems raised by changes *within* social systems differ from those raised by changes *of* social systems, they can nevertheless be dealt with within the same conceptual framework. I will now try to show that the notion of *relative deprivation,* which was developed to account for certain aspects of the behavior of groups and individuals differentially located in relatively stable social structures, serves equally well to deal with problems of abrupt social change and deep-going social conflict. More particularly, I shall attempt to show that it can help account for differential homicide rates in the contemporary United States as well as for differential participation rates in violent action during revolutions.*

* Charles Tilly's work in the sociology of revolution, more particularly his self-conscious utilization of the concepts of urban sociology in the eluci- dation of problems of the French Revolution, seems to have been moti- vated by concerns similar to my own. See in particular his masterly *The Vendée,* Cambridge, The Harvard University Press, 1964.

IT HAS BEEN A SOCIOLOGICAL COMMONPLACE EVER SINCE Emile Durkheim that deviant behavior is unevenly distributed throughout the social structure. The fact that the rates of such behavior are socially patterned has been the most effective sociological argument against the view that deviance results from biological impulse or idiosyncratic propensity. A great deal of empirical evidence is now available that class position, ethnic belongingness, and occupational status are effective indicators for the prediction of rates of deviance. In addition, sociological concepts such as the notion of relative deprivation[1] help to interpret these statistical regularities and afford insights into the ways in which, to quote Merton, "social structures exert a definite pressure upon certain persons in a society to engage in non-conforming rather than in conforming conduct."[2]

Eruptions of illegitimate violence, just as other forms of deviance, are unequally distributed in society. The rates of homicide, for example, vary in the United States in terms of ethnic as well as class belongingness, region, age, and sex.[3] An attempt will be made to show that even when the external social controls that normally operate in a society breakdown, the drastically increased incidence of violence is also not random.[4]

1. On this concept cf. R. K. Merton, *Social Theory and Social Structure.* New York, The Free Press, 1957, pp. 227 ff.
2. *Ibid.*, p. 132. This paper relies heavily on Merton's theoretical guide lines, especially on Chapters IV, V, IX, and X, *ibid.* Another major stimulus for this paper came from the seminal work of A. F. Henry and J. F. Short, *Suicide and Homicide.* New York, The Free Press, 1954.
3. In this paper homicide has been chosen as an indicator of violence. Other indicators, such as aggravated assault, might have been chosen as well. The results would not have differed materially.
4. In the following, violence is to be understood in terms of illegitimate violence only. I am not concerned here with the legitimate exercise of violence by agents of the state. In other words, I am not concerned with the violent behavior of a police officer in the pursuit of law enforce-

THE INCIDENCE OF HOMICIDE

The relation between high degrees of frustration and murderous violence has been discussed at length in the literature. A recent study of the life history of murderers concludes that "the murderers appear to have been terribly frustrated during their early lives . . . the frustration to which each had been subjected seemed much greater than that of the average person."[5] It seems to be the consensus among most students of the subject that high degrees of frustration account for the majority of homicides. Yet obviously murder is only one among several reactions to frustration. Aggression resulting from frustration may be directed against the self; or it may be repressed or sublimated, i.e., subjected to internalized social control. Hence two related questions must be asked: (1) Which categories of persons in a society are likely to suffer structurally induced frustrations greater than those experienced by average members?; and (2) In which social strata are we likely to find that internalized social controls are not strong enough to prevent high rates of homicidal aggression? The first question can be discussed in terms of differential status positions. An answer to the second will focus on processes of socialization in various social strata.

If there is merit in the contention that low-status position is a determinant of homicide, one would expect that in the lower class rates of homicide are higher than in the upper class. This is indeed consistently the case. Palmer finds that of the fathers of the 51 New England murderers in his sample, 53

---

ment. Only if a police officer exceeds the duties of his office and hence exercises illegitimate violence does he come within the purview of my discussion.

5. S. Palmer, *A Study of Murder*, New York, Thomas Y. Crowell, 1960, p. 8.

per cent come from the lowest rung of a 5-class scale.[6] Similarly, Porterfield found that the mean annual homicide rates in Fort Worth, Texas, was 1.06 per 100,000 population for the lower class but only 0.26 in the upper class.[7]

There are no nationwide statistics about the relation between class and homicide but there are other indicators of the relative status of categories with high homicide. Homicides are more frequent in the economically underdeveloped areas of the American South than they are in the North. Indeed, these regional differences are startling. The 1961 rates for murder and non-negligent manslaughter were 8.2 in the South Atlantic region as against 1.4 in New England.[8] The Mississippi rate was 10.3 in contrast to the Connecticut rate of 1.0 Generally, as one moves from the economically developed and high-status areas of the North to the low-status and underdeveloped areas of the South, the probability of homicide increases. The regional underdogs in the national status structure have considerably higher homicide rates than the regional top dogs.

6. In Hollingshead and Redlich's study of New Haven, the lowest class comprises only 17.8 per cent of the population; in Lloyd Warner's study of Newburyport only 25.4 per cent are found in this class. Only rough approximations between Palmer's New England sample and these two cities are permissible, but the general thesis of class differentials in homicide seems sustained by the date. This is especially so if one realizes that only about one tenth of the fathers of the murderers were in Class I, II, and III. This is significantly lower than the class distribution in the population would make one expect since over three-tenths of the residents of New Haven and over four-tenths of Newburyport were in those three higher classes. See Palmer, *ibid.,* p. 34, 209.

7. A. L. Porterfield, "Suicide and Crime in the Social Structure of an Urban Setting." *Am. Soc. Rev.* 17:341–49, 1952. This refers to the class position of victims, not murderers, but since most homicides are committed by murderers belonging to the same class as their victims, the class differences are meaningful in our context.

8. Uniform Crime Reports—1961, Washington, D.C.: U.S. Department of Justice, 1961, pp. 34–36.

It is often said that the higher proportion of Negroes in the South accounts for the higher Southern homicide rates. This is not the case. Even when the effect of race is held constant, homicide rates in the South are still considerably higher than in the North. Yet the high Negro rates of homicide deserve comment in their own right. Negroes are assigned lowest position in all three major dimensions of the status system: ethnicity, class, and education. We should expect that the ensuing cumulative frustrations result in extremely high Negro homicide rates. This is indeed the case. Although Negroes comprise only approximately 10.5 per cent of our total population, 2,154, i.e., 60 per cent, of all city arrests for murder and non-negligent manslaughter in 1961 were Negroes and only 1,493 were white.[9] The discrepancy between Negro and white homicide rates exists in all regions of the country. In Birmingham, Alabama, where Negroes account for 40 per cent of the population, they committed 84.9 per cent of the murders between 1937 and 1944. Negroes in Massachusetts constitute only 1 per cent of the population but committed about 10 per cent of the homicides. In up-state New York, the homicide rate in the twenties was 2.8 per 100,000 for Caucasians and 30.4 for Negroes.[10]

These data may suffice to substantiate the view that lower

9. *Ibid.*, p. 97.

10. H. A. Bloch, and G. Geis, *Man, Crime, and Society,* New York, Random House, 1962, p. 263. The higher rates for homicide among Negroes relative to whites in various sections of the country does not tell the whole story, however. Negro homicide rates vary in different regions together with white rates so that the Negro rates are highest in the states like Alabama where the white rate is also high (41.1 per 100,000 for Negroes as against 11.6 for whites), whereas in states where white rates are low the Negro rates are also lower. The Negro rate in Maine (3.2 per 100,000) is considerably lower than the Caucasian rates in Alabama (11.6), although it is considerably higher than the Caucasian rate in Maine (1.9). See *ibid.*, p. 262.

position in the status hierarchy of American society and the frustrations that lower position brings in its wake lead to higher homicide rates. Yet this demonstration still remains incomplete if it is realized that not all low-status groups in America show high homicide rates. Females have a lower status than males, yet female homicide rates are considerably lower. The young have a lower status than the middle-aged, yet they commit fewer homicides than their elders. Similarly, there is some evidence that the homicide rates among certain subgroups that occupy a very low-status position in America, as deviant religious sects, is quite low. To elucidate this matter one needs to move from the notion of *absolute deprivation* to a consideration of *relative deprivation*.

The notion of relative deprivation has been developed in recent sociological theorizing to denote the deprivation that arises not so much from the absolute amount of frustration as from the experienced discrepancy between one's lot and that of other persons or groups that serve as standards of reference. Whether or not superordinate groups or persons are taken as standards of reference by subordinate groups or individuals depends, at least in part, on whether the unequal distribution of rights and privileges is considered illegitimate by them. Negatively privileged groups or individuals may not develop the awareness that they are deprived of rights and privileges.[11] In a caste society, for example, members of the lower caste, considering this system justified for religious reasons, may not feel frustrated by it. If the privileges of the superordinate groups are not considered legitimately attainable by their subordinates, lower-status people compare themselves only with each other and not with members of higher-status groups.

11. Cf. Merton, *op. cit.*, esp. chapters VII and IX. Cf also L. A. Coser, *The Functions of Social Conflict*. New York, The Free Press, 1956, esp. pp. 32–38.

In contrast, in societies such as ours, in which upward social mobility is said to be accessible to all, yet where in fact mobility is blocked for significant sections of the population, the bottom dogs in the status hierarchy compare their lot to that of the top dogs. Persons measure their status and the deprivations that it entails against the superior rights and privileges that they visualize as being enjoyed by the superordinate strata. Thus it stands to reason that, for example, American Negroes are especially frustrated because they contrast the success ideology inculcated by schools and mass media to the reality of continued discrimination. Hence among them, as among other low-status groups discussed so far, relative deprivation is likely to be high. This helps to account for their higher homicide rates more adequately than the notion of absolute deprivation, for it clarifies the fact that in social structures that do not institutionalize social mobility, homicide rates do not necessarily follow the American pattern.

The notion of relative deprivation also helps us understand why other low-status categories, such as women and the young, do not show high homicide rates. To put the matter in a nut shell: the young know that they will grow older, move up in the age hierarchy, and enjoy the perquisites of higher age status in the future; hence their lower relative deprivation. Women similarly do not tend to feel relatively deprived but for opposite reasons: equality with men seems unattainable and different status among the sexes seems legitimate to both sexes. This accounts for the fact that women experience smaller degrees of relative deprivation. The young tend to accept the higher status of their elders because they know that one day they will be like them. Women accept the higher status of men because they believe that they will never be like them. Thus assurance of success just as assurance of lack of success may equally shield one against a sense of frustration. Similarly, sectarian subgroups who have withdrawn from involvement with the larger society in the name of a set of exclusive values do not compare their lot with that of members of the outside world and hence do not feel deprived.

This reasoning seems to account adequately for the fact that although women occupy lower statuses vis-à-vis men, their homicide rate is distinctly lower. (Of all city arrests for murder and non-negligent manslaughter in 1961, 834 were women and 3,791 were men.)[12] It also explains why the young, although having lower-status positions than their elders, still have relatively low homicide rates. (Only 8.3 per cent of the city arrests for murder and non-negligent manslaughter in 1961 were of persons under 18 years of age.)[13]

12. Uniform Crime Reports, *op. cit.,* p. 96. It should be noted, furthermore, that to the extent women do achieve a status more nearly equal to that of men, to the extent that they no longer accept their lower status and compete for higher status, to that extent their crime rates approach the male rates. Thus in America the crime rates of females are closer to those of males in cities than in small towns. In Western Europe and the United States these rates are closer to the male rates than in countries like Japan and Algiers where the lower status of females is still clearly and fully institutionalized. Cf. E. Sutherland, and D. Cressey, *Principles of Criminology*. New York, Lippincott, 1955, pp. 112–113.

13. Uniform Crime Reports, *op. cit.,* p. 95. It might be objected that our reasoning concerning the relatively low degree of violence among the young is refuted by the extent of juvenile delinquency in the United States. This is, however, not the case. In the first place sensational reportings about juvenile delinquency often distorts the facts in the popular imagination. While persons under 18 do indeed constitute a major proportion of city arrests for certain offenses against property such as larceny and auto theft (49.8 and 61 per cent, respectively) they do not commit a very high proportion of crimes against persons. The homicide figures were already quoted. Similarly, only 13 per cent of all city arrests for aggravated assault were of persons below the age of 18. Even the figure for forcible rape. (19.1 per cent), although higher, does not back up the popular misconception that such crimes are mainly committed by juvenile offenders. (Cf. Uniform Crime Reports, *op. cit.,* p. 95.)

In addition, juvenile delinquency is in the main limited to specific

Having accounted for differential homicide rates in terms of the related notions of frustration and relative deprivation, the second question can now be discussed: Frustrations can be dealt with in many ways other than homicide or other forms of interpersonal violence. They are often responded to with suicide or with successful repression or sublimation. Why do people in lower-status positions select more often violent aggression as a way of dealing with their frustrations?

THE EFFECTS OF DIFFERENTIAL SOCIALIZATION

Psychoanalytic theory seems to be divided on the effects of parental severity on superego formation. Anna Freud and Aichhorn[14] seem to suggest that parental severity leads to inadequate superego formation. Sigmund Freud taught that "the severity which a child's superego develops in no way corresponds to the severity of the treatment it has itself experienced. It seems to be independent of the latter."[15] However, recent cross-cultural evidence and some experimental work[16] tend to support the view that excessive severity is likely to hinder the formation of a strong superego, whereas permissive child-

---

areas in modern cities in which ethnic and class discriminations have created especially tense situations among especially deprived youngsters amidst an urban middle-class culture in which only success meets with applause and defeat invites contempt. These youngsters suffer from particular acute humiliations and frustrations because of their lower class and ethnic status. Low socioeconomic and ethnic status rather than youthfulness per se seems to lie at the bottom of most juvenile delinquency. It would be a major mistake to generalize from these special situations about the younger population as a whole.

14. A. Aichhorn, *Wayward Youth*. New York, The Viking Press, 1935, pp. 202–203; A. Freud, *The Ego and the Mechanisms of Defense*. New York, International Universities Press, 1946, Chapter IX.

15. S. Freud, *Civilization and Its Discontents*. (Trans. J. Riviere) London, The Hogarth Press, 1930, p. 116–17.

16. See Henry and Short, *op. cit.*, Chapter VII.

rearing techniques, which emphasize the loss of love rather than punishment as a means of discipline, are associated with a high degree of internalization, a heightened sense of guilt, that is, with a strong superego. Were child-rearing techniques distributed at random throughout the social structure, there would be no reason to expect structured variations in superego formation in the population. But this is not the case. Socialization processes are class-patterned, and the bulk of the evidence seems to indicate that working-class and lower-class child-rearing practices are more punitive than middle-class patterns.

In an excellent analytical summary of the many studies of the relation between social class and socialization in America, Bronfenbrenner[17] concludes: "The most consistent finding . . . is the more frequent use of physical punishment by working-class parents. The middle-class, in contrast, resort to reasoning, isolation, and . . . 'love-oriented' discipline techniques." Bronfenbrenner does not only find consistent class differences in child-rearing practices, but he also finds a differential effectiveness of these techniques. Summarizing the results of two large-scale studies in Boston and Detroit, he says: " 'Love-oriented' or 'psychological' techniques are more effective than other methods for bringing about desired behavior. Indeed, both groups of researchers concluded on the basis of their data that physical punishment for aggression tends to increase rather than decrease aggressive behavior . . . these findings mean that middle-class parents, although in one sense more lenient in their discipline techniques, are using methods that are actually more compelling."

17. U. Bronfenbrenner, "Socialization and Social Class Through Time and Space." In: *Readings in Social Psychology,* Eleanor Maccoby, Theodore Newcomb and Eugene Hartley, Eds.: New York, Henry Holt and Co., 1958.

Additional evidence comes from a study by Kohn[18] in which parental values and the exercise of parental authority are related to social-class position. Kohn finds that "middle-class parents . . . are more likely to ascribe predominant importance to the child's acting in terms of internal standards of conduct, working-class parents to the child's compliance with parental authority." In other words, middle-class parents are mainly concerned with developing internalized control in the child and with enforcing attitudinal conformity;[19] working-class parents, in contrast, are mainly concerned with behavior conformity, i.e., with external compliance. The working class wishes to instill respectable conduct in its children, the middle class is concerned with inculcating moral standards. The working class focuses attention on the act itself, the middle class on the actor's intention. This different emphasis on types of expected conformity helps to explain why, as Henry and Short[20] have shown, high degrees of frustration tend to lead to different types of deviant behavior in different classes. Where conformity is enforced externally, the agents of frustration remain external to the individual. In contrast, where standards for conformity are internalized, the individual perceives himself as the agent of his own frustrations. These findings make it possible to supplement the results arrived at earlier: not only is aggressive acting out in general and the rate of homicide in particular connected with the relative deprivation of various status categories in the social

18. M. L. Kohn, "Class and Parental Values. *Am. J. Soc.* 64:337–51, 1959; "Social Class and the Exercise of Parental Authority." *Am. Soc. Rev.* 24:352–66, 1959. Cf. also M. Gold, "Suicide, Homicide, and the Socialization of Aggression." *Am. J. Soc.,* 63:651–661, 1958.

19. On the distinction between behavioral and attitudinal conformity. Cf. R. K. Merton, "Conformity, Deviation and Opportunity Structure." *Am. Soc. Rev.* 24:177–88, 1959; R. L. Coser,: "Insulation from Observability and Types of Social Control." *Am. Soc. Rev.* 26:28–39, 1961.

20. *Op. cit., passim.*

structure, but also persons in the lower-status categories tend to have lower built-in barriers against the acting out of external aggression.

THE EVIDENCE FROM EXTREME SITUATIONS

Evidence from situations in which the normal social controls have broken down shows that even in such relatively unpatterned and unpredictable situations the comparative rates of aggressive deviance are predictable. Lower-status categories are disproportionately involved in mob actions and in acts of violence during revolutions.

Competent observers seem to agree that in the eighteenth and nineteenth centuries—the major revolutionary period in modern Europe—the urban lower classes suffered extremes of poverty and deprivation. They also tend to agree that these classes were hardly considered part of the moral fabric of the society in which they lived. Although it would be hazardous to make dogmatic statements about differences in the internalization of norms in the various strata of the population during this period, it seems probable that the guiding norms and values were most imperfectly internalized in the lower class, which was in significant ways excluded from the moral community of the nation. Furthermore, in any class-differentiated society the upper classes tend to have internalized more strongly the guiding normative standards, for these are, to a significant extent, *their* standards. The ruled are always more subject to external constraints than their rulers.

A true sociology of revolutions still remains to be written, yet whatever evidence I have been able to uncover points to the fact that revolutionary crowds were made up with a majority of lower-status people. The social composition of the participants in revolutionary violence is not related to the social and political character of the revolution. The barricades of the "bourgeois" revolutions seem to have been manned by roughly similar proportions of lower-class individuals as those of "proletarian" revolutions. In the French Revolution the extremely poor population was hardly represented among the *Jacobins*, yet the men who actually fought in the streets and stormed the Bastille were drawn in their overwhelming majority from the Parisian *sans-culottes*—from the workshop masters, craftsmen, wage earners, shop keepers, and petty traders.[21] In contrast, the political leaders came from the commercial bourgeoisie, the professions, or liberal aristocracy.

This was not an atypical phenomenon. A student of the city mob in the eighteenth century concludes:[22] "Who, then, were the 'mob'? Its main strength lay in the strata commonly described on the continent as the 'little people,' particularly those of certain cohesive and ancient quarters of the city like the Faubourg St. Antoine in Paris, the Trastevere in Rome or the Mercato in Naples. It was a combination of wage-earners, small property owners, and the unclassifiable urban poor." The revolutions of the early nineteenth century did not differ fundamentally from those of the eighteenth.

Students of revolutions have often suggested that revolutionary outbreaks can best be accounted for in terms of what has been called relative deprivation. De Tocqueville, for example, wrote that:[23] " . . . the French found their position insupportable, just where it had become better . . . A people, which has supported without complaint, as if they were not felt, the

21. G. Rudé, *The Crowd in the French Revolution.* Oxford, England, Clarendon Press, 1959, esp. pp. 178 ff.
22. E. J. Hobsbawm, *Social Bandits and Primitive Rebels.* New York, The Free Press, 1959, p. 113.
23. De Tocqueville's *L'Ancien Regime,* trans. M. W. Patterson, Oxford, England, Basil Blackwell, 1949, p. 186.

most oppressive laws, violently throws them off as soon as their weight is lightened. The social order destroyed by a revolution is always better than that which immediately preceded it . . . The evil, which was suffered patiently as inevitable, seems unendurable as soon as the idea of escaping from it is conceived."

In other words, only when hopes have been raised do deprived strata tend to react with revolutionary vigor against a regime that seems to frustrate the achievement of these hopes. Yet this explanation holds for all strata that participated in the revolutions and would not seem to account for the differential rates of participation in revolutionary violence.

From this reasoning one might conclude that the lowest strata of the population, who lived without hope in prerevolutionary days, were therefore predisposed to apathy rather than active revolt. This is indeed so, but one needs to realize that the very outbreak of a revolution is likely to raise the hopes and expectations of deprived classes. They now feel that what was an impossible aspiration in the past is such no longer. When the status order is toppling, the absolutely deprived may suddenly realize that what seemed impossible yesterday has become possible today. Any revolution is a revolution of rising expectations; it transforms absolute deprivations into relative deprivations. Moreover, since the lower class tends to be bound more exclusively by external restraints, their removal through the revolution furnishes a socially sanctioned outlet for agression.

There is some evidence of the import of relative deprivation in a more recent revolution, the Hungarian Revolution of 1956. A perceptive analyst of these events writes:[24] "Those who had the amplest ground for complaint were not the most prone to rebel. People who had lost everything tended to

24. P. Kecskemeti, *The Unexpected Revolution.* Stanford, Stanford University Press, 1961, p. 117.

be demoralized and passive, whereas revolutionary activity originated with groups who were partly privileged and partly frustrated. . . . In fact, disappointed expectations are particularly likely to result in violent hatreds." I stated previously that the gulf between structurally induced expectations and reality is apt to lead to a high sense of relative deprivation among certain groups in the American cultural setting in which the idea of open channels of mobility is part of the ideology although it is hardly realized in reality. Hungary presented a similar picture. This was predominantly a workers' revolution because the industrial workers had been led to believe that this was "their" state and that they would hold a dominant position, only to find out that they were actually subject to relentless regimentation and exploitation. Similar considerations also explain the high rates of participation among writers and students in that revolution. Both categories had indeed a somewhat privileged social position, yet suffered acutely from the loss of personal int grity and forced indoctrination. They had been led to expect that intellectual roles would carry highest honor and prestige only to find in practice that they had to submit to the dictates of unintellectual party bureaucrats.

The appraisal of revolutionary violence is broadly in accord with the previous appraisal of homicide rates; yet two significant differences appear. It will be remembered that the homicide rates of the young and of women, although these are lower-status categories, nevertheless, are lower than the rates of their superordinates in the respective sex and age hierarchy. But in revolutionary violence, women and the young play a very pronounced role. The active participation of women is noted by all students of the French Revolution. In fact, in certain key revolutionary events, such as the March on Versailles of October, 1790, and in later food riots, women were predominant. Writes Rudé: "On the morning of October 5 the revolt started simultaneously in the central markets and the Faubourg Saint-Antoine; in both cases women were the leading spirits."[25]

I know of no detailed breakdowns of the age of participants in violent crowds during the French Revolution. (Rudé gives some data indicating that their "average age" was in the thirties, but he does not indicate the range.) But, in the case of the Hungarian Revolution the data are unambiguous; here the very young played very active roles so that some observers have talked of a veritable "children's crusade." "To a very considerable extent," says Kecskemeti,[26] the street battles were fought by the young: students, apprentices, school children. A good many older people participated too, but it seems certain that the struggle would not have been sustained as long as it was if it had not been for the death-defying, desperate determination of the very young."

What explains the fact that, at least in certain revolutionary events, women and the young played a considerable role? Here one may suggest that situations of normlessness differ significantly from the normatively structured situations which were discussed when homicide was considered. In the latter case women, having internalized the acceptance of their lower status, tend to experience relatively low relative deprivation. The matter is quite different, however, when normative restraints and traditional expectations have been shattered. It is as if many were to say to themselves, "If all these extraordinary actions have become possible, then it is perhaps permissible to entertain the extraordinary idea that women need no longer accept their inferior status and can aspire to become like men." In this case, also, the revolution turns absolute deprivation into rela-

25. Rudé, *op. cit.*, p. 73. On the participation of women in the Paris *Commune* of 1871, see Edith Thomas, *The Women Incendiaries,* New York, Braziller, 1966.
26. Kecskemeti, *op. cit.*, pp. 112 ff.

tive deprivation by raising the hopes of the underdogs in the sex hierarchy. Moreover, and perhaps above all, a revolutionary situation provides the occasion for women to indeed act like men. It offers opportunities for the assertion of equality which were previously unavailable.[27]

The case of the high participation of the young in revolutionary activity can be explained in similar terms. In routinized social situations the young may feel that, although they suffer status deprivations from their elders, the course of time will rectify these felt injustices. But in periods of revolutionary normlessness, or in highly anomic and disorganized situations, normal expectations can no longer be entertained.

The breakdown of tradition creates in the young two seemingly contradictory expectations: the fear that the gradual advancement in the age hierarchy is put into question, and the hope that it is no longer necessary to wait the requisite number of years for the rewards of maturity. Insecurity about the future and hope for the present leads behavior that so far had been future-oriented to be replaced by present-oriented activity. For the young as well as for the women, the revolution provides a setting for the triumph of human action over biology.

The composition of the participants in the only major form of mass violence that continues to occur in recent American history, urban race riots, shows a consistently higher rate in the lower-status categories. Participants in race riots, both Negro and white, are of predominantly low status, such as the unemployed, the unskilled or little educated. As in revolutions, here also women as well as the young tend to play a very active part. The composition of the modern rioters is so similar to that of

27. Finally, it seems worthwhile mentioning that it was in revolutionary situations impinging more directly on female activities that women took an especially active part. Food riots in response to scarcity or high prices showed an especially high involvement of women in violent and aggressive behavior.

earlier revolutionaries that no special discussion is required.[28]

Relative deprivation accounts for seemingly contradictory findings about two categories of lower status, the women and the young. Although in normal periods their rates contrast with the relatively high violence rate among other lower-status categories, this is not the case in revolutions and mob violence in which participation of the young and of women tends to be remarkably high. This is because revolutions transform the absolute deprivation of the young and of women into relative deprivation so that in these situations all relevant lower-status categories tend to have a disproportionately high rate of participation in violence.

28. Cf. A. D. Grimshaw, "A Study in Social Violence, Urban Race Riots in the United States." Unpublished doctoral dissertation, Graduate School of Arts and Science, The University of Pennsylvania, 1959, mimeo. This is the best general survey of the subject.

4

Some Social Functions of Violence

The common view of things social, being rooted most often in a moralistic perspective, seems to assume that when something is useful, makes some contribution, or has some social function, it must necessarily be a good and "nice" thing; and conversely, that "bad" actions can have only evil consequences. In this common view, good effects must stem from pure motives, and evil intentions lead to evil results. The impact of the deed, so it is assumed, must somehow be in tune with the motives and characteristics of the doer.

Much sociological thought has been devoted to the rejection of this simplistic view. Social scientists from Wilhelm Wundt to Max Weber and Robert K. Merton have highlighted the fact that large areas of social life become understandable only when we consider the unanticipated consequences or latent functions of social action, and when we distinguish between an actor's intention and the consequences of his action. They have shown that social actions may have effects wholly or partly at variance with what they were originally intended to accomplish. Furthermore, functional analysis has been able to show that many frowned-upon and tabooed social activities may nevertheless perform a variety of social functions.* This type of analysis has

* Cf. Robert K. Merton, *Social Theory and Social Structure*, New York, The Free Press, 1957, especially Chapter I. For a concrete illustra-

taught us to distinguish sharply between motive and consequence as well as between moral evaluation and sociological assessment.

Even when social commentary has successfully emancipated itself from a crude moralistic perspective in such matters, it tends but too often to fall into a related error. There is a tendency to ignore the fact that actions that seem in the short run to lead to dysfunctional consequences might in the long run still be conducive to the emergence of highly functional adjustments. Too many sociologists, I fear, echo Senator Robert Kennedy when he recently stated, "The course of violence would be terribly, awfully wrong: Not just because hatred and violence are self-defeating. . . . They strike at the very heart of obedience to law, peaceful progress, and political cooperation which are man's last, best hope for a decent world."† The underlying assumption in these and similar statements always seems to be that what is distasteful in its immediate impact must also, almost by definition, be socially undesirable in its long-range effect. Whereas such sentiments might be understandable when expressed by a politician, they are less excusable when made by social scientists who are presumably able to detach themselves from the immediacy of events and to set their analyses in contextual frames.

The following pages are meant to question moralistic assumptions and foreshortened thinking by showing that types of violence that are morally disapproved or judged to be destructive may nevertheless have a number of societal functions that, on balance, may turn out to be positive. Just as other types of deviance to be discussed later in this volume may make major contributions to the smooth operation of a society, so violence, distasteful though it may be on other counts, may perform definite social functions.

This chapter attempts to illustrate the sociological analysis of violence by reference to three selected functions: violence as an

---

tion see Kingsley Davis, "The Sociology of Prostitution," *Am. Soc. Review*, II, (Oct. 1937) pp. 744–755.

† *New York Times*, Oct. 24, 1966, p. 16.

area of achievement, violence as a danger signal, and violence as a catalyst. In the first case violence serves specified functions for its practitioners. In the second, the community at large derives advantages from violent action. In the third, violence is analyzed in terms of its functional impact on publics and audiences of nonparticipants.

THE FOLKLORE OF PSYCHOLOGY HAS IT THAT ANIMALS IN experimental studies display systematically different behavioral characteristics depending on the investigator. Rats described by American observers are seen as frenetically active, given to a great deal of motor activity, forever dashing in and out of mazes, always trying to get somewhere—though not always certain of exactly where. In contrast, experimental animals seen through the lens of German investigators, seem given to long and intense periods of pensive deliberation and musing cogitation.

This jest highlights an important truth. There *are* systematic differences in the ways a particular scholarly community at a given moment in time chooses to approach the manifold data with which it is confronted. In sociology, for example, even if most American social theorists would readily agree in the abstract that conflict as well as order, tension as well as peaceful adjustment characterize all social systems in varying degrees, social theory actually has settled mainly for a remarkably tame and domesticated view of the social world. This is so despite the fact that European social thinkers such as Marx, Weber, and Simmel, upon whose works so much of American theorizing depends for its inspiration, had an entirely different orientation.

It seems as if American social science, developing in a society that, its birth through revolution notwithstanding, has only known one major internal upheaval throughout its history, has failed to be sensitized to the pervasive effects of violence, conflict, and disorder that to the European thinker were facts that they could not but be acquainted with intimately. Whereas to the European thinker the fragility of the social fabric and the brittleness of social bonds seemed self-evident experiences, American social science proceeded from a world view in which social violence was at best seen as a pathological phenomenon. As Arnold Feldman has recently argued:

Violence is conceived as being *incidental* to the basic character of social structures and processes. Indeed the very conception of social structure ordinarily excludes the source of structural destruction.[1]

As long as American sociology confined its attention mainly to a limited view of the contemporary American scene, its neglect of conflict and violence was, perhaps, none too disabling, at least until recently. But at present, when sociology has happily awakened to the need of doing comparative studies of social structures in both geographical space and historical time, this domesticated vision of the social world can be severely hampering. In addition, it seems that even the proper study of American society can no longer profit from exclusive emphasis on models and constructs in which conflict and violence are deliberately or unwittingly minimized. Just as analyses of, say, contemporary South Africa, Latin America, or Southeast Asia, or of seventeenth-century England or nineteenth-century France, would be patently unrealistic if they ignored the functions of political violence, so it has become increasingly evident that such ignoring would be just as unrealistic in the study of the current racial scene in the United States.

For a number of years I have urged a correcting of the traditional balance in theoretical and empirical emphasis in studies of social conflict and social order and have suggested that it is high time to tilt the scale in the direction of greater attention to social conflict.[2] Though much of my work was more generally concerned with the wider topic of social conflict rather than with the somewhat narrower area of social violence, a number

1. Arnold S. Feldman, "Violence and Volatility: The Likelihood of Revolution," *Internal War*, ed. Harry Eckstein, New York, The Free Press, 1964, p. 111.
2. Lewis A. Coser, *The Functions of Social Conflict*, New York, The Free Press, 1956.

of propositions previously advanced apply to violence as well. There is no need, therefore, to reiterate them in this paper. Instead, I shall focus selectively on but a few functions of social violence: violence as a form of achievement, violence as a danger signal, and violence as a catalyst. It is to be understood that this is by no means an exhaustive list of the functions of violence, nor will its dysfunctions be dealt with in this paper.

VIOLENCE AS ACHIEVEMENT

Certain categories of individuals are so located in the social structure that they are barred from legitimate access to the ladder of achievement, as Merton has argued in convincing detail.[3] Moreover, as Cloward and Ohlin[4] have shown more recently, certain categories of persons may find themselves in structural positions which effectively prevent them from utilizing not only legitimate channels of opportunity but criminal and illegitimate channels as well. I shall argue that when all such channels are barred, violence may offer alternate roads to achievement.

Cloward and Ohlin take as a case in point adolescents in disorganized urban areas who are oriented toward achieving higher positions and yet lack access to either conventional or criminal opportunity structures. "These adolescents," they argue,

> seize upon the manipulation of violence as a route to status not only because it provides a way of expressing pent-up angers and frustrations but also because they are not cut off from access to violent means by vicissitudes of birth. In the world of violence, such attributes as race, socioeconomic position,

3. Robert K. Merton, *Social Theory and Social Structure* (rev. ed.), New York, The Free Press, 1957, chaps. 4 and 5.
4. Richard A. Cloward and Lloyd E. Ohlin, *Delinquency and Opportunity*, New York, The Free Press, 1960.

age, and the like are irrelevant; personal worth is judged on the basis of qualities that are available to all who would cultivate them. The acquisition of status is not simply a consequence of skill in the use of violence or of physical strength but depends, rather, on one's willingness to risk injury or death in the search for "rep."[5]

In the area of violence, then, ascriptive status considerations become irrelevant. Here, the vaunted equal opportunity, which had been experienced as a sham and a lure everywhere else, turns out to be effective. In the wilderness of cities, just as in the wilderness of the frontier, the gun becomes an effective equalizer. Within the status structure of the gang, through a true transvaluation of middle-class values, success in defense of the "turf" brings deference and "rep" that are unavailable anywhere else. Here the successful exercise of violence is a road to achievement.

Nor need we rest consideration with the case of juvenile delinquency. One can make the more general assertion that in all those situations in which both legitimate and illegitimate socioeconomic achievement seems blocked, recourse to aggressive and violent behavior may be perceived as a significant area of "achievement." This may help to explain the ideal of *machismo* in the lower classes of Latin America. Here, as in the otherwise very different violence in disorganized urban areas of American cities, men tend to feel that only prowess in interpersonal violence or in aggressive sexual encounters allows the achievement of personal identity and permits gaining otherwise unavailable deference. Where no social status can be achieved through socioeconomic channels it may yet be achieved in the show of violence among equally deprived peers.

Somewhat similar mechanisms may be at work in the intrafamilial aggression and violence of American lower-class

5. *Ibid.*, p. 175.

fathers. These men tend to compensate for inadequate rewards in the occupational world at large by an aggressive assertion of male superiority within the little world of the family—as Donald McKinley has recently argued with much cogency.[6] The disproportionately high rate of interpersonal violence among Negro males may yield to a similar explanation. Since Negroes are assigned lowest position in all three major dimensions of the American status system—ethnicity, class, and education— and since their mobility chances are nil in the first and minimal in the second and third, it stands to reason that achievement in the area of interpersonal violence might be seen as a channel leading to self-regard and self-enhancement—at least as long as conflict with the dominant white majority seems socially unavailable as a means of collective action. This does not preclude that violent acting out may not also at the same time call forth a feeling of self-hatred for acting in the stereotypical manner in which the Negro is accused of acting by the dominant white.

Revolutionary violence, both in the classical revolutions of the past and in the anticolonialist liberation movements of the present, can also be understood in this manner. Participation in such violence offers opportunity to the oppressed and downtrodden for affirming identity and for claiming full manhood hitherto denied to them by the powers that be. Participation in revolutionary violence offers the chance for the first act of participation in the polity, for entry into the world of active citizenship. In addition, participation in acts of violence symbolizes commitment to the revolutionary cause. It marks to the actor, but also to his circle, the irrevocable decision to reject the *ancien régime* and to claim allegiance to the revolutionary movement. This has been well described by the late Frantz Fanon, an active participant in the Algerian movement of

6. Donald G. McKinley, *Social Class and Family Life,* New York, The Free Press, 1964.

liberation and one of its most powerful ideological spokesmen. "For colonial man," he writes,

> violence incarnates absolute *praxis*. . . . The questions asked of militants by the organization are marked by this vision of things. "Where did you work? With whom? What have you done?" The group demands that the individual commits an irreversible deed. In Algeria, for example, where almost all of the men who called for the struggle of national liberation were condemned to death or pursued by the French police, confidence in a man was proportional to the degree of severity of his [police] case. A new militant was considered reliable when he could no longer return to the colonial system. It seems that this mechanism was at play among the Mau Mau in Kenya where it was required that each member of the group strike the victim. Hence everyone was personally responsible for the victim's death. . . . Violence once assumed permits those who have left the group to return to their place and to be reintegrated. Colonial man liberates himself in and through violence.[7]

The act of violence, in other words, commits a man symbolically to the revolutionary movement and breaks his ties with his previous life and its commitments. He is reborn, so to speak, through the act of violence and is now in a position to assume his rightful place in the revolutionary world of new men.

Similar considerations may also account for the otherwise puzzling fact that women, normally much less given to violence than men, have played leading roles in classical revolutionary movements and in such modern liberation movements as that of Algeria. Here, as in all the other cases considered, violence equalizes and opens to the participants access to hitherto denied areas of achievement.[8]

7. Frantz Fanon, *Les Damnés de la Terre,* Paris, Francis Maspero, 1961, pp. 63–64.
8. I dealt with this in a somewhat different framework in Chapter 3.

VIOLENCE AS A DANGER SIGNAL

The late Norbert Wiener once remarked that cancer is so peculiarly dangerous a disease because it typically develops through its early stages without causing pain. Most other diseases, by eliciting painful sensations in the body, bring forth bodily signals which allow early detection of the illness and its subsequent treatment. Pain serves as an important mechanism of defense, permitting the medical readjustment of bodily balance which has been attacked by disease. It seems hardly far-fetched to apply this reasoning to the body social as well.

A social dysfunction can, of course, be attended to only if it becomes visible, if not to the total community, at least to certain more sensitive and more powerful sectors of it. But the sensitive usually lack power, and the powerful often lack sensitivity. As Merton has phrased the issue, there are latent social problems, "conditions which are . . . at odds with values of the group but are not recognized as being so,"[9] that can become manifest, and hence subject to treatment, only when particular groups or individuals choose to take cognizance of them. Merton urges that it is the task of the sociologist to make latent social problems manifest; at the same time he stresses that

> those occupying strategic positions of authority and power of course carry more weight than others in deciding social policy and so . . . in identifying for the rest what are to be taken as significant departures from social standards.[10]

Granted that the social perceptions of those in power and authority may be influenced by social scientists, calling attention to previously neglected problems, it would be an indulgence in

9. Robert K. Merton, "Social Problems and Social Theory," *Contemporary Social Problems,* ed. Robert K. Merton and Robert A. Nisbet, New York, Harcourt and Brace, 1962, p. 709.
10. *Ibid.,* p. 706.

unwarranted Comtean optimism to assume that such enlighten-
ment will at all times be sufficient to alert them. It is at this
point that the signaling functions of social violence assume
importance.

Although there are individual, subcultural, and class variations in the internalized management and control of anger in
response to frustration, I take it to be axiomatic that human
beings—other than those systematically trained to use legitimate or illegitimate violence—will resort to violent action only
under extremely frustrating, ego-damaging, and anxiety-produc-
ing conditions. It follows that if the incidence of violence increases rapidly, be it in the society at large or within specific
sectors of it, this can be taken as a signal of severe maladjustment. I would further suggest that this signal is so drastic,
so extremely loud, that it cannot fail to be perceived by men in
power and authority otherwise not noted for peculiar sensitivity
to social ills. This is not to say, of course, that they will necessarily respond with types of social therapy that will effectively
remove the sources of infection. But I suggest that outbreaks of
social violence are more apt than other less visible or sensitive
indicators at least to lead them to perceive the problem.

To be sure, outbreaks of violence can be seen as mere
manifestations of underlying conditions. Yet this view neglects
the contribution that outbreaks make to the change of conditions. Two illustrations will have to suffice. Conventional historical and sociological wisdom has it that the British Chartist
movement of the first half of the last century and the often
violent and destructive popular movements which preceded it
were but manifestations of temporary imbalances brought by
the Industrial Revolution upon the British social and political
scene. These imbalances, it is argued, were progressively eliminated through a variety of social-structural changes, more
particularly through an increase in structural differentiation that

gradually provided the homeostatic forces that led to the re-stabilization of British society in the second part of the nineteenth century.[11] In this perspective, Chartism was a symptom of a temporary pathological condition, and its defeat highlighted the return to equilibrium and stability.

This view seems to be seriously deficient, if for no other reason than that it ignores the impact of Chartism and related movements on the political decision-makers. It ignores, in other words, the determining contribution of this movement. Far from being but an epiphenomenal manifestation of temporary maladjustment, Chartism had a direct impact by leading to a series of reform measures alleviating the conditions against which it had reacted. Violence and riots were not merely protests: They were claims to be considered. Those involved in them assumed that the authorities would be sensitive to demands and would make concessions. And it turned out that they were right.[12]

Historians will hardly deny that the condition of the laboring poor, and more particularly the industrial working class, between the beginning of the Industrial Revolution and the middle of the nineteeth century was appalling. Nor is it subject to debate that for a long time these conditions were barely perceived by those in power. Finally, it is not to be doubted that legislative remedies, from factory legislation to the successive

11. Cf. Neil J. Smelser, *Social Change in the Industrial Revolution,* Chicago, University of Chicago Press, 1959 and the same author's *Theory of Collective Behavior,* New York, The Free Press, 1963. In the latter work, social movements are seen as always involving the "action of the impatient" who "short-circuit" the process of social readjustment by "exaggerating reality," see pp. 72–73. In this perspective one might be justified in concluding that had impatient Christians not short-circuited the adjustment process in ancient Israel, the Jews would have readjusted in time—and spared the world the spectacle of much later impatient religious action.

12. Eric J. Hobsbawm, *The Age of Revolution,* London, Weidenfels and Nicholson, 1962, p. 111.

widening of the franchise and the attendant granting of other citizenship rights to members of the lower classes,[13] came, at least in part, in response to the widespread disorders and violent outbreaks that marked the British social scene for over half a century. Let me quote from Mark Hovell, one of the earliest, and still one of the best, of the historians of the Chartist movement. "The Chartists," he writes:

> first compelled attention to the hardness of the workmen's lot, and forced thoughtful minds to appreciate the deep gulf between the two nations which lived side by side without knowledge of or care for each other. Though remedy came slowly and imperfectly, and was seldom directly from Chartist hands, there was always the Chartist impulse behind the first timid steps toward social and economic betterment. The cry of the Chartists did much to force public opinion to adopt the policy of factory legislation in the teeth of the opposition of the manufacturing interests. It compelled the administrative mitigation of the harshness of the New Poor Law. It swelled both the demand and necessity for popular education. It prevented the unqualified victory of the economic gospel of the Utilitarians. . . . The whole trend of modern social legislation must well have gladdened the hearts of the ancient survivors of Chartism.[14]

The often violent forms of rebellion of the laboring poor, the destructiveness of the city mobs, and other forms of popular disturbances which mark English social history from the 1760's to the middle of the nineteenth century, helped to educate the governing elite of England, Whig and Tory alike,

13. Cf. T. H. Marshall, *Class, Citizenship and Social Development,* New York, Doubleday Anchor Books, 1965.
14. Mark Hovell, *The Chartist Movement,* London, Longmans, Green, 1918, pp. 210–211. See also Edouard Dolléans, *Le Chartisme,* Paris, Marcel Rivière, 1949.

to the recognition that they could ignore the plight of the poor only at their own peril. These social movements constituted among other things an effective signaling device that sensitized the upper classes to the need for social reconstruction in defense of a social edifice over which they wished to continue to have over-all command.[15]

My second example concerning violence as a danger signal will be brief since it deals with recent experiences still vivid in social memory: the civil rights movement and the war against poverty. The plight of the American Negro and of the urban poor until recently had a very low degree of visibility for the bulk of the white population and the decision-makers on the American scene. Much of it was physically not visible in the sense that it took place in segregated areas not customarily visited by "good people." Much of it, on the other hand, though physically visible, was yet not socially perceived. The sociology of social perception, a sociology elucidating why people some-times look and why they sometimes look away, it may be re-marked in passing, still is to be written. Be that as it may, the shock of recognition, the jolt to conscience, occurred only when the Negroes, through by-and-large nonviolent action in the South and through increasingly violent demonstrations and even riots in the North, brought the problem forcibly to the attention of white public opinion and the white power structure. To be sure, a whole library of books has been written on the dehumanizing consequences of the racial caste system. Yet all this became a public issue only after a number of large-scale

15. On the politics of rioting and crowd action see, among others, George Rudé, *The Crowd in History,* New York, John Wiley & Sons, 1964; *The Crowd in the French Revolution* by the same author, also his *Wilkes and Liberty,* Oxford, Clarendon Press, 1962; Eric J. Hobsbawm, *Labouring Men,* London, Weidenfels and Nicholson, 1964 and his earlier *Social Bandits and Primitive Rebels,* New York, Free Press, 1959.

social conflicts, beginning in Montgomery, Alabama, helped to highlight the situation. No doubt, the slow process of structural differentiation might have taken care of the problem some time in the indeterminate future. In fact, something was done about it here and now mainly because Negroes, no longer satisfied with promises and having gained some advances, now raised their level of expectations indicating in a quite drastic manner that they were no longer prepared to wait, that they wanted *Freedom Now.* (I shall return to the topic in the last part of this paper.) Much as one might deplore the often apparently senseless violence displayed in such racial riots as those in Los Angeles, one cannot help feeling that they, too, constituted quite effective signaling devices, perhaps desperate cries for help after other appeals had been unavailing. They indicated a sickness in the body social which demands immediate remedy if it is not to undermine social order altogether.

VIOLENCE AS A CATALYST

Marx once remarked: "The criminal produces an impression now moral, now tragic, and hence renders a 'service' by arousing the moral and aesthetic sentiments of the public," Marx here anticipated by many years similar formulations by Durkheim and Mead stressing the unanticipated functions of crime in creating a sense of solidarity within the community.[16] Here I shall argue a related idea, namely, that not only criminals, but law-enforcing agents also, may call forth a sense of solidarity against their behavior. More particularly, the use of extralegal violence by these officers may, under certain circumstances, lead to the arousal of the community and to a

16. For the relevant quotations from Marx, Durkheim, and Mead, see "Some Functions of Deviant Behavior," in this volume.

revulsion from societal arrangements that rest upon such enforcement methods.

It is common knowledge that the violence used by sheriffs and other Southern officers of the law against Southern Negroes engaged in protest activities and voting-registration drives has had a major impact upon public opinion and federal legislation. The fact is that such methods had been relied upon by Southern police for a very long time without any marked reaction against them. Why, then, did they suddenly become counterproductive? Two major factors seem to account for this reversal. First, modes of control involving the extralegal uses of violence worked well as long as the acts in question could be committed with a minimum of publicity and visibility. They became suicidal when they were performed under the glare of television cameras and under the observation of reporters for national newspapers and magazines.

Everett Hughes, in discussing the Nazi case, has argued that all societies depend for their maintenance on a certain amount of "dirty work" by shady agents of the powers that be, and he added that such dirty work is usually performed far from the sight of "good people."[17] Indeed, the usefulness of those doing the "dirty work" may well come to an end when it must be performed in full view of "good people." If, as Hughes argues, those who do the dirty work "show a sort of concentrate of those impulses of which we are or wish to be less aware," then it stands to reason that they cease to be useful if they have to operate in full view. The solid middle-class citizens of Nazi Germany seem initially, by and large, to have been unconcerned with what was being done to the Jews; even the public degradation of Jews in city streets seems to have left them unaffected.

17. Everett C. Hughes, "Good People and Dirty Work," *Social Problems,* X, 1 (Summer 1962), pp. 3–11.

But the Hitler regime showed very good judgment indeed in carefully hiding and camouflaging its later murderous methods. One may doubt that the death camps could have been operated except in secret. Similarly, solid middle-class citizens in both North and South may have been aware of the extralegal uses of violence habitually resorted to by Southern sheriffs and police. Yet as long as such knowledge did not intrude too much in their visual field, they remained unconcerned. Matters changed drastically when these inhuman methods were fully exposed to the public at large. Now visibility could no longer be denied. Had these officials become conscious of the changed circumstances under which they were now forced to operate, they might well have abandoned these methods in favor of more subtle means of intimidation. As it turned out, they were subject to the "trained incapacity" upon which Veblen and Kenneth Burke have commented. They adopted measures in keeping with their past training—and the very soundness of this training led them to adopt the wrong measures. Their past training caused them to misjudge their present situation.[10] The very exercise of violence that had been productive of "order" in the past now produced a wave of public indignation that undermined the very practice.

The matter of publicity, powerfully aided by the recent "communication revolution," though crucially important, is not the only one to be considered here. It is equally relevant to observe that violent tactics of suppression tend to be much less successful when used against people who are publicly committed to the principle of nonviolence. Violence by the police, even extralegal violence, may be approved, or at least condoned, when it can be justified by reference to the supposed

18. Kenneth Burke, *Permanence and Change,* New York, New Republic, 1936, p. 18.

actual or potential violence of the offending criminal. That is, such behavior seems to be justified or condoned when there exists, or seems to exist, a rough equivalence between the means used by both sides. A tooth for a tooth tends to be a maxim popularly applicable in these cases. But the matter is very different when the presumed offender is committed in principle to a politics of nonviolence. The nonviolent resisters in the South, as distinct from other cases where nonviolence was not based on principle, had consciously assumed the burden of nonviolence. That is, they had made a commitment to the public not to have recourse to violence. When violence was used against them, this hence came to be seen as a breach of a tacit reciprocal commitment on the part of those they opposed. What is ordinarily perceived as a multilateral relationship in which both sides actually or potentially use violence, came now to be perceived as unilateral violence. This impression was still accentuated when acts of official or semiofficial violence were being directed against ministers, that is, against men who enjoy specific mandates and immunities as men of peace.

For these reasons, extralegal violence habitually used in the South to maintain the caste system turned out to be a most effective triggering device for measures to abolish it. One need, perhaps, not go so far as to argue, as Jan Howard has recently done,[19] that the very effectiveness of the nonviolent methods used depended on the assumption or expectation that it would encounter violent reactions that would arouse the public conscience. The violent reactions did not have to be anticipated. But it was nevertheless one of the latent functions of Southern violent response to the nonviolent tactics used to lead to the arousal of a previously lethargic community and to a general sense of indignation and revulsion.

19. In *Dissent* (January–February 1966).

Nor is the Southern case unique. Even in earlier periods extralegal violence on the part of law-enforcement agencies has often been suicidal. The Peterloo Massacre of 1819 in Manchester, when a crowd of listeners to speeches on parliamentary reform and the repeal of the Corn Laws was charged by soldiers who killed ten and injured hundreds, became a rallying cry for the reformers and radicals. The wholsale massacre of participants in the French Commune of 1871 created a sense of intimate solidarity, but also of alienation from society at large, among large sectors of the French working class. In these latter cases the impact was not on the total society but only on particular sectors of it, but in all of them the show of violence on the part of officialdom was suicidal in so far as it transformed victims into martyrs who became symbols of the iniquity and callousness of the rulers.

Lest it be understood that I argue that unanticipated and suicidal uses of violence are limited to cases involving law-enforcement agents alone, let me remark, even if only in passing, that there are clearly other groups within society whose resort to violence may under specifiable circumstances bring forth similar suicidal consequences. In particular, when minority groups appeal to the public conscience and attempt to dramatize the fact that they are treated with less than justice and equity, their resort to violence may effectively hamper their cause. They must depend in their appeal on winning to their side previously indifferent and unconcerned sectors of the public. Resort to violence, however, even though it may serve as a danger signal, is also likely to alienate precisely those who are potential recruits for their cause. Hence groups such as the Black Muslims and other extremist Negro organizations may, if they resort to violence, bring about suicidal results by turning previously indifferent or potentially sympathetic bystanders into hostile antagonists.

The preceding discussion has indentified and examined a series of cases in which violence may perform latent or manifest functions. The approach was meant to be exploratory and tentative rather than exhaustive and systematic. It is hoped, however, that enough has been said to show that the curiously tenderminded view of the social structure that has generally predominated in American social theory is seriously deficient and needs to be complemented by a more tough-minded approach.

5

Internal Violence as a Mechanism for

Conflict Resolution

The preceding chapter dealt with a few selected functions of violence for several different groups and communities; this chapter focuses specific attention upon the uses of violence for deprived and excluded sectors of the population and stresses the importance of violence as a mechanism for conflict resolution when non-violent channels for the expression of group desires and demands are socially unavailable.

Following Robert K. Merton's lead, I attempt to show here that "*apparently* irrational behavior may *at times* be found to be positively functional for the group."* I distinguish two categories: (1) Cases in which closer inspection reveals that though outside observers have attributed irrationality to the actors involved, and though such violent behavior may indeed have been extraordinary, threatening, and anxiety-provoking to observers and victims, it was not necessarily irrational from the point of view of the actors. (2) Cases in which a certain amount of irrational behavior can indeed be found, but where that behavior nevertheless serves latent positive functions for the group engaged in conflict.

* Robert K. Merton, *Social Theory and Structure, op. cit.,* p. 65.

Although the first case is sufficiently spelled out in the chapter, the second case may need a few additional comments here. In the Introduction I briefly alluded to Ralf Dahrendorf's statement that organized conflict groups tend to use less violent means of combat than those that lack organization. Such cases of violence as the race riots in Watts can be better understood if this proposition is taken in conjunction with my earlier statement in *The Functions of Social Conflict* that when group members are deeply involved with one another, conflicts are likely to mobilize a very high degree of their energies and be very intense in character.

In urban ghettos like Watts we usually find a very low rate of associational participation. These ghettos tend to lack organizational structure and the inhabitants tend to be deprived of the multifaceted group life that characterizes middle-class and, to some extent, even working-class life styles. The ghetto dweller is deprived of the social support that comes from involvement in a variety of groups. As a consequence, he has a rather restricted role-set, being involved only with relatively few persons in relatively unsegmented relationships. It seems fairly well established that complex role-sets and segmented types of relationships with others are conducive to a multiplicity of conflicts that, however, are generally not very intense since they typically mobilize only a segment of the personality and do not polarize the population into the same two camps on all issues. But when, as in the case of the ghetto dweller, the individual is involved with relatively few others, when social participation is severely limited, the chances are much higher that conflicts, if they occur, assume higher degrees of both intensity and violence. In such communities social energies are bottled up; they hence may explode upon occasion in outbreaks in which realistic and nonrealistic elements are intertwined and fused. The lack of social participation, the unavailability of associational ties and the consequent restriction of the role-set of persons living in a ghetto community may help to account for the peculiar violence and the peculiar intensity of the riots that have marked the racial scene in recent years.*

* Some of the ideas adumbrated here grew out of discussions with my Brandeis colleague Samuel E. Wallace. For further clarification of the implications of simple and complex role-sets for personality development see, Rose Laub Coser, "Role Distance, Sociological Ambivalence, and Transitional Status Systems," *Am. Journal of Sociology,* LXXII, 2 (Sept. 1966), pp. 173–187.

INTERNAL VIOLENCE WITHIN A SOCIAL SYSTEM MAY BE SEEN as a response to the failure of established authority to accommodate demands of new groups for a hearing. It is a danger signal as well as a means by which such groups make their demands heard. "Rebellions," writes William Kornhauser, "are ways of making demands on authority, whether for changes of specific acts or rulers or of structures of authority. They are alternatives to established ways of making demands on authority in an orderly manner . . ."[1] They may be "a way of performing political functions in the absence of political structures capable of accommodating political demands."[2]

All political structures tend to provide channels for the expression of claims and grievances of the underlying population, yet it can be taken as axiomatic that these channels, having been designed to register power balances of the past, tend to be insufficient when it comes to accommodating claims of new groupings not previously considered as political actors worthy of having their voices heard and their contributions counted. In other words, the channels of political communication tend to be so constructed that they admit access only to those social forces that have succeeded in making their voices heard in the past. When new social forces appear on the arena they often find themselves blocked from these channels and hence remain unable to actualize their potential force. They feel excluded from participation in the political dialogue. I should like to argue that when this is the case the actual or threatened use of violence must be seen not only as a signaling device by which the new groups indicate their dissatisfactions and grievances to those in power,[3] but also as an indicator of the seriousness of

1. William Kornhauser, "Rebellion and Political Development" in Harry Eckstein, ed., *Internal War,* New York, The Free Press, 1964, p. 142.
2. *Ibid.*
3. Cf., "Some Social Functions of Violence," in this volume.

their commitment, of their will and their ability to have their voices heard and counted.

I take it to be axiomatic that men—other than those systematically trained in the use of legitimate or illegitimate violence—will resort to violent action only under extremely frustrating, ego-damaging, and anxiety-provoking conditions. It follows that the threat to resort to violence on the part of aggrieved groups is likely to be perceived by those in power as a very serious indicator of maladjustment; it follows further that there must be a very strong commitment by aggrieved actors if they are to make a credible threat of violence. It stands to reason that the actual use of violence requires even stronger commitment.[4] The threat of violence and, even more so, its actual use, indicate that aggrieved groups "really mean it." Violence whether acted out or threatened serves to symbolize to those in power and to the community at large that aggrieved groups and individual actors are willing to forego the gratifications that flow from peaceful acceptance and internalization of existing norms and to launch themselves on the unchartered seas of rebellion. To reject the wont and use of a political community and to threaten or actually to commit violence requires considerable psychic energies; it therefore testifies to unbearable frustration and is an indicator of very serious commitment as well.

When such breaking away from the established ways of the political community occurs, it is to be expected that a variety of highly irrational activities will mark the behavior of rebellious actors. This has been amply shown in such studies as that by Norman Cohn[5] of the millenarian cults among displaced artisans and peasants of the late Middle Ages and

4. Cf. H. L. Nieburg, "Uses of Violence," *The Journal of Conflict Resolution,* VII, 1 (March 1963), pp. 42–54.
5. Norman Cohn, *The Pursuit of the Millennium,* Fairlawn, N.J., Essential Books, 1957.

that by Richard Hofstadter[6] of the paranoid political style of threatened and displaced groups on the American scene. But it would be a major mistake to assume that irrationality is necessarily the only impellant to violence. One might even argue with the historian E. P. Thompson that "abject 'adjustment' to suffering and want at times may indicate a sense of reality as impaired as that of the chiliast."[7]

The distinction between realistic and unrealistic conflict, which I proposed some time ago, may serve us well here.[8] Conflicts that arise from frustration of specific demands and from estimates of gains of the participants, and which are directed at the presumed frustrating object, can be called realistic conflicts, insofar as they are means toward a specific end. Nonrealistic conflicts, on the other hand, are not occasioned by the rival ends of the antagonists, but by the need for tension release of at least one of them. If this distinction is kept in mind, serious analytical mistakes can be avoided. In particular, such a distinction allows us to eschew the common error of interpreting every outbreak of violence as senseless and irrational. To sustain such claims it must be shown that such outbreaks function simply as tension releases and are not focused on specific frustrating targets. I would contend that this is by no means always the case. I will illustrate this contention by discussing two examples, the machine-breaking movements in England during the early Industrial Revolution and the recent riots in the Watts section of Los Angeles. I choose these examples deliberately because in both cases the presumption of the purposeless and senseless character of violence seemed almost self-

6. Richard Hofstadter, *The Paranoid Style in American Politics,* New York, Alfred A. Knopf, 1965.

7. E. P. Thompson, *The Making of the British Working Class,* New York, Vintage Books, 1966, p. 50.

8. Lewis A. Coser, *The Functions of Social Conflict, op. cit.,* p. 48 ff.

evident to most observers and social analysts. What applies in these extreme cases will apply *a fortiori* in less extreme instances. Both examples concern outbreaks of violence at levels below that of the national political system. This latter case will be discussed in a later part of this paper.

Until recently, the Luddite movement and the more widespread machine-wrecking movements which marked British history during the Industrial Revolution have usually been considered utterly irrational outbreaks of violence, a "pointless, frenzied, industrial jacquerie."[9] Most social historians, writing from the perspective of a later phase in the history of modern industrial society, failed to make sense of these violent and disorganized outbursts and thus interpreted them as frenzied and desperate revolts of handloom weavers, knitters, and artisans against the new machinery which displaced them. Machine wrecking was interpreted as a projection of pent-up hatred against the new machines, as an irrational eruption of indiscriminate aggression by men who did not understand the new industrial world into which they had been forced within a very short span of time.

Recent reinterpretations of machine wrecking in early industrial England by such social historians as George Rudé, E. P. Thompson, and E. J. Hobsbawm[10] throws a very different light on these events. Hobsbawm in particular advances a very suggestive thesis.[11] He distinguishes two different types of machine breaking, neither of which could be said to be senseless and irrational. One type did indeed express hostility against the new labor-saving machines. Even so, it was selective in its

9. E. J. Hobsbawm, "The Machine Breakers," *Past and Present,* 1 (1952), pp. 57–67.
10. George Rudé, *The Crowd in History,* New York, John Wiley and Sons, 1964; E. P. Thompson, *op. cit.;* E. J. Hobsbawm, *op. cit.*
11. Hobsbawm, *op. cit.,* pp. 58–59.

choice of target and by no means indiscriminate. (Writes E. P. Thompson, the foremost contemporary student of early labor organizations in England, "Luddism in Nottingham, as in Yorkshire, was highly selective. Those frames only were broken which manufactured under-price or 'cut-up' work; when goods were slashed in the loom or when seized from the carrier's cart, the 'cut-ups' were destroyed while those with proper selvedges were left undamaged.")[12] The second type of machine breaking, however, "implies no special hostility to machines as such, but is, under certain conditions, a normal means of putting pressure on employers or putters out . . . This sort of wrecking was a traditional and established part of industrial conflict in the period of the domestic and manufacturing system, and the early stages of factory and mine." Hobsbawm uses the felicitous phrase "collective bargaining by riot" to describe this type of machine wrecking. By this he means that in a period when trade-union activity was repressed and therefore ordinary collective bargaining was impossible, the workers would resort to machine-wrecking violence in order to impose their demands on their employers. Far from being irrational and nonrealistic outbursts, these were, in fact, highly realistic acts aimed at expressing specific demands. Machine wrecking served both as a means of pressure on employers and of solidarity among the workers.

Against comparatively small local employers, destruction of property or the constant threat of such destruction often was a rather effective means of securing a bargain. For underpaid workers, without unions and without strike funds, the danger of strike-breaking was always acute. In such cases the breaking of machinery was at least a temporary guarantee that the plant could not be operated. This type of machine breaking was a technique that, at a stage in which no legitimate trade-

12. E. P. Thompson, *op. cit.*, p. 534.

union channels for bargaining were open, permitted the marshaling of otherwise unavailable power against employers and also increased unity among the workers. Bargaining by riot was a crude mechanism of conflict resolution in a period when other such mechanisms tended to be socially unavailable. It turns out upon inspection that it was, at least in part, a rational conflict strategy rather than an outbreak of irrational and senseless destructiveness and violence.

My second example concerns the riot in the Watts section of Los Angeles in August, 1965. Press commentary at the time as well as almost all subsequent writing has been almost unanimous in stressing the irrational character of this riot. Although most commentators have noted that such factors as high unemployment rates, inadequate schools, and dilapidated housing could be said to have set the stages for the riots, almost all of the commentators still felt that the behavior of the rioters was totally senseless. As the official McCone Report on the investigation of the causes of the riot puts it: "The rioters seem to have been caught up in an insensate rage of destruction."

Yet, subsequent discussions of the riot, notably by the eminent Negro civil rights leader Bayard Rustin[13] and by the University of California sociologist Robert Blauner[14] throw a different light on the case. The riot appears to have stemmed, at least in part, from frustrated efforts of the community to call attention to its plight. It seems to have been a cry for help in a situation where other means to draw attention to the community's distress seemed socially unavailable. The following incident reported by Rustin is worth quoting in

13. Bayard Rustin, "The Watts 'Manifesto' and the McCone Report," *Commentary*, Vol. 41, 3 (March 1966) pp. 29–35. For a good journalistic account of the Watts riot, see Jerry Cohen and William Murphy, *Burn, Baby, Burn!*, London, Gollancz, 1966.

14. Robert Blauner, "Whitewash over Watts," *Trans-action*, III, 3 (March–April 1966), p. 3 ff.

some detail: "At a street-corner meeting in Watts when the riots were over, an unemployed youth of about twenty said to me: 'We won.' I asked him: 'How have you won? Homes have been destroyed, Negroes are lying dead in the streets, the stores from which you buy food and clothes are destroyed, and people are bringing you relief.' His reply was significant: 'We won because we made the whole world pay attention to us. The police chief never came here before; the mayor always stayed uptown. We made them come.' Clearly it was no accident that the riot proceeded along an almost direct path to City Hall."[15] This young Negro, in any case, believed that the riot had been a potent signaling device, compelling the attention of those in power as no previous call for help had managed to do.

Nor was the violence always indiscriminate and "insensate." Wherever a store owner identified himself as a Negro, the mob passed the store by. Even a few white businesses that had shown sympathy for their Negro clientele were spared, while stores notorious for high prices and shoddy quality or hostile behavior toward Negro customers were looted and destroyed. What is more, public buildings serving the community such as libraries and schools were only minimally damaged. More remarkably still, although liquor stores and pharmacies were broken into, the liquor and narcotics were destroyed, not stolen. There was indeed a good deal of stealing in other stores, but it tended to be utilitarian rather than indiscriminate.

All these facts hardly support the dominant image of a minority of Watts' population having run amok. The crowd's selectivity in its choice of targets, as well as the behavior of the looters, contradict this. Moreover, the community as a whole tended to react to the riot with a great deal of understanding and even of sympathy. Even though many members

15. Rustin, *op. cit.*, p. 30.

of the community criticized specific acts of looting and killing, they nevertheless seemed in the majority to have felt that the rioters in some sense expressed their own grievances. "In the countless interviews and feature stories that appeared in the press and television, Watts Negroes were more likely to explain and justify the rioters rather than to condemn them . . . And months after the rioting a poll conducted by ABC Television found the proportion of Watts residents who felt that the summer's events had helped the Negroes' cause was twice as much as those who felt it had hurt them"[16]

What seems to have occurred at Watts was an effort of an active minority within the Negro ghetto, supported by a mass of nonparticipants, to announce their unwillingness to continue accepting indignity and frustration without fighting back. In particular, they were communicating their desperation through violent acts since no other channels of communication seemed open to them.

The riots, moreover, did not only represent a general call for help; they also centered upon specific issues. One of these was concerned with the fact that white policemen and other officials treated Watts as if it were "occupied territory," denying any kind of local autonomy to its inhabitants. When the rioters manifested their hatred of policemen, firemen, and other officials, they made a claim for indigenous control of the community. "They were asserting a claim to territoriality," writes Blauner, "an unorganized and rather inchoate attempt to gain control over their community, their turf. . . . On the collective level the revolt seems to represent the crystallization of community identity through a nationalistic outburst against a society felt dominating and oppressive.[17]

The dominant image of pure senselessness of the Watts

16. Blauner, *op. cit.,* p. 8.
17. *Ibid.,* pp. 8–9.

riots can hardly be sustained. The conflict was directed at the improvement of conditions and at securing human rights. From this point of view, the conflict was realistic. Indeed, nonrealistic conflict stems from frustrations caused by agents other than those against whom the conflict is waged—the well-known scapegoating behavior is a case in point. It consists in a displacement onto a target other than the frustrating individuals or groups. The violence in Watts can hardly be called a "displacement." It was directed at the agents of frustration—the whites, the police, the "exploiters."

Yet, there was also much senselessness. If we distinguish between the sources of the conflict and its manifestations, or between the goals sought and the means used, it becomes clear that the latter were nonrealistic in that there seemed to be no possibility to consider alternatives to destructive violence. For it is precisely the mark of nonrealistic conflict that there is no alternative conceivable to the means that are being used. The acting-out is compelled, as it were, by a driving force of its own and becomes an end in itself. In Watts, the affective energies mobilized in the conflict, as well as the lack of perceived institutional mechanisms for nonviolent adjustments, combined to press for resort to acts that to a considerable extent were self-defeating. What was involved was indeed a marshaling of collective strength, an assertion of collective power in attempts to gain a hearing and to assert a claim to control, but the structural position of the Watts population was such that nonrealistic rather than realistic conflict tactics were resorted to.

The Watts population, just as to a large extent the Negro population generally, does not participate in the overall pluralistic societal pattern in which a citizen is a member of many groups, all sewn together, so to speak, through the various small conflicts they conduct with one another. In a segmental society, individuals in their respective groups bring to their various conflicts only a part of themselves, without involving the inner core of their being, without putting at stake their very identity. Under these conditions, a rational evaluation as to appropriate means and alternatives of action is possible. But the fight of the Negro in Watts and elsewhere has become an all-out unsegmented struggle, in which indeed his very identity *is* at stake.

The fact that the Negro population of Watts had been denied participation in the wider society and had had no occasion to get involved in that multiplicity of associations and hence of criss-crossing conflicts which characterize American society as a whole led to an intensity and bitterness of conflict that would otherwise not have occurred. When surrounding society proves incapable of flexibility in dealing with aggrieved groups, conflicts tend to "assume peculiar intensity due to the total involvement of the personality and the accumulation of suppressed hostilities."[18] The more intense a conflict, the higher the chances of admixtures of nonrealistic elements into what may, at the origin, have ben quite realistic contentions. The absence of community structure in Watts, the absence of community channels to the municipal authorities, help explain the peculiar intensity and violence of the outburst.

The cases considered so far, though having obvious national political implications, were limited in the main to nonpolitical sectors or local political systems. It now remains to analyze the impact of violence or the threat of violence on the larger political system.

In the modern industrial societies of the West the incidence of political violence has been successfully minimized, and violence on the part of excluded groups or strata has become comparatively rare. But only those with an atrophied historical

18. Coser, *The Functions of Social Conflict, op. cit.,* p. 79.

imagination fail to realize that the state of affairs is of very recent date in the West, and only those who restrict their vision to the contemporary West can overlook the fact that this is by no means a condition which prevails today in the largest part of the world.

In Western democratic societies—with the significant exception of the situation of American Negroes, who have only begun to create their own pressure and struggle organizations —channels typically exist for the assertion of various group interests within the framework of political legitimacy. But this is not the case in most other contemporary societies, and it has not been so in the Western past.

To make oneself understood and to get others to listen is contingent upon the possession of power to give force to one's argument. A group that is not able to assert its interests will not gain consideration of its claims. As William Graham Sumner once put it, "No doctrine that a true adjustment of interest follows from a free play of interest can be construed to mean that an interest which is neglected will get its right."[19]

The assertion of interest can ordinarily proceed on a nonviolent basis in those social systems in which channels for such assertions have been legitimized. But where this is not the case, the chances are high that violence will be one of the ways in which interest is being asserted.

Only where full citizen rights have been conquered by all significant strata of the population, that is, only where there exist open channels of political communication through which all groups can articulate their demands, are the chances high that the political excercise of violence can be successfully minimized. Where this is not the case the political use of violence is a recurring potentiality. Where political structures

19. William Graham Sumner, *What the Social Classes Owe to Each Other*, New York, Harper Bros., 1883, p. 89.

are incapable of accommodating all political demands there is an ever-present chance that violence will be resorted to by those who feel that they cannot get their voice heard, as well as by those who have a vested interest in suppressing this voice.

Precisely because in such polities the threat of violence is never absent, the contending groups find it hard to commit themselves to principled nonviolence. "The actual demonstration of violence must occur from time to time in order to give credibility to its threatened outbreak, thereby gaining efficacy for the threat as an instrument of social and political change."[20] Strikes, political demonstration, and the like are used in order to give credibility to the capacity of the attacking group to engage, if need be, in more drastic forms of disorder.

It would be a major analytical error to argue that groups threatening violence or actually engaged in violence can be disregarded, because they are typically small in numbers. If we are concerned with historical change we must attend to articulate minorities at least as much as to habitually inert and mute majorities. Given the psychic costs that are always involved in the uses of violence, it is to be expected that only relatively small numbers of men will at any given time be ready to engage in a politics of violence. For only a few will the psychic rewards of violence outweigh the cost. But the very fact that they are able to break with the habitual wont and use of the political game gives them a specific weight that is out of proportion to their sheer numbers.

Relatively small groups given to a politics of violence differ from larger groupings by requiring full commitment. They tend to absorb and preempt the whole personality of their numbers whereas larger groups require only a weaker type of participation in group activities. In larger groups, members will be involved with only a segment of their personalities

20. Nieburg, *op. cit.,* p. 44.

rather than as whole human beings. The sect-type group committed to a politics of struggle, on the other hand, is "greedy," it demands the wholesale commitment of the members' personality in the service of the cause.[21] Hence numerically small groups of this militant type, by being able to mobilize the energies of their members to the fullest, can exert influence quite disproportionate to their numerical insignificance.

These considerations help explain the crucial importance of militant struggle groups. Even if political movements in many countries, especially in the New Nations are typically split between a moderate wing, committed in principle to a politics of nonviolent compromise, and a militant wing willing, if the occasion demands it, to threaten violence or actually to use it, it would be a mistake to view these wings in separation. In fact, a very subtle dialectical interplay is likely to be operative between them. The leader of the reformist and conciliatory wing is likely to depend in his strategy on the existence of the militant wing which he opposes in principle. He is supposed to bargain with the authorities, and since he cannot himself threaten violence, it is advantageous for him to point out that more radical and militant elements will take over if he is unsuccessful. He will claim that the demands he voices must be accepted, otherwise he will no longer be able to control his people. As H. L. Nieburg puts it shrewdly, "While playing this role, the reformist leader is not unhappy to have his prophesies fulfilled by a few psychotic teenagers. . . . The irresponsible elements are, of course, disowned, but the bargaining power of the responsible leaders is enhanced."[22] The very stance of a

21. *The Sociology of Georg Simmel,* transl. and ed. by Kurt H. Wolff, New York, The Free Press, 1950, pp. 92 ff., and Coser, *The Functions* . . . . , *op. cit.,* pp. 95 ff.

22. Nieburg, *op. cit.,* p. 51. Cf. also Thomas Schelling, *The Strategy of Conflict, op. cit.,* esp. chapters 2 and 3.

numerically weak minority might hence have the unanticipated consequence of strengthening the bargaining power of the moderate leadership. When this increased bargaining power brings results it is likely to enhance the status of the moderates —though it might also temporarily benefit the extremists. There is hence the chance in such movements as the American Civil Rights Movement or the struggle by Jewish organizations against the British government in Palestine or the rise of the British Labor Movement that a subtle division of labor takes place between extremists and "responsible" elements. The Black Moslems, the Irgun, and the extreme wing of the Chartist movement were committed to the threat or the actual exercise of violence. Moderates rejected such methods—and profited by exploiting them for their own purpose. The interplay between moderates and extremists in the contemporary French nationalist movement of Quebec provides another instance in point. Had there been no terrorist and extremist wing, one feels, the provincial government would have had to invent it. (It stands to reason that if the authorities prove inflexible and fail to make concessions, the chances are high that the militant wing will in fact take over and escalate demands as well as violent techniques. This is the Kerensky pattern well known to any student of revolutions.)

I have dwelt on the above at some length in order to illustrate the point that even apparently irrational and senseless acts of violence and destruction engaged in by small and desperate minorities may have widespread adjustive consequences and positive social functions for deprived social groups and for the larger social system in which they are embedded.

Those in power and authority generally tend to have a propensity to regard any incidence of political violence as a prelude to revolution and the total subversion of the political edifice. It behooves the social scientist to point out to them that this is a profoundly mistaken view of the matter. Just as the physician would be foolish were he to attend only to the elimination of a fever without paying due attention to the underlying organic causes that have brought it about, so the policy-maker would indeed be ill-advised were he to concentrate his efforts at the suppression of violence without attending to the underlying systemic malfunctioning to which it attests. Just as the detection of bodily ills would be very difficult indeed were an abnormal increase in bodily temperature not available as a major index to underlying bodily difficulties, so the detection and treatment of disorders in the body social can be enchanced if policy-makers are attentive to the impact and incidence of violence in a body social which lacks less drastic indicators for measuring group frustrations and dissatisfactions.

The great visionary poet William Blake wrote half a century before Freud that "Unacted desire breeds pestilence." Enacted desire, on the other hand, even if, in the absence of alternative channels, it be expressed through social violence, may help clear the air.

6

Some Functions of Deviant Behavior
and Normative Flexibility

The dialectical relation between conflict and order, between stability and change, is a major theme throughout this book. This chapter treats it in regard to the special problems of deviance.

One cannot even form the notion of order without the contrasting notion of disorder, nor can conformity be conceived without a contrasting concept of deviance against which conformity can be measured. We know a light is *on* only if we know what it is for a light to be *off.** Conformity and deviance, in other words, are complementary notions and they use useful tools for sociological investigation only if this complementarity it kept always in mind. If either the one or the other is absolutized, analysis is likely to end up in blind alleys.

The fact that deviance may be destructive of groups and larger social systems needs hardly much documentation. Thus, as Albert Cohen has written, ". . . the most destructive impact of deviance on organization is probably through its impact on *trust,* on confidence that others *will,* by and large, play by the rules."†

* I borrow this phrase from Bruce Mazlish's characterization of the Hegelian dialectic in his *The Riddle of History,* New York, Harper & Row, 1966, p. 147.

† Albert Cohen, *Deviance and Control,* Englewood Cliffs, N.J., Pren-

When participants have committed some resources to an enterprise and have invested in it, they have done so under the
assumption that if they play by the rules of the game, so will
others. If they lose trust in the others playing by the rules and
living up to expectations, they will tend to withdraw. Without a
certain degree of trust in others, social life would be impossible.
Hence, too high levels of deviance, to the extent that they
undermine basic trust, undermine the very possibility of collective
life.

Although the destructive possibilities of high levels of
deviance must be kept firmly in mind in any sociological analysis,
it would be a major mistake to conclude from this that all
deviance is necessarily dysfunctional. Just as Durkheim showed
in his classical analysis that a certain amount of crime in a
society is not only "normal" but has positive functions for that
society, so it is necessary to stress that certain degrees of deviance
may make positive contributions to the vitality of smaller groups
and social systems alike.

The chapter that follows does not aim at presenting a full
inventory of all possible functions of deviance. It attempts,
instead, to sensitize the sociological reader to the need for further
search for such functions by analyzing at least some of them.
Among the latent functional contributions examined here are the
role of the deviant in arousing the community to the consequences
of the breach of its norms, and the fact that deviance may be considered the very "ground" of normalcy. Various structural and
situational circumstances that lead the group to tolerate or even to
foster deviance are considered. Criminal deviance is distinguished
from nonconformist innovating behavior; and various types of innovating departures from normalcy are considered from the dual
viewpoint of structurally-induced motivation and of impact on
group structure.

---

tice-Hall Inc., 1966, pp. 4–5. Cohen is among the relatively few writers on
deviance who are well aware of its positive as well as its negative contributions.

MOST CONTEMPORARY SOCIOLOGICAL THEORIZING ABOUT deviant behavior has tended to focus on mechanisms of social control. The analysis of instances in which behavior that violates institutional expectations may be considered functional for an ongoing social system has been largely neglected. This paper tries to highlight some functions of deviance for social structures. This does not deny, of course, the dysfunctions of deviance, but only suggests that an exclusive emphasis on these may result in inadequate and distorted analysis.[1]

CONSEQUENCES OF DEVIANCE FOR INTERNAL GROUP RELATIONS

We have known ever since Durkheim that crime alerts the common conscience and contributes to the revival and maintenance of common sentiments by arousing the community to the consequences of infringements of rules. "Crime," he wrote, "brings together upright consciences and concentrates them."[2] It will also be remembered that Mead wrote in a similar vein: "The criminal . . . is responsible for a sense of solidarity, aroused among those whose attitude would otherwise be centered upon interests quite divergent from each other." "The attitude of hostility toward the lawbreaker has the

1. This paper was substantially completed during the author's stay at the Institute for Social Research, Oslo, Norway, under a Fulbright Senior Research Scholarship. I wish to express my appreciation to a number of European colleagues, too numerous to mention, whose critical reading of an earlier draft of this paper was most helpful. I owe a special debt to Johan Galtung, of the University of Oslo and the Institute for Social Research, Oslo, to Yrjö Littunen, School of Social Sciences, Tampere, Finland, and to Robert K. Merton, of Columbia University, who made a number of very valuable suggestions.
2. Emile Durkheim, *Division of Labor in Society*, New York, The Free Press, 1947, p. 102.

unique advantage of uniting all members of the community."[3] Durkheim and Mead both state that, though an individual criminal act elicits negative sanctions, crime also has positive consequences for the society or group since the breach of a norm calls attention to its importance for the common weal. Like bodily pain serves as a danger signal calling for the mobilization of energies against the source of disease, so crime, these writers argue, alerts the body social and leads to the mobilization of otherwise inactive defense mechanisms.

Durkheim and Mead are often quoted in current theorizing, yet their pertinent insight on the functions of crime has been somewhat neglected. Thus Parsons focuses attention on mechanisms of social control that serve to check deviant behavior but fails to consider possible contributions that deviance may make to the system in which it occurs. He distinguishes types of deviance that "fall within the range of permissiveness which should be considered normal to people under certain strains" and "a vicious circle of gratification of deviant wishes [leading to the] undermining of the main value system."[4] But he does not consider those deviant acts that, though not considered "normal to people under strain," reinforce rather than undermine the social system. We shall see in a later part of this paper that different types of deviant behavior must be discussed in terms of their differential impact. Even if we should agree, for the purpose of discussion, that deviants are always motivated to defy the group's norms, nothing requires us to assume that such

3. George Herbert Mead, "The Psychology of Punitive Justice," *American Journal of Sociology*, XXIII (1928), 557–602, esp. p. 591. Cf. also Marx's parallel formulation: "The criminal produces an impression now moral, now tragic, and renders a 'service' by arousing the moral and aesthetic sentiments of the public." Quoted in Bottomore and Rubel (eds.), *Karl Marx*, London, Watts & Co., 1956, p. 159.

4. Talcott Parsons, *The Social System*, New York, The Free Press, 1951, p. 512.

acts may not have the unanticipated consequence of strengthening those norms.

Durkheim and Mead see the functional consequences of deviance in the strengthening of the group that results from the collective rejection of the deviant. This assumption is indeed borne out by much of small-group research. An article summarizing much of the research findings in this field states, for example: "When a member deviates markedly from a group standard, the remaining members of the group bring pressures to bear on the deviate to bring him back to conformity. If pressure is of no avail, the deviate is rejected and cast out of the group."[5] Statements such as these seem to imply, though the authors do not explicitly say so, that deviations from standards lead to the mobilization of the group's energies. But small-group research has not adequately considered the possibility that the repression of deviance may not in all cases be functional for the group. Moreover, it has not been shown that all types of groups will reject deviance under all circumstances. These two variables—"strengthening of the group" and "rejection of the deviant"—call attention to four possible cases: (1) the deviant is opposed and the group is strengthened—the situation discussed by Durkheim and Mead; (2) the deviant is tolerated or even accepted and the group is strengthened; (3) the deviant is rejected and the group is weakened; and (4) the deviant is not rejected and the group is weakened. The last case is relatively unproblematical, but the other three have not been given sufficient systematic attention in sociological theorizing, although empirical evidence about them is available.

5. Harold H. Kelley and John W. Thibault, "Experimental Studies of Group Problem Solving and Process" in *Handbook of Social Psychology,* ed. Gardner Lindzey, Cambridge, Mass., Addison Wesley Publishing Co., 1954, II, 768.

1. *The deviant is opposed and the group is strengthened.* In the process of uniting itself against deviance, the community not only revives and maintains common sentiments but creatively establishes moral rules and redefines "normal" behavior. "Each time the community brings sanctions against a detail of behavior . . . it sharpens the authority of the violated norm and redefines the boundaries within which the norm exercises its special jurisdiction."[6] Thus the criminal, the scapegoat, the mentally ill, in their diverse ways, allow the group to reaffirm not only its social but also its moral identity, for they establish signposts which serve as normative yardsticks.[7] Deviance "establishes the point beyond which behavior is no longer within acceptable reach of the norm, and in this way gives substance and authority to the norm itself."[8]

Thus, definition of what is considered normal in the group takes place with reference to what is considered deviant, and morality is given its content through the contrast provided by

6. Kai T. Erikson, "Social Margins: Some Notes on the Sociology of Deviance" (paper read at the fifty-fifth annual meeting of the American Sociological Association, New York, 1960).

7. W. E. H. Lecky wrote about the prostitute: "herself the supreme type of vice, she is ultimately the most efficient guardian of virtue" (quoted by Kingsley Davis, "Prostitution" in Robert K. Merton and Robert A. Nisbet [eds.], *Contemporary Social Problems,* New York, Harcourt, Brace & World, Inc., 1961, pp. 262–88). Davis shows the close connection between prostitution and the maintenance of traditional family patterns.

8. Erikson, *op. cit.* Cf. also V. W. Turner's parallel formulation: "The norm derives strength and definition from condemnation of its breach in the public situations of ritual and law. The deviant, the haphazard and the contingent can only be recognized to be such where consensus to what is typical, orthodox, regular exists. And vice versa" (*Schism and Continuity in an African Society,* Manchester, Manchester University Press, 1957, p. 329). This is of course what Hegel meant when he asserted that "no step in philosophy was possible" unless it was recognized that the positive and the negative gain their "truth only in their relation to each other so that each contains the other within it" (*Wissenschaft der Logik,* Lasson ed., Leipzig, Felix Meiner, 1923, II, 54–56).

that which is not moral. We touch here upon a dialectical relation that Gestalt psychology has discussed in detail with respect to perception. Figures cannot be perceived except in relation to grounds setting them off. In the same way, normalcy can hardly be perceived except against the ground of deviance; to be "good" makes sense only in relation to being "bad."

It is with the body social as it is with individuals: Moral indignation against deviants serves to purge the righteous from a sense of their own sins and unworthiness and helps sustain their moral identity. Such indignation may well serve as a reaction-formation, securing the ego against the repressed impulse to identify with the criminal.[9] It is against the ground of criminal deviance that the righteous achieve the comforting affirmation of their normality. Inasmuch as "our" innocence is contingent upon "their" guilt, dereliction by others provides occasion for self-congratulations.

But dereliction by others also provides occasion for self-examination. Thus, when a crime is committed in the community, religious leaders use the occasion to exhort the congregation to reexamine themselves and "purify their souls." Deviance is taken as a warning that there is something foul in the state of Denmark that needs correction—correction not only on the individual level but in the social realm as well. Thus, Stewart and Helen Perry have shown that in the mental hospitals deviant patients may, by their acting out, "act as a fire alarm for the ward." By upsetting the social equilibrium of the ward, the "fire-alarm patient" may highlight such defects as understaffing, staff overwork, and the like and thus dramatize the need for remedial action.[10] Bureaucratic organizations are

9. Cf. Anna Freud, *The Ego and the Mechanisms of Defense,* New York, International Universities Press, 1946, pp. 117 ff.

10. Stewart E. Perry and Helen Swick Perry, "Deviant Behavior, Function and Dysfunction on the Psychiatric Ward" (paper read at the Eastern Sociological Society meetings, April 23–24, 1960, Boston, Mass.).

familiar with similar situations in which the failure effectively to control behavior in terms of official goals will be used by practitioners as a convincing means for appealing for increased resources. Thus many organizations (as well as many role incumbents) have a vested interest, though rarely acknowledged, in the very deviant behavior that they are set up to combat, for deviance provides the reason for their existence: Increases in deviance may help them to highlight the need for strengthening the organization (or the department in the organization) to cope more effectively with disturbing behavior.

2. What has been said so far about reactions to deviance—be it a spontaneous, that is, a non-deliberate "pulling together" of group members, or deliberate policy—refers to those instances in which deviant behavior leads to its rejection. The second case is that of *tolerance or acceptance of the deviant with concomitant strengthening of the group.* There are groups in which deviants provide the occasion for a reaffirmation of values without incurring rejection. Thus in a seminal paper, Dentler and Erikson give illustrations from Quaker work camps and Army Basic Training Squads where deviants do indeed "become critical referents for establishing the end points (of the range of possibilities judged permissible within the group's boundaries)" —the figure-ground effect discussed earlier—and where "the deviant is someone about whom something should be done, and the group, in expressing this concern, is able to affirm its essential cohesion and indicate what the group is and what it can do."[11] However, in these cases the occasion for affirmation of cohesion does not come from rejecting the deviant but rather from protecting him: he "becomes the ward of the group. . . . In a setting in which having buddies is highly valued, he is unlikely to receive any sociometric choices at all. But it would be quite

11. Robert A. Dentler and Kai T. Erikson, "The Functions of Deviance in Groups," *Social Problems*, VII, No. 2 (Fall, 1959), 98–107.

unfortunate to assume that he is therefore isolated from the group or repudiated by it: an accurate sociogram would have the deviant individual encircled by the interlocking sociometric preferences, sheltered by the group structure."[12]

It would seem that in some groups tolerance of deviance is a function of a specific value system: among Quakers, "tolerance" is a salient component of the ideology. In tolerating or protecting a deviant, they practice what they publicly profess. (It may even be said that such groups do, in fact, need social objects upon whom "tolerance" can be exercised because they provide the occasion for testing and confirming their values.)

If it is objected that tolerance of deviance in army units is merely a manifestation of opposition to official army goals, that is, part of a collective effort to "get back" at army authority, this only confirms the analytical point: by setting itself off against an intolerant environment, the group exercises tolerance precisely with regard to those individuals who would otherwise be the victims of the very environment whose values the group rejects. In both cases—Quaker camps and army units—acceptance of deviance is contingent upon the value system of the group. What Kelley and Thibault say about the rejection of deviance applies to its tolerance as well: "Generally, the same factors responsible for the emergence of group standards will also in large measure be responsible for the motivations to enforce conformity to them."[13] Thus in the groups discussed by Dentler and Erikson, the practice of tolerance—whether positively stated as a "way of life" as among Quakers, or stated in opposition to the intolerance of army authorities as in army units—would seem to be a basis for the emergence or strengthening of group standards and would therefore be the guiding principle that moti-

12. *Ibid.,* p. 105.
13. Kelley and Thibault, *op. cit.,* p. 766.

vates the responses of group members to non-conformity among them.

3. So far, the assertion has been made that deviants offer to group members the opportunity to reaffirm common values, be it by providing an occasion to oppose them collectively (case 1), or by bringing about a situation in which their acceptance or tolerance serves as an affirmation of beliefs held in common (case 2). In these cases, the groups were strengthened. There are groups, however, for whom *rigid and repeated rejection of deviants has serious dysfunctional consequences* (case 3). Rigidly structured sects or radical political organizations of the sectarian type provide examples in point. Even a cursory perusal of the history of the Trotskyist movement leaves no doubt about the fact that the lack of ability to tolerate deviance led to further and further fragmentation of the movement. Religious sects provide similar examples.

To be sure, in such groups each single case of negative sanctions against deviant behavior led, at the moment the act of sanctioning occurred, to a reaffirmation of values among those who remained faithful. Yet, rejection of nonconformity as an ongoing organizational activity was disruptive as a *process* in that in the long run it weakened the group in relation to its external environment.

This calls attention to the need to consider the relation between the group within which deviance occurs and the external context.

CONSEQUENCES OF DEVIANCE FOR GROUP RELATIONS WITH THE OUTSIDE

In the first two situations discussed—one of rejection and the other of tolerance of the deviant—our concern was with relationships within the group. It now turns out that what may be functional for the group in one respect—that is, the reaffirmation of its norms—may turn out to be detrimental in another respect, namely, in its relation to the outside. To consider only the internal consequences of deviance and of responses to it, that is, to limit analysis to the group processes within given subsystems without paying attention to the group's relations with the outside, is a common pitfall in sociological theorizing, especially in small-group research. In contrast to much of such research, Kelley and Shapiro set up an experimental group in a situation in which the group's norms were discordant with outside reality.[14] In this situation conformity to these norms tended to be detrimental to the success of the group. (Situations similar to those contrived in the laboratory are likely to occur when disparate rates of change impinge on a group and lead to cultural lags and dysfunctional resistances of vested interests.)

It turned out that in these experimental groups deviation from the norms did not call forth rejection. This case is, in this respect, more similar to case 2 discussed above, for here also deviance is accepted. Whereas in the Quaker camps deviance may be *implicitly* welcomed as an occasion for group members to live up to professed values, in these experimental groups deviant behavior seems to have been *explicitly* welcomed as an occasion for better adaptability to outside reality. Indeed, it turned out that in these groups persons who deviated from the group's norms were also those who were judged to be highly acceptable as co-workers.

A consideration of the external environment for the understanding of internal dynamics of deviance and responses to it makes it possible to throw more light on the behavior of the Quaker camps and army units discussed earlier. There also the

14. Harold H. Kelley and Martin M. Shapiro, "An Experiment on Conformity to Group Norms Where Conformity Is Detrimental to Group Achievement." *American Sociological Review,* XIX (1954), 667–77.

relation with the outside would seem to be one important determinant of inside responses: In Quaker groups and army camps alike, the norms that guide the behavior of members toward deviants seemed to consist in *countervalues* to patterns prevailing on the outside. Thus in Kelley and Thibault's groups, as in the groups studied by Dentler and Erikson, outside reality was an important determinant—whether as a spur for adaptation or for opposition to it—of the responses to deviant behavior within.

The evidence so far indicates that the widely accepted notion that groups always reject deviance is, at the least, open to question. To be sure, deviance may be *proscribed* as in the examples of criminal behavior used by Durkheim and Mead. Yet, a deviant redefinition of norms may be *permitted,* as when the value system of the group prescribes tolerance. It may be *preferred,* as when it is accepted as a means for better adaptability of the group.[15]

Deviant behavior may also be *prescribed,* as during periodic feasts when the participants are expected to infringe the norms of ordinary behavior.[16] These, however, are instances where it would be deviant not to deviate; that is, they are special instances of conformity that do not concern us here.

The recognition that departure from the norms may be preferred, permitted, or proscribed raises two related problems: (1) The license to deviate is differentially distributed among members of a group. For example, there is tolerance of deviance for special role incumbents such as the "star," the "stranger," or

15. These variations in social control have been identified and discussed by Robert K. Merton in his "Social Structure and Anomie," *Social Theory and Social Structure* (rev. ed.), New York, The Free Press, 1957, esp. p. 133.

16. Roger Caillois, "Theory of the Festival" in *Man and the Sacred,* New York, Free Press, 1959.

the "fool";[17] or there is some expectation of deviance for some group leaders who are supposed to be flexible and to depart from the norms to further the tasks of the group. (2) Another important problem raised by the differential response to deviance is the need to distinguish between different types of deviant behavior.

DEVIANCE AND INNOVATION

So far the concept of deviance has been used here in accordance with its definition in most contemporary sociological work.[18] An overarching concept of this kind has the distinct merit of drawing attention to the structural similarities of a variety of behaviors which might otherwise seem but little related. Yet at the same time, it has the disadvantage of obscuring distinctions which might be crucial in certain contexts.[19] Thus Merton distinguishes nonconformity from such other kinds of deviant behavior as crime or juvenile delinquency. Criminal

17. Georg Simmel, "The Stranger," in *The Sociology of Georg Simmel*, trans. and ed. Kurt H. Wolff, New York, The Free Press, 1950; and Orrin E. Klapp, "The Fool as a Social Type," *American Journal of Sociology*, LV (1949), 157–62.

18. Cf. Albert K. Cohen, "The Study of Social Organization and Deviant Behavior," in *Sociology Today*, ed. Merton *et al.*, New York: Basic Books, 1959, pp. 461–84.

19. It was a distinct step forward to conceptualize the sick and the criminal as deviants from the institutionalized norms on the ground that both roles called forth social control mechanisms designed to restore "health." Nevertheless, as Vilhelm Aubert and Sheldon Messinger have recently argued ("The Criminal and the Sick," *Inquiry* [Oslo], I, No. 3 [Autumn, 1958], 137–60), these roles are also crucially dissimilar insofar as, among other things, the sick is conceived as one who cannot be held responsible for his failure to perform previously assumed roles, while the criminal is not perceived in terms of inability but rather as having been able to act differently had he chosen to do so.

behavior is impelled by private and self-centered motives that are by definition antisocial. Innovating dissent of a nonconforming minority, on the other hand, may be manifestly intended to serve group interests in a more effective manner than the conforming majority. "These kinds of 'deviant behavior' differ structurally, culturally and functionally."[20]

Although both the nonconformist and the criminal defy normative expectations, they are profoundly dissimilar: the nonconformist's dissent "is not a private dereliction, but a thrust toward a new morality (or a restoration of an old and almost forgotten morality). . . ."[21] I have argued elsewhere in a similar vein that "When all forms of dissent are [considered] criminal by definition, we are in the presence of a system which is ill-equipped to reveal fully the extent to which nonconformity, as distinct from crime, involves the striving toward an alternative moral basis rather than moral deviation."[22]

To be sure, the behavior of the nonconformist may bring forth community reactions similar to those occasioned by criminal violations of the norms, yet the innovations he proposes, allegedly in the interest of the group's welfare, are likely to be evaluated in their own right, if only by a minority. This is why, as distinct from the case of the criminal, there is likely to be buried under layers of hostility a certain measure of respect for the disinterested dissenter. Being oriented toward the collectivity, he is led to seek and to find an audience within it. The innovator sends a message intended to be picked up and diffused. His behavior proceeds, so to speak, in broad daylight in

20. Merton, *op. cit.*, p. 360. Cf. also his "Social Problems and Sociological Theory" in Merton and Nisbet (eds.), *op. cit.*, pp. 697–737.

21. Merton, *op. cit.*, p. 363 *et passim*.

22. "Durkheim's Conservatism and Its Implications for Sociological Theory," in this volume. Cf. also Roger Nett, "Conformity-Deviation and the Social Control Concept," *Ethics*, LXIV (1953), 38–45.

order to attract a maximum audience. Whereas the criminal seeks to minimize the chances of detection, the innovator seeks maximum publicity for his message. One may argue with an innovator but hardly with a criminal.[23]

Just as with various types of deviance, the innovations that the nonconformist proposes for the consideration of the group may be prescribed or proscribed with various degrees of tolerance, depending on the structured and normative context. Moreover, they may be wittingly favored by the group or the group may unwittingly be favored by them.

When innovation is highly valued, as, for example, in scientific societies, innovating behavior must be considered a special type of conformity rather than deviation. In the context of the institution of science, innovations and discoveries, provided they satisfy the criteria of evidence, are highly valued variants that permit the goals of the group to be more adequately met— though even here the innovator may at first encounter the resistance of vested interests.[24]

On the other hand, in groups that place no value on innovation, an innovating response will be considered truly nonconformist. In contrast to the case of the criminal, however, at least some of the group's members might perceive that the innovator intends to perform a positive task for the group. This might then lead to a conflict within the group over the issue raised. If this happens, the innovator has transformed individual

23. Gandhi distinguished between criminal and civil disobedience in terms of the concept of publicity. Civil disobedience, to him, was by definition public action.

24. Cf. Robert K. Merton, "Social Conformity, Deviation and Opportunity-Structures," *American Sociological Review,* XXIV, No. 2 (April, 1959), 177–89, esp. p. 181. Cf. also Herbert Menzel, "Innovation, Integration, and Marginality," *American Sociological Review,* XXV, No. 5 (October, 1960), 704–13.

nonconformity into group conflict and has raised it from the idiosyncratic to the collective level.

Thus, pressures for innovation are likely to result in the emergence of social conflicts within a system. Such conflicts, as I have shown elsewhere, may be highly functional for that system.[25] Dewey has noted that "conflict shocks us out of sheeplike passivity, and sets us at noting and contriving . . . it is a *sine qua non* of reflection and ingenuity."[26] The innovator's behavior may serve to reduce the chances that adherence to the routines of yesterday render the group unable to meet the challenges of today. The innovator may thus be a pace-setter and a setter of new standards. By attacking vested interests in the habitual, the innovator helps insure that the group does not stifle in the deadening routines of ritualism.

What is said here of group processes indeed applies to every productive interaction as well. Interaction does not merely consist of mutual filling of expectations but in ever renewed innovating contributions. In much current theorizing it is assumed that the equilibrium of a group is a function of the extent to which group members habitually conform to each other's expectations. The maintenance of complementarity between the interaction orientations of alter and ego is said to be the mark of a stable social system.[27] "This model seems to assume," Gouldner has noted, "that each of a sequence of identical conforming acts will yield either the same or an increasing degree of appreciation and satisfaction and will thus elicit the same or increasing amounts of reward."[28] Yet, "later conforming actions are worth

25. "Social Conflict and the Theory of Social Change," in this volume.
26. John Dewey, *Human Nature and Conduct,* New York, Modern Library, 1930, p. 300.
27. Talcott Parsons, *op. cit.,* pp. 204–5 *et passim.*
28. Alvin M. Gouldner, "Organizational Analysis," in *Sociology Today,* pp. 423 ff.

less than earlier ones, in terms of the rewards or propensity to reciprocate which they elicit." When conformity is taken for granted, the propensity to reciprocate is weakened in the long run. Homans also states this principle of satiation, a version of marginal utility: "The more often a man has in the recent past received a rewarding activity from an other, the less valuable any further unit of that activity becomes to him."[29]

The Finnish sociologist Yrjö Littunen has formulated an "optimal frustration" hypothesis: "Persons who have to maintain a monotonous interaction pattern for a long period of time tend to become bored with each other. This phenomenon of *social fatigue* may be understood as a situation where there is no excitement in the interaction to maintain the cohesiveness, to increase liking."[30] Although sustained conformity may bring the reward of smooth adjustment to expectations, it also brings the penalty of boredom. That is why apathy and monotony may lead a person to "seek a frustration which his energy potential can adequately balance and overcome."[31] This hypothesis, which Littunen developed on the basis of the psychological research of Hebb and Thompson,[32] gains added theoretical relevance with Gouldner's recognition that a system built upon the habituation of conforming responses may be said to contain built-in tenden-

29. George Homans, *Social Behavior*, New York, Harcourt, Brace & World, Inc., 1961, p. 55.

30. *Income-Security Values at Different Levels of Frustration* (Transactions of the Westermarck Society, IV, No. 4, Copenhagen: Ejnar Munksgaard, 1959), pp. 234–35 ff. Cf. also Goethe's "Nichts ist schwerer zu ertragen als eine Reihe von schoenen Tagen."

31. Littunen, *op. cit.*, p. 224. Cf. also Marx's statement: "The criminal interrupts the monotony and security of bourgeois life. Thus he protects it from stagnation" (*op. cit.*, p. 159).

32. D. O. Hebb and W. R. Thompson, "The Social Significance of Animal Studies," in *Handbook of Social Psychology*, I, 532–61.

cies toward a high level of entropy. It is high social entropy that the innovator, as an agent of change, helps to prevent.

NORMATIVE FLEXIBILITY AND
INNOVATING ROLES

In monolithic structures role requirements may be so rigidly defined that only fully conforming role performance will be tolerated; in less rigid structures, on the other hand, a measure of diversity may be tolerated at various levels in the system.[33] For example, low-ranking deviants may perform important functions for the group. This was the case in the groups discussed earlier, about which Dentler and Erikson have argued that low-ranking members who deviate from the group's norms "become critical referents for establishing the end points" of the range of possibilities judged permissible within the group's boundaries.[34]

Such considerations direct attention to the relation between status, group structure, and the acceptance of innovation by the group.

Deviant behavior as well as innovation varies within different social structures. Furthermore, the social structure puts pressure on some of its status-occupants to engage in innovating rather than in conforming behavior.[35] For example, as Veblen

33. Daniel J. Levinson, "Role, Personality, and Social Structure in the Organizational Setting," *Journal of Abnormal and Social Psychology,* LVIII (1959), 170–80. Cf. also Erving Goffman's discussion of "Role Distance" in his *Encounters,* Indianapolis, Bobbs-Merrill Co., 1961.

34. *Op. cit.* Cf. also E. Paul Torrance, "Function of Expressed Disagreement in Small Group Processes" in A. Rubenstein and C. Haberstroh (eds.), *Some Theories of Organization,* Homewood, Ill., Dorsey Press, 1960, pp. 250–57.

35. Robert K. Merton, "Social Structure and Anomie," *op. cit.,* pp. 131–60.

and Simmel,[36] among others, have pointed out, marginal individuals are likely to be highly motivated to engage in innovating behavior because they are structurally induced to depart from prevailing social norms. "With the least opportunity for full participation in the most valued activities of their own society,"[37] they may be stimulated to make new responses that depart from the habitually required. Being less tied to the system of wont and use that regulates the lives of insiders, they may see alternatives of action that escape the latter's attention. The structural circumstance of their exclusion from some of the prized values of the group may make the marginal man more sensitive to the lacunae that may well remain hidden from "well-adjusted" members of the group. If he wishes to gain acceptance among insiders, he will be motivated to propose innovating means designed to allow the group to reach its goals more effectively than before.

There are also positions in a group other than those of marginal men that motivate innovating departures from the norms. For example, the status of leader requires the ability to adjust to new circumstances. The rank and file may take the customary for granted, but a break of wont and use may enhance the reputation of the leader. The flexibility required in leadership roles may entail greater or lesser departures from otherwise expected behavior so that a certain amount of license to deviate and to violate norms is built into the very definition of leadership.

36. Georg Simmel, "The Stranger," *op. cit.;* and Thorstein Veblen, "The Intellectual Preeminence of the Jews," in his *Essays in Our Changing Order,* pp. 219–31.

37. H. G. Barnett, *Innovation—the Basis of Cultural Change,* New York, McGraw-Hill Book Co., 1953, p. 404. Cf. also Karl Mannheim, *Man and Society in an Age of Reconstruction,* London, Routledge & Kegan Paul, 1940, esp. pp. 56–57, as well as Robert Park's "Introduction" to E. V. Stonequist, *The Marginal Man,* New York, Charles Scribner's Sons, 1937.

Homans, who had argued in an earlier work that "the higher the rank (or status) of a person within a group, the more nearly his activities conform to the norms of the group,"[38] stated more recently, after discussing, among others, the above-quoted study by Kelley and Shapiro, that "we now have experimental evidence that it is not just the members of low status, but members of high status as well, who are prone at times to non-conformity."[39] It will be remembered that in these groups deviant behavior helped the group to adapt to the outside. This suggests that the pressure on the leader to engage in innovating behavior may derive from the structural circumstance that he is the group's representative to the outside. He stands at the point of interchange between in-group and out-group. A leader may be considered a special case of the marginal man: having the task to relate his group to the demands of the environment, he is oriented, at the same time as he is the group's representative, toward extra-group values.

In view of these requirements of leadership, it is not always clear whether the leader's innovation can be called "deviant" at all. Though it involves adoption of new procedures, innovation in this case still takes place within normative limits. Just as with

38. Homans, *The Human Group*, New York, Harcourt, Brace & Co., 1950, p. 141.

39. *Social Behavior*, p. 346. Recent experimental work throws doubt on the idea that the relation between status and conformity is ever a simple one. J. E. Dittes and H. H. Kelley showed, e.g., that individuals who felt acceptable in a group felt freer to express disagreements publicly, while those with a low sense of acceptance were much higher in their *public* than in their *private* conformity "Effects of Different Conditions of Acceptance upon Conformity to Group Norms," *Journal of Abnormal and Social Psychology*, LIII [1956], 100–107). Cf. also Herbert Menzel, "Public and Private Conformity under Different Conditions of Acceptance in the Group," *Journal of Abnormal and Social Psychology*, LV (1957), 398–402.

groups in which innovation is highly prized, so in situations in which the leader's departure from institutionalized procedures is part of the system of expectations, what may be considered deviation from one point of view may well be considered conforming behavior from another.

Yet leaders are often also permitted some deviant behavior that neither increases the group's adaptation to the outside nor otherwise directly benefits the group in any way. Simply by virtue of otherwise showing prized qualities, a leader accumulates what Hollander has called "idiosyncrasy credit."[40]

One would assume that the more task-oriented a group, the less its tolerance of deviant behavior that interferes with the attainment of the group's goal. This may well be so, but if a leader is seen as important for the attainment of these goals, or even for their partial attainment, the group may tolerate individual deviation when it is seen as balanced by positive contributions. A man may lose credit for deviations, but only when his credit balance is exhausted will he be removed. If he continues to amass credit in the eyes of the members through group-approved activities, he attains a threshold permitting deviations from common expectations. This may explain, at least in part, why a leader may be given greater leeway for deviating behavior than his followers: His having accumulated highly visible merit gives him a leeway in behavior not granted to less meritorious members; the group will take from "him" what it will not take from "them." Task orientation and tolerance of deviance are therefore not necessarily mutually exclusive.

The term "idiosyncrasy credit" readily brings to mind the image of a "would-be" innovator, who is tolerated because of other contributions, yet whose innovating message is largely

40. E. P. Hollander, "Conformity, Status and Idiosyncrasy Credit," *Psychological Review*, LXV (1958), 117–27.

ignored by the group. This is not necessarily so. "Idiosyncrasy credit" because of high achievement does not merely imply high tolerance of otherwise unacceptable behavior; it also implies that members of the group will listen more readily.

THE TIME DIMENSION OF INNOVATION

Innovations must not only be analyzed in terms of the structural circumstances under which they occur but also in terms of their impact over time. They must be located in social time as well as in social space.

A type of behavior that might at first be perceived by the group as an attack on its norms and values might at a later time be considered in a different light. If this happens during the lifetime of the innovator he is likely to experience a sharp change in status; he will then reap the rewards of an action that was at first negatively sanctioned. The innovator is then co-opted, perhaps even against his will, into the ranks of the upholders of conformity. If, on the other hand, he obtains recognition only after his death, the lifelong heretic becomes, in effect, a posthumous saint. The Catholic church, with its amazing flexibility, has been especially adept at this process of social transmutation in which, through a remarkable alchemy, its victims have been transformed into patron saints so that Joan of Arc in due time became Saint Joan. As Merton has observed: "In the history of every society . . . some of its cultural heroes have been regarded as heroic precisely because they have had the courage and the vision to depart from norms then obtaining in the group. As we all know, the rebel, revolutionary, nonconformist, individualist, heretic, and renegade of an earlier time is often the culture hero of today."[41] The Jewish prophets, those holy demagogues, were feared, despised, and outcast by the religious and secular powers

41. Merton, *Social Theory*, p. 183.

of their day. Yet, as Max Weber has noted, "it is completely inconceivable that without a profound experience of a confirmation of the prophetic words of doom . . . the belief of the people was not only unbroken by the fearful political fate, but in a unique and quite unheard of historical paradox was definitely confirmed. The entire inner construction of the Old Testament is inconceivable without its orientation in terms of the oracles of the prophets. These giants cast their shadows through the millennia into the present."[42]

42. Max Weber, *Ancient Judaism,* trans. and ed. Hans H. Gerth and Don Martindale, New York, The Free Press, 1952, p. 334.

II

SOCIAL THEORY

AND SOCIAL CONFLICT

7

Karl Marx and Contemporary Sociology

Karl Marx is the classical theorist of social conflict. His whole contribution is based on the premise that collective interests and concomitant confrontations of power are central determinants of social process. The chapter that follows attempts to highlight this key component of Marx's work. It is not an assessment of his whole contribution, but rather a more modest attempt to emphasize one major aspect of his work that seems important for sociological inquiry today.

In the complex thought of Karl Marx there are many different strains that have been stressed at different times. With ideas of the past it is as with general history; "Every generation," wrote Carl L. Becker, "writes the same history in a new way, and it puts upon it a new construction. . . . We build our conceptions of history partly out of our present needs and purposes. The past is a kind of screen upon which we project our vision of the future."* Every generation reinterprets its intellectual inheritance and appropriates those ideas of past thinkers that are most peculiarly in tune with present needs. This is why mere inventories of our inheritance of ideas are never enough; we need to select

* Carl L. Becker, "What are Historical Facts," in Hans Meyerhoff, Ed., *The Philosophy of History in Our Time,* Garden City, New York, Doubleday Anchor Books, 1959, pp. 132–133.

and to sift if we are truly to incorporate inherited ideas into our present thought structures and thus make them our permanent possessions.

As a complicated and multi-faceted thinker, Karl Marx has been especially subject to the propensity of different periods and different groupings to refashion his image in accord with their own needs. Thus the generation of Lenin would hardly recognize *their* Marx in the psychologized version of Marx's message that is projected by certain contemporary thinkers. Indeed, this process recently has been pushed to absurdity when, for example, Erich Fromm sees Marx as being mainly concerned with the psychological alienation of modern man and relates him to Zen Buddhism in his alleged concern for the curing of souls. For Marx, the alienation of modern man was not a psychological condition to be cured, but a consequence of social contradictions that could be abolished only through class conflict.

Marx's stress on the function of social interests in the historical process can serve as a counterargument to those who claim that a functional orientation precludes concern with power and social change. These strictures may indeed be warranted when normative functionalism is under consideration, but I see no reason why other types of functional analysis might not be able to deal with these factors. Indeed, an eminent modern anthropologist of the functional school, the late S. F. Nadel, felt that "command over one another's actions" and "command over existing benefits or resources" were the main criteria to be used in the analysis of social roles and social structures.* The fact remains, however, that current sociological theorizing, whether functional in orientation or not, has too often neglected the dimensions of power and interests. The incorporation of certain of Marx's key ideas into the body of current theory will, I feel, be an important corrective in this respect. It will help right a balance that has been inclined excessively in the direction of normative integration and homeostatic balance.

* S. F. Nadel, *The Theory of Social Structure*, New York, The Free Press, 1957, p. 115.

EVERY SOCIOLOGICAL THEORY TYPICALLY RESTS ON SOME key variables that are thought to account in major part for the functioning of social systems. More particularly, norms and values, power, and interests may be said to be central factors on which various sociological theorists have focused their attention. The relative weight given to these factors, however, and their specific combinations, varies considerably. Thus, whereas normative functionalism, from Durkheim to Parsons, emphasizes common norms and values, it slights the importance of the allocation of scarce power and scarce resources as major explanatory variables. Conversely, Paretian sociology, although not unaware of the importance of the normative order as well as of economic determinants, focuses its major attention on the contest for power. Marx's sociology, in turn, though by no means oblivious of the functions of norms and values, is mainly concerned with the systematic consequences of the unequal allocation of scarce resources within a social system, one of these consequences being the unequal allocation of scarce power. Marx's major independent variable in the study of social systems turns out to be the character of interests that are systematically generated by the structure of productive relations, that is by a given system of allocation of scarce resources. Marxian sociology focuses on class interests just as Paretian sociology focuses on the striving for power, and normative functionalism on common-value integration.

Concentration on one set of variables, although it may be exceedingly valuable and productive of insights, always carries with it the inherent danger of wittingly or unwittingly slighting the importance of others. The fallacy of believing that explanations for a certain set of data are adequate for all scientific purposes lurked especially large in the case of major creative social theorists who felt justifiably that "their" variables did indeed have a great deal of explanatory power. They were prone to believe that, as Talcott Parsons has argued in his first book, their logically closed system of theory referred to an empirically closed system.[1] This is why it behooves later generations of sociologists continuously to reassess their heritage and to attempt to determine the degree to which preponderant emphasis on one or the other set of variables may not hinder the understanding of the full operation of social systems even as it may brilliantly illuminate certain of their aspects.

Even though, and perhaps just because, theorizing in the dominant mode of normative functionalism has permitted American sociology to reach a level of sophistication hitherto unattained in any other sociological enterprise, it is time to help redress the balance by emphasizing the explanatory value of neglected conceptualizations of the factors of interests and power. This is, I take it, why Marx's sociology should again be accorded serious attention both as a corrective for certain prevailing emphases and as a major theoretical scheme in its own right.

Marx's analytical focus on the ways in which the relationships between men are shaped by their relative positions in regard to the means of production, that is, by their differential access to scarce resources and scarce power, carries with it, it stands to reason, an emphasis on clash, conflict, and contention as constitutive elements of any differentiated society. Marx was aware of the fact that unequal access must not at all times and under all conditions lead to active struggles, as his description of the century-long stasis of societies operating under Asiatic modes of production testifies. He nevertheless assumed that the potential for social conflict is inherent in every differentiated society since it systematically generates conflicts of interests be-

1. Talcott Parsons, *The Structure of Social Action*, New York, The Free Press, 1949, p. 476.

tween persons and groups differentially located within the social structure.

To Marx, societal equilibrium was a special case of disequilibrium, whereas to current normative functionalism, disequilibrium is a special case of equilibrium. This is why it turns out that social change has typically presented special difficulties to normative funtionalism whereas, in contrast, in the Marxian mode of analysis it is difficult to account for continued societal functioning under relatively stable conditions. The notion of intrinsic contradictions within the social order has been a mainstay of Marxist types of explanations, whereas current normative functionalism has clung to the idea of the integration of all component actors within a common system of norms and values. It is in this respect also that a reexamination of the Marxian scheme has some urgency. Even if there are certain relatively stable social systems for the analysis of which the integrative model would seem appropriate, sociologists would deprive themselves of a most valuable tool for the understanding of social systems such as those, say, of present-day South Africa,[2] Latin America, or the American South, were they to forego the opportunity of utilizing certain approaches that Marxian sociology provides for them. Not that opposed sociological theories variously premised on the ubiquity of social order or of social conflict are likely to be most productive in the long run, but a mature theoretical scheme will have to take both factors into account if it is to elaborate a full theoretical armatorium. This is another reason why I suspect that a reexamination of Marxian sociological categories can only benefit the further development of modern sociological theory.

A prerequisite for the understanding of the Marxian con-

2. Cf., Pierre L. van den Berghe, *South Africa, a Study in Conflict,* Middletown, Conn., Wesleyan Univ. Press, 1965.

cept of class interests is the realization that Marx was not concerned with the maximization of individual self-interest upon which utilitarian interest theories commonly rest. He was not concerned with the private drives and propensities of individuals but rather with the collective interests of particular categories of men playing their peculiar roles on the social scene. "Individuals are dealt with only in so far as they are the personifications of economic categories," he says in the Preface to *Kapital*, "embodiments of particular class relations and class interests." Or, to put it into modern language, Marx was concerned with the way in which specific positions in the social structure tended to shape the social experiences of their incumbents and to predispose them to actions oriented to maximize their collective life chances.

Class interests in Marxian sociology are not given *ab initio*. They develop through the exposure of the incumbents of particular social positions to particular social circumstances. Thus competition divides the personal interests of "a crowd of people who are unknown to each other" in early industrial enterprises. "But the maintenance of their wages, this common interest which they have against their employer, brings them together again in the same idea of resistance-*combination*. Thus combination has always a double aim, that of putting an end to competition among themselves, to enable them to compete as a whole with the capitalist."[3] This is why Marx made fun of those utilitarian economists who were wont to wonder why workers might sacrifice a substantial part of their wages during strikes or in the effort to build a union. This behavior, Marx contended, could be easily understood if it was realized that these workers, far from maximizing their short-run private interests, were engaged

3. Quoted in Karl Marx, *Selected Writings in Sociology and Social Philosophy*, ed. by T. B. Bottomore and Maximilien Rubel, New York, McGraw-Hill Book Co., 1964, pp. 186–187.

in building organizations that could defend their long-term collective interests.

The collective or class interests which were in the center of Marx's concern were not simply *given,* they did not as such call forth action directly. Interests provided meaningful motivation for action only if translated into a collective assessment of the communality of life chances. This could arise only under specified conditions of which the most important one is communication between individuals similarly placed in the social structure. "The small peasants," he writes with regard to the French peasantry of the middle of the nineteenth century, "form a vast mass, the members of which live in similar conditions, but without entering into manifold relations with one another. Their mode of production isolates them from one another, instead of bringing them into mutual intercourse. . . . Insofar as millions of families live under economic conditions of existence that divide their mode of life, their interests, and their culture from those of the other classes and put them into hostile contrast to the latter, they form a class. Insofar as there is only a local interconnection among these peasants, and the identity of their interests begets no unity, no national union, and no political organization, they do not form a class."[4]

To Marx, then, potential common interests of a particular stratum can be said to derive from the location of that stratum within a particular social structure. But potentiality is transformed into actuality, *Klasse an sich* into *Klass fuer sich* only when communication, common involvement in common struggle, and the formation of a consciousness of common fate ties individuals to a cohesive class that consciously articulates common interests. A cohesive class requires of its members the commonly assumed burden of letting the demands of class

4. Quoted in Lewis A. Coser and Bernard Rosenberg, *Sociological Theory,* 2nd Ed., New York., The Macmillan Co., 1964, p. 396.

action take priority over the urges of private self-interest. Class action channels and restrains self-interest. It is a form of social control and hence helps class integration. It has disciplinary functions.

Moreover, Marx was well aware that "particular individuals are not 'always' influenced in their attitude by the class to which they belong."[4a] That is, he admitted that particular individuals may not be interested in their class interests. Whether individuals would indeed transcend their individual self-interests and develop class interests was hence to Marx an empirical question—though he assumed, of course, that most of them would indeed do so. He showed hardly any concern with the processes of individual social mobility, since to him non-transcended individual interests, though they might hinder the formation of collective interests, were not a historically transforming social force.

In contrast to the utilitarians, who see self-interest as a regulator of harmonious society, Marx sees individual self-interest as destructive of class interest in general, and leading specifically to the self-destruction of capitalism. The very fact that each capitalist acts rationally in his own self-interest leads to the destruction of the interest common to all. Capitalists are doomed since their structural position does not permit them to arrive at a consistent assertion of common interests. As Raymond Aron has recently said, "For Marx, each man working in his own interest, contributes both to the necessary functioning and to the final destruction of the regime."[5] The very fact that the competitive mode of production of capitalism does not allow the emergence of a common class interest except as a defensive mechanism, the fact that capitalist entrepreneurs, due to their

4a. Quoted in Karl Marx, *Selected Writings, op. cit.,* p. 202.
5. Raymond Aron, *Main Currents in Sociological Thought,* New York, Basic Books, 1965, pp. 134–135.

structural position, are unable to transcend individual competition among themselves, leads them to their doom. Correlatively, the workers are seen as the agents of change and of destruction of the capitalist order precisely because their structural condition predisposes them to transcend their individual interests and to evolve a consciousness of common class interests.

Marx allowed that capitalists also found it possible to transcend their immediate self-interest, but he thought this possible only in the political and ideological rather than in the economic sphere. Capitalists, divided by their economic competition among themselves, evolved a justifying ideology and a political system of domination that served their collective interests. Political power and ideology thus seem to be serving the same functions for capitalists that class consciousness serves for the working class. But this symmetry is only apparent. To Marx the economic sphere is always the finally decisive realm. And within this realm, the bourgeoisie is always the victim of the competitiveness of its very mode of economic existence. It can evolve a consciousness, but it is always a "false consciousness," that is, a consciousness that does not transcend its rootedness in an economically competitive mode of production. The bourgeoisie engenders a repressive state machinery, but this machinery cannot come to grips with an economic process based on self-interest. Hence neither the bourgeois state nor bourgeois ideology can serve truly to transcend bourgeois self-interest in the same manner as working-class consciousness transcends the self-interests of the underprivileged.

Marx's analytical focus was on those points in the social structure at which a transformation of individual interests into collective interests could be predicted. He concluded that the structural position of the bourgeoisie did not let it attain a true collectivization of interests whereas the very position of the working class brought forth true collectivization.

Marx directs our attention to the differential distribution of resources and power and the chances that such differences will lead to the emergence of social conflicts over their retention, alleviation, or abolition. He argues that these conflicts will bring about the transcendence of self-interest among the deprived. Marx focuses attention upon those social processes in which alienative tendencies and counter-ideologies among the deprived are systematically generated by the distribution of statuses and powers upon which the social organization rests.

In the Marxian view, the nuclear cell of capitalist society, the factory, embodies within it that fatal contradiction of interests that will lead to the destruction of the capitalist enterprise. The capitalist mode of production is premised upon unequal access to resources on the part of different classes and it is equally premised on an unequal access to power. The institutional framework of capitalism is built upon systematic inequalities that, in turn, through their cumulative impact upon the life chances of the actors involved, lead to the activization of alienative tendencies among the deprived strata and ultimately to the breakdown on the capitalist system.

One need not share Marx's certainties, or at least hopes, concerning the breakdown of the capitalist system, in order to recognize the importance of the analytical tool he has provided for us. In fact, nothing seems lost for sociological purposes if Marx's deterministic scheme is couched in a probabilistic framework. One need not agree that unequal life chances must lead to a common consciousness and common political action in capitalist or any other society and yet accept the notion that one is most likely to find alienative and disruptive tendencies among those whose life chances have been impaired by the operation of a particular system. Similarly, it is profitable to investigate to what degree countercultures develop through communication and contact with men involved in similar social situations and located in similar structural positions that are depriving them of significant life chances. At the very least Marx has provided us with a program of research for investigating systematically those factors that might lead to the transformation of social system through the mobilization of the energy of those whom it exploits.

It is probably true, as Arnold Feldman has recently argued, that Marx "often correctly identified the contradictions within industrial societies, but that he uniformly overestimated the extent to which such contradictions could only be resolved through revolution of counterrevolutions."[6] But it is hardly difficult, though Marx would have disapproved, to separate Marx's eschatological hopes from his analytical scheme.

Marx remains the most powerful analyst of asymmetrical relationships. In contrast to the social theorists who cling to a harmony model of society and stress symmetry in the mutual orientation of actors, Marx is concerned with the facts of unilateral dependence and hence of exploitation, and the denial of reciprocity. Complementarity can be found in every type of society, even in a totalitarian one. Autocrats and dictators engage in complementary interactions with their subjects, even while they exploit them. In fact, institutionalized exploitation, the "right to something for nothing," to use Veblen's telling phrase, is usually hidden under a veil of claims to the complementarity of the roles of rulers and ruled. Marx helps to reject these conceits. He shows why, when economic resources or power positions are unequal, the resultant relationship is likely to be unbalanced, unilateral rather than multilateral.[7]

We have seen so far that Marx's social theory focuses atten-

6. Arnold Feldman, "Violence and Volatility" in *Internal War*, ed. by Harry Eckstein, New York, The Free Press, 1964, p. 126.
7. Cf., Alvin Gouldner, "The Norm of Reciprocity," *American Sociological Review*, April, 1960, Vol. 25, 2, esp. pp. 165 and 169.

tion on three interrelated conceptualizations. He stresses the importance of common interests and analyzes structural conditions that lead to the emergence of such common interests; he discusses the ways in which particular positions within the social structure predispose toward the development of alienative tendencies, and he analyzes unilateral relations of power as they emerge out of unequal access to scarce resources and scarce positions of power. These analytical concepts remain of high value even though Marx's concrete predictions as to, for example, an impending socialist revolution in highly developed industrial societies have been proven invalid. Unfortunately, those who opposed Marx for ideological reasons as well as his own followers and epigones have tended to focus their attention on concrete historical examples and predictions rather than on the concepts that informed Marx's analysis of social structure. This becomes evident if we confront Marx's conceptualization with certain present-day events. Let me give a few concrete illustrations:

Marx certainly had very little to say, concretely, on the turning point in American race relations that we experience today. Yet a Marxian type of analysis would be most helpful for its understanding. The fact that American sociology was so ruefully unprepared for the civil rights revolution of the last few years is connected with its systematic neglect of social conflict and of the mobilization of power and interests in racial contentions. Being wedded to the belief that only increased understanding between the races and successful mobilization of guilt about the American dilemma among the dominant racial majority would lead to the gradual erosion of prejudice and discrimination, American sociology was by and large unprepared for the emergence of a situation in which a major part of the initiative for change did not come from the white man but rather from the black. American sociology has systematically neglected analysis of the conditions that gradually led to the emergence of a new self-consciousness among younger Negroes and to the development not only of alienative tendencies in the Negro community but of a militant type of alienation as well. Much professional embarrassment might well have been avoided had attention been paid to certain Marxian leads; for example, to the process of communication through which individuals gradually came to submerge their initially separate and competitive self-interests in favor of overriding common interests and collective actions for revolutionary change in the status order. Similarly it would have been less easy to brush off Marxian leads as useless nineteenth-century utilitarianism had it been grasped that Marxian sociology, far from being predicated on the idea that human actors are always predisposed to act in terms of individual self-interest, is concerned with precisely those climactic situations in which men transcend self-interest and accept the sacrifices involved in the struggle for collective interests. It would hardly have come as a surprise to Marx that so many Negroes are disposed to sacrifice their own individual life chances, to postpone present satisfaction in the collective pursuit of common long-range goals. He knew that only men who articulate their common interests through common action have a chance to change their collective destiny.

The usefulness of the Marxian perspective does not stop with the understanding of the posture of the underprivileged within a specific social structure. It can be of equal help, as Marx himself showed, to understand the orientations of those who have vested interests in the maintenance of the social order. One need not neglect the importance of legal norms, of national values, and of appeals to conscience to grasp the impact on the Southern *status quo* of such mundane matters as the flow of federal funds, the prospective sales of bond issue, the direction of the flow of new capital into private enterprise. In the South one also finds principled racists who happen not to be interested in their economic interests, but the majority of Southern dominants *are* so interested. The threat faced by businessmen of losing customers or credit, or the threat faced by politicians of losing votes if dependent on a large Negro constituency, are efficient solvents of the cake of Southern custom. Even a cursory reading of the daily news about the South—and the North as well—revives the conviction that it is entirely too early to relegate Marxian thinking to the heap of historically obsolete dogmatic constructions. We still ought to listen to the man who wrote, "Morality, religion, metaphysics, and other ideologies, and their corresponding forms of consciousness, no longer retain . . . their appearance of autonomous existence. . . . It is men, who, in developing their material production and their material intercourse, change, along with their real existence, their thinking and the products of their thinking. Life is not determined by consciousness, but consciousness by life."[8]

Marx suffered from the misfortune of having been born in the nineteenth and not in the twentieth century, and much of his thinking is inevitably historically obsolete. In fact, I believe that a thinker who was so concerned with emphasizing the principle of historical specificity would have been the first to agree. Many of Marx's problems are no longer ours, few of his solutions can be ours, and even his methods of analysis are only partly usable today. More particularly, messianic and eschatological elements loom large in the Marx's overall work and must be eliminated if his contribution to the science of society is to be recognized and utilized.

Moreover, it seems necessary to reject Marx's reductionist tendencies, his propensity, for example, to see in the political order only a reflection of the economic order.

Marx's economic reductionism, as Ralf Dahrendorf, among

8. *Karl Marx, op. cit.*, p. 75.

others, has shown,[9] led him to neglect the analysis of those power relations that are not derived from property relations. To Marx, power flowed from command over economic resources; he did not entertain the idea that command over economic resources might result from access to powerful positions. He understood, to cite Ignazio Silone's insightful quip, the role of plutocrats but was unable to foretell the advent of the "cratopluts" of the twentieth century.

Similarly, Marx's powerful analysis of unilateral relationships and his theory of exploitation remained too narrowly focused on the economic framework. Let me end with a quote from a young sociologist, himself clearly not a Marxian, Donald McKinley: ". . . perhaps Marx was, in part, right. His focus on exploitation was, however, too narrowly economic, and his predicated aggressive counterresponse, too narrowly political. Perhaps more importantly, the exploitation in a highly industrialized and differentiated society is of an emotional and moral nature and the alienated and aggressive response is of a like kind —family disorganization, crime, and political apathy."[10]

Here, as elsewhere, Marx did not go far enough, no doubt. But it behooves us to push farther in a direction in which he did some pioneering exploitations. The cumulative enterprise of scientific inquiry is best served if we honor the contributions of our ancestors by selectively incorporating them into the body of our theories, while utilizing their leads to penetrate into realms that, to them, were yet virgin territory.

9. Ralf Dahrendorf, *Class and Class Conflict in Industrial Society,* Stanford, Calif., Stanford University Press, 1959.
10. Donald McKinley, *Social Class and Family Life,* New York, The Free Press, 1964, p. 266.

8

Durkheim's Conservatism

and Its Implications for Sociological Theory

My intent in the preceding chapter was to show how certain aspects of Marx's work, especially his focus on social conflict, can fruitfully be incorporated into current sociological theory and help enrich it. In this complementary chapter I pursue an opposite strategy by attempting to document the fact that Durkheim's conservative orientation prevented him from taking due cognizance of a variety of societal processes, among which social conflict is most conspicuous, that could not be incorporated into his overall theoretical scheme. I attempt to indicate in what ways such theoretical blinders impoverished his sociology.

The chapter speaks for itself and needs no extended commentary. It is worthwhile to record, however, that my critical attitude toward certain shortcomings of Durkheim's overall theory is by no means rooted in a general rejection of his approach. I regard Durkheim as one among the four or five major figures whom sociology has so far produced. My first encounter with sociology as a scholarly discipline took place at the *Sorbonne* under the guidance of two of Durkheim's close disciples, Célestin Bouglé and Paul Fauconnet. The Durkheimian tradition has continued to be one of the central influences on my own intellectual development.

Although the pages that follow attempt to demonstrate how Durkheim's conservative orientation deflected his attention from a number of significant areas of investigation, among which social conflict and social change loom perhaps largest, I fully concur with Robert A. Nisbet's judgment when he wrote that, "More than any other figure in the history of sociology, Emile Durkheim seems to embody what has proved to be conceptually most distinctive in the field and most fertile in its contribution to other modern disciplines."*

* Robert A. Nisbet, *Emile Durkheim,* Englewood Cliffs, N.J., Prentice-Hall, 1965, p. 1.

"A WAY OF SEEING IS ALWAYS A WAY OF NOT SEEING."[1] It is clear that Durkheim saw much, and many writers have recently reminded us of it. My task here, though complementary, is different: I shall attempt to establish that Durkheim's conservatism significantly limited his perception of society. I would hold with Max Weber that "the choice of the object of investigation and the extent or depth to which this investigation attempts to penetrate into the infinite causal web, are determined by the evaluative ideas which dominate the investigator and his age."[2] Since Durkheim was unusually explicit in stating his values, it is possible to trace in some detail the manner in which they limited the extent or depth of his investigation in certain areas, just as they helped him open up other areas to fruitful and often entirely new investigation.

In spite of all the adverse criticism that it contains, this essay is written in praise of Durkheim. I know of no better way to celebrate the work of a master of the past than to account for the limitations of his work. No one knew better than Durkheim that progress in science can be achieved only through the selective elimination as well as the selective preservation of past contributions.

As one studies the numerous hostile criticisms of Durkheim's sociology,[3] one is struck by the fact that many, though not all, of them share a limited number of common themes.

1. This is Kenneth Burke's dictum in *Permanence and Change* (New York, New Republic, Inc., 1935), p. 70.

2. *On the Methodology of the Social Sciences,* ed. and trans. Edward A. Shils and Henry A. Finch (New York, The Free Press, 1948), p. 84.

3. See, for example, Roger Lacombe, *La méthode sociologique de Durkheim,* Paris, Félix Alcan, 1926; Emile Benoit-Smullyan, "The Sociologism of Emile Durkheim and His School," in *An Introduction to the History of Sociology,* ed. Harry Elmer Barnes, Chicago, University of Chicago Press, 1948; Jules Monnerot, *Les faits sociaux ne sont pas des choses,* Paris, Gallimard, 1946.

It is said that Durkheim was so fascinated by the study of cohesion that he neglected to study the phenomena of conflict; that he was so absorbed in the study of society as a whole that he did not deal adequately with the subgroups and subdivisions that make up the total society; that he neglected the individual and his claims because he concentrated upon the society and its claims; that he stressed the cohesive function of religion without considering its divisive features; that he did not duly appreciate the import of social innovation and social change because he was preoccupied with social order and equilibrium; and that he neglected to analyze power and violence in the body politic because he was overly concerned with the factors which make for agreement.

In what follows I shall make an attempt to show that these shortcomings, assuming for a moment that his critics are correct, are not due to fortuitous circumstances, such as the exigencies of a particular research situation, but that they can be accounted for to a large extent in terms of Durkheim's abiding conservatism. To the extent that I can support this interpretation, I may be able to contribute to the sociological interpretation of his sociology.

I shall, of course, not be concerned with Durkheim's conservative ideas as such, but only with the way in which these ideas obscured, for him, certain fruitful sociological problems. Theoretical orientations result from a series of decisions by a theorist concerning what he considers problematical. Such decisions lead him to adopt particular theoretical frameworks and to ignore others. Durkheim's conservatism, accordingly, led him to make a series of decisions regarding theory that crucially influenced the direction of his research.[4]

By conservatism, I mean an inclination to maintain the

4. Of course, what is said here about conservatism would also be true of liberalism or radicalism in other cases.

existing order of things or to reenforce an order that seems threatened. For the conservative, as Karl Mannheim has argued, "everything that exists has a positive and nominal value merely because it has come into existence slowly and gradually."[5] The conservative does not reject all change; he insists only that change must be slow and gradual and that it must never endanger the social order.

There can be no doubt that Durkheim, though a "liberal" in the political arena, considered himself a conservative in this sense; he often reiterated his conviction that social reform ought to be introduced with the utmost care so that it does not damage the fabric of society. The science of ethics, he believed, "does teach us to treat [reality] with extreme caution, imparting to us a conservative attitude."[6] There will be times, he wrote, when "everything is not all it ought to be, and that, consequently, will be the time to intervene." But this intervention must always be limited and piecemeal: "It has for its object, not to make an ethic completely different from the prevailing one, but to correct the latter, or partially to improve it."[7]

Before considering in detail the shortcomings of Durkheim's theory, let us recall briefly that his whole contribution to theory was itself a result of his concern as a conservative with the conditions of the French society of his time. The problem of order preoccupied Durkheim from his earliest writings to the last pages of the *Introduction à la morale*, a paper he wrote shortly before his death. Directly or indirectly, all of his writings are related to his problem.

5. Karl Mannheim, *Ideology and Utopia*, New York, Harcourt, Brace and Co., 1936, pp. 211–12.
6. *The Division of Labor in Society*, trans. George Simpson, New York, The Free Press, 1948, p. 35.
7. *Ibid.*, pp. 35–36.

Durkheim wrote during a period of social disorganization. When he was a student, the Third Republic was in its infancy. Deeply attached to the new republican society and yet aware of the weak foundation upon which it rested, Durkheim felt that it was his central task to contribute to the development of a new French republican moral order. Even though he was utterly devoted to the idea of establishing a science of society, Durkheim nevertheless believed that this science would have no value if it did not eventually lend itself to practical application. "We should judge our researches to have no worth at all," he wrote, "if they were to have only a speculative interest."[8] "A science that deserves that name," he stated in his last paper, "must result in an art: otherwise it would only be a game, an intellectual distraction, pure and simple erudition."[9]

There is no need here to document further the well-known connection between Durkheim's program of study and his moral and political orientation. Harry Alpert[10] and several others have shown that Durkheim's thoughts were centered upon the problems of his time; they have shown how close the relationship is between Durkheim the moralist and Durkheim the sociologist. I agree with Robert A. Nisbet, who, after tracing some of the similarities between Durkheim's themes and those of the French conservatives that preceded him, remarks that "what Durkheim did was to take the conservative view of society out of what was essentially a speculative framework of inquiry and translate it into certain hypotheses, which he sought to verify"[11] I shall now show that this led Durkheim to neglect certain other types of hypotheses and in consequence

8. *Ibid.,* p. 33.
9. "Introduction à la morale," *Revue philosophique,* LXXXIX (1920), 84.
10. Harry Alpert, *Emile Durkheim and His Sociology,* New York, Columbia University Press, 1939.
11. "Conservatism and Sociology," *American Journal of Sociology,* LVIII (1952), 165–75.

made him unable to account for a wide range of social facts. The discussion must begin with a consideration of Durkheim's views on social order and disorder.

Alfred North Whitehead once wrote that periods of transition, although they manifest "the misery of decay," also show "the zest of new life."[12] Durkheim would have understood only the first part of this statement. He often referred to the Saint-Simonian distinction between critical and organic periods of history, a distinction that in his opinion marked "an important progress in the philosophy of history."[13] But it is remarkable that Durkheim, although his sociology arises out of an awareness of the crises of his age, never really attempts to analyze such crises in their own terms. They are always seen as departures from the expected order and equilibrium; they are pathological, and thus devoid of any inherent worth. Just as to Durkheim any type of nonconformity is criminal by definition, so critical periods, periods of social disequilibrium, are by definition aspects of social pathology. Such a definition prevents the study of these crises in terms of the opportunities they offer for the emergence of alternatives to the existing order. At best, Durkheim believed, the sociologist can only suggest how the patient may be cured by the judicious application of carefully (that is, conservatively) defined remedial action: "The duty of the statesman is no longer to push the patient toward an ideal that seems attractive to him, but his role is that of the physician: He prevents the outbreak of illness by good hygiene, and he seeks to cure them when they have appeared."[14]

The liberal or radical thinker contrasts an ideal state with a real state. Durkheim, to the contrary, substituted the distinction between the normal and the pathological for the disjunc-

12. *Adventures of Ideas,* New York, Mentor Books, 1955, p. 15.

13. *Le socialisme,* Paris, Félix Alcan, 1928, p. 312.

14. *The Rules of Sociological Method,* ed. George E. G. Catlin, New York, The Free Press, 1950, p. 75.

tion between the ideal and the real—a distinction that was not as "scientific" as he thought it was, since normality may itself be considered a fact or a value—and thus introduced bias toward conservatism. This bias predisposed him to consider any attempt to make the world more nearly resemble an ideal world a wanton disregard of the facts of social life. Such a procedure is likely to make the sociologist less able to understand social innovation. It is true, of course, as Gaston Richard and others have pointed out, that Durkheim does not always follow his own prescription.[15] For example, he states in *The Division of Labor* that all generally existing forms of the division in his times are pathological, even though he considered the general to be the normal. In *The Division of Labor*, the normal turns out to be a utopian fiction and not general at all. Durkheim's very inconsistencies reveal that his method did not permit him fully to understand periods of transition.

Durkheim believed disorder was a special case within a generally ordered system. To him, just as to the classical economists, disequilibrium is only a special instance of a general equilibrium. His commitment to the idea of a state of order prevented him from considering the alternative that obtains in the Keynesian approach in economics—that equilibrium might be a special case of a general disequilibrium. With such an approach, conflict and change would be considered the rule, stability and order the exception, perhaps even the "pathological" exception.[16] "Transitional states" would not be seen

15. Gaston Richard, "La pathologie sociale d'Emile Durkheim," *Revue internationale de sociologie*, XXXVIII (1930), 123; see also Achille Ouchy, "Les sociologies et la sociologie," *Revue internationale de sociologie*, XLVII (1939), esp. pp. 482–84.

16. Cf. Ralf Dahrendorf, "Struktur und Funktion," *Kölner Zeitschrift für Soziologie*, VII (1955), 491–519, esp. 510–14. See also the author's *The Functions of Social Conflict*, New York, The Free Press, 1956, and "Social Conflict and the Theory of Social Change," in this volume.

as exceptional but, at least in the modern world, the rule. This is not the place to discuss the respective merits of these alternative approaches, but one may at least ask whether an orientation similar to that of Keynes in economics is not likely to reveal elements that the "classical" orientation obscures.

With his idea of an ordered state of affairs, it is not surprising that Durkheim deals but little with those aspects of social life that concern division, strife, conflict. In this he is clearly within the general conservative tradition: The conservative thinks in terms of the "whole," ignoring antagonisms and struggles between the "parts"; whereas these struggles are central to the thought of the change-oriented radical or liberal.[17] Nor should it surprise us that Durkheim's morphology tends to be a morphology of the total group. Gunnar Myrdal has laid bare the shortcomings of his approach in his well-known criticism of William Graham Sumner's method. Although Sumner's and Durkheim's theoretical orientations are widely divergent, the bias toward conservatism which they share seems to account for similar shortcoming in theory. Myrdal writes:

> Sumner's construction contains a valid organization and offers a useful methodological tool for studying primitive cultures and isolated, stationary folk communities. . . . The theory is, however, crude and misleading when applied to a modern Western society . . . it is likely to conceal more than to expose. It conceals what is most important in our society: the changes, the conflicts, the absence of static equilibria, the lability in all relations even when they are temporarily, though perhaps for decades, held at a standstill.[18]

17. Cf. Karl Mannheim, *op. cit., passim,* and "Conservative Thought," *Essays on Sociology and Social Psychology,* New York, Oxford University Press, 1954, pp. 74–164.
18. *An American Dilemma,* New York, Harper & Bros., 1944, II, 1032.

This is a harsh judgment; nevertheless one cannot but feel that by and large it also applies to Durkheim's work. This may help to explain why, though deeply indebted to that work, modern sociology seems to have utilized less of its heritage from Durkheim than has anthropology. (It must be remarked, however, that even nonliterate societies are much less homogeneous than Durkheim has supposed. Conflicts between subdivisions, between age classes, kinship units, and residential groups are, even there, the rule rather than the exception.) [19]

Durkheim's general neglect of conflicting subgroups in modern society is perhaps nowhere as evident as in his neglect of class phenomena. This is especially striking since he wrote extensively on professional groups. Classes are always conflict groupings whereas professional organizations are not. Only in the very last pages of his *The Division of Labor,* a subject matter that would seem to require close attention to the sociology of class relations, does Durkheim mention class conflicts—or, for that matter, classes—at all, and then only in order to affirm that when organic solidarity replaces mechanical solidarity there is a diminution of social inequalities and hence a reduction of class differentiation.

Durkheim always rejected socialism, though he knew socialist theory quite well and though a great number of his friends, such as Jean Jaurès, were among the leaders of French socialism. Marcel Mauss, his relative, intimate friend, and collaborator, writes:

> All his life he was disinclined to become an adherent of socialism properly speaking because of certain aspects of its activities: its violent character, its class character, its working-class orientation, and also its political and "hack" character.

19. Cf. Max Gluckman, *Custom and Conflict in Africa,* New York, Free Press, 1956. See also Armand Cuvillier, "Durkheim et Marx," *Cahiers internationaux de sociologie,* IV (1948), 75–97, esp. 79.

> Durkheim was profoundly opposed to any class war . . . he wanted only changes that would profit the total society and not only one of its parts, even if this were a powerful and numerous part.[20]

The point here is obviously not to reproach Durkheim for not having become a socialist, but rather to indicate that his rejection of socialism was based not so much—perhaps not all— on its economic program, for which he often expressed some sympathy, but rather on the fact that it was the doctrine of a conflict group, benefiting, he believed, a part, not the whole. He found the harmonious socialism of the Saint-Simonians much more attractive. This explains Durkheim's neglect of the study of class phenomena: They appeared to him *a priori* divisive and disintegrating.

For Durkheim, the "social question" was a moral question, a question that involved the relation of individuals to the social whole, not the contention for power, status, and wealth. The following quotation will provide sufficient evidence.

> It is not a question of putting a new society in the place of that which exists, but to adapt the latter to new social conditions. It is no longer a question of classes, of the opposition of the rich to the poor, of entrepreneurs to workers, as if the only possible solution were to diminish the portion of one in order to increase that of the other. What is needed in the interest of the one and the other is the necessity to contain from above the appetites of both, and thus to put an end to the state of disorganization, of maniacal agitation, which does not stem from social activity, and which makes it suffer. In other words, the social question posed this way is not a question of money or of force; it is a question of moral agents. What dominates it is not the state of our economy, but rather the state of our morality.[21]

20. Introduction to Durkheim, *Le socialisme,* p. viii.
21. *Ibid.,* p. 297.

We shall have to come back to the insistence on the necessity of containing individual desires which informs so much of Durkheim's writing; at present we need only note his quite explicit refusal to deal with the "social question" in terms of contentions for scarce power and scarce wealth. Durkheim's sociology here closely followed in the path of his moral philosophy. He did not believe that contentions for power and wealth touched upon the significant moral issues that preoccupied him; consequently, his sociology did not in any real sense take cognizance of them. His sociology was the poorer for it.

Durkheim was forced to assume that the major social norms generally express the sentiments of the total society. He never seriously entertained the idea that they might only express the sentiments of a specific stratum with it. If it is affirmed *a priori* that the major social norms express the sentiments of the total collectivity, then one cannot recognize conflicting norms within a society; one cannot take cognizance of clashing values; one is unable to understand, as Roger Lacombe has pointed out, that certain subordinate social strata may accept a norm only because it is imposed upon them by violence or because they passively submit to it, whereas it is the genuine expression of the moral sentiment of only a superordinate stratum.[22]

All this is not to say, of course, that Durkheim was unaware of the existence of subgroups within a society. His intense concern with professional and family groupings reminds us of this fact. However, and this seems important, he sees the various norms of subgroups only as complementary, as having a specific place in a hierachy. He did on occasion speak of a "decentralization of moral life," and discussed the fact that "the priest and the soldier have different duties" and that occupational moralities vary in different branches of industry. Yet he was convinced

22. Lacombe, *op. cit.,* p. 73.

that there existed a hierarchy among the different groups and institutions, and hence among the duties peculiar to them. Thus professional morality was "lower" than state morality, and domestic morality lower than either. This is not the place to discuss the dubious foundation of a "scientific morality" that pretends that it has established scientifically that one's duty to one's family is necessarily inferior to one's duty to the state; one needs only to point out that, here again, Durkheim, though recognizing that there may be a clash of values and norms between various subgroups in a society and that loyalties and allegiances to various institutions may be at variance, dismisses this consideration by affirming that hierarchy is the central scientific fact and that infringements upon the hierarchial principle can be due to pathological factors only.[23] To Durkheim a divided society can be neither normal nor moral. The "good" society is cohesive. There may be deviation and criminality on its fringes, as there are red-light districts within a metropolitan area, but its main constituent groups, far from contending, must complement each other in a disciplined conformity to the overriding norms of the whole. It is not surprising that a postwar generation to whom class divisions, revolutions, and wars had become "normal" social phenomena found that Durkheimian sociology was an unsuitable instrument for the analysis of their social world.[24]

Consideration of a few of Durkheim's definitions may enable us to grasp the relationship between his conservatism and his shortcomings in theory. The matter of initial definitions,

23. For Durkheim's main discussion in this connection, see *L'Education morale,* Paris, Félix Alcan, 1925, esp. pp. 83 ff., and "Morale professionelle," *Revue de métaphysique et de morale,* XLIV (1937), 527–44, 711–38, esp. 535–36. See also the excellent essay by Georges Gurvitch, "La morale de Durkheim," in *Essais de sociologie,* Paris, Recueil Sirey, 1939.

24. Cf. Monnerot, *op. cit.,* esp. pp. 75–76, 88–91.

as Harry Alpert has remarked, is all-important for Durkheim.[25] It is for him the most indispensable condition of scientific proof and verification. But, as Alpert has also pointed out, it is precisely here that Durkheim's methodological approach is weak indeed. To him definitions were by no means merely tentative working tools to be discarded or changed during the course of research; he assumed, instead, that a definition could disclose a truth rooted in the nature of things. Hence definitions may be considered more important in the assessment of Durkheim's system than in an appraisal of a thinker more adequately aware of their tentative function and of the crucial role of the definer. His definitions may not give us, as Durkheim believed, a "firm foothold on reality," but they can give us a kind of privileged access to his own cast of mind. A few examples may serve to illustrate this.

Let us take Durkheim's famous definition of crime as all acts which present "the external characteristic that they evoke from society the particular reaction called punishment. . . . We call every punished act a crime."[26] Such a definition could have been adopted only by a thinker whose general orientation is fundamentally conservative. For under this definition, as Lucien Goldman has remarked,[27] is subsumed the action of Jesus in ejecting the merchants from the temple, as well as the activities of a Thomas Muenzer and a Lenin, on the one hand, and of a highway robber, on the other. Such subsuming of what would appear to the non-conservative thinker essentially dissimilar phenomena may indeed appear quite natural to a conservative, who places everything that disturbs the social order in the same category. The failure to discriminate between heter-

25. Alpert, *op. cit.,* esp. pp. 114 ff.
26. *The Rules of Sociological Method,* pp. 35–36.
27. *Sciences humaines et philosophie,* Paris, Presses Universitaires de France, 1952, pp. 21–22.

ogeneous phenomena is not likely to be scientifically productive. I am, of course, aware that Durkheim did not consider crime an abnormal occurence, and that he did in fact—with rather obvious embarrassment and strained reasoning—attempt in a number of places to distinguish between crime and the intellectual dissent of, for example, Socrates.[28] It is true, nonetheless, that he never departed from his definition of crime, thus maintaining that, in spite of certain difficulties in the application of his concepts, all acts that evoke societal punishment are basically similar. When all forms of dissent are thus criminal by definition, we are in the presence of a system that is ill-equipped to reveal fully the extent to which nonconformity, as distinct from crime, involves the striving toward an alternative moral basis rather than moral deviation.[29]

To Durkheim, "undisciplined and irregular people" were "morally incomplete"; in his belief, "it is impossible to consider moral those practices which are subversive of the society in which they are observed; because it is everywhere a fundamental duty to ensure the existence of the fatherland."[30] Given

28. Cf., for example, *L'Education morale,* pp. 60–61, and *Sociology and Philosophy,* trans. D. F. Pocock, London, Cohen and West, 1953, pp. 64–65.

29. This is, of course, not meant to deny that it might not be necessary for the purpose of a particular study to distinguish between crime and nonconformity, but only to indicate that failure to distinguish between them on the conceptual level prevents the sociologist from perceiving their distinctive functions. Cf. for the above distinction Robert K. Merton's lucid discussion in his *Social Theory and Social Structure* (rev. ed.), New York, Free Press, 1957, pp. 360–68. See also Roger Nett, "Conformity-Deviation and the Social Control Concept," *Ethics,* LXIV (1953), 38–45; L. G. Brown, *Social Pathology,* New York, F. S. Crofts Co., 1942, esp. pp. 70 ff.; and Lewis A. Coser, "Social Conflict and the Theory of Social Change," in this volume.

30. *De la division du travail social,* Paris, Félix Alcan, 1893, p. 21. All translations are the work of the author unless reference is made to a specific translation.

these premises, the lines that divide genuine pathological failure from nonconformity are, of course, blurred. Thus Durkheim was not able to ask whether a high percentage of conformists may not be pathological failures as well, and whether individuals cannot adhere pathologically to the approved patterns of society as easily as to disapproved patterns. There is, after all, something which might be called the "mad orthodoxy" of the mentally ill, and prison inmates often have quite "proper" political views.

Durkheim's definition of the state affords us another example of the effects of a conservative bias on one's definitions and hence on one's theoretical orientation. I have mentioned Durkheim's reluctance to discuss, or even to take full cognizance of, power and violence. This becomes especially obvious in his definition of the state. Whereas Weber, to whom struggle, conflict, and contention are in the very center of social life, defined the state as a human group "that (successfully) claims the monopoly of the legitimate use of physical force within a given territory,"[31] one finds in Durkheim's definition no reference to the authoritative enforcement of will but rather a curiously abstract and intellectualistic conception of the state. The state is to him "a group of functionaries *sui generis* within which representations and directives which engage the collectivity are being elaborated." Not the whole of the collective consciousness is incarnated in the state; "it is only the seat of a special and delimited consciousness, but a consciousness higher and clearer, having a more lively feeling of itself." It was a mistake, Durkheim believed, to identify the state with the executive power: "The state executes nothing." "All the life proper of the state is not spent in exterior action, in movements, but rather in deliberations, that is, representations." Administrative

31. *From Max Weber,* ed. H. H. Gerth and C. Wright Mills, New York, Oxford University Press, 1953, p. 78.

action must be distinguished from state activity. They differ as the muscular system does from the central nervous system. "The state is, rigorously speaking, the organ of social thought." "Its essential function is to think."[32]

Defining the state as he does, it is not surprising that Durkheim never succeeded in analyzing or even in taking theoretical cognizance of the role of governmental force and violence or of political power and coercion. He relegated all of that to the "muscular system," and it seemed, in a sense, *infra dignitatem.* Being so deeply concerned with buttressing the authority of the secular republican state, he may, in fact, have felt that to pay attention to the mechanics of power might undermine that respect for the state that he attempted to implant. He took the disenchantment with religious symbols in his stride; but disenchantment with the symbols of secular authority, he may have felt, could contribute only to further anomie. He was exclusively concerned with those functions of the state that would make it appear as a kind of brain trust, the special seat of the more rarefied and self-conscious collective ideas. Given Durkheim's initial decision to build a sociology that would help to reestablish the threatened order of the Third Republic, given his lifelong endeavor to elaborate a secular morality that would serve to strengthen the foundations of the republican regime, it was perhaps understandable that he focused attention only on the positive functions of the state. The fact remains that what may perhaps have been a gain for the political practice of the regime turned out to be a loss for sociological theory. A system of sociology that proved incapable of dealing with the facts of state power, that framed its definitions in such a way that these facts could not be properly indentified, was to remain a truncated system. Even

32. *Leçons de sociologie,* Paris, Presses Universitaires de France, 1950, pp. 61–63.

though it may have been adequate for a limited understanding of the "Republic of Professor"—as the Third Republic has sometimes been called—it could hardly aid comprehension of the era of the total state that began after Durkheim's death. We cannot reproach Durkheim for lacking the gift of prophecy, but we might reproach him for not having grasped the irreducible facts of power so glaringly obvious in the living past of his own age. If he had had the tough-minded detachment of a Marx or a Weber, his contribution might have been of value to the understanding of an era that was in crucial ways different from his own. As it was, his tender-minded attachment to the institutions of Republican France proved to be a fatal handicap.

Durkheim's definition of the term "society" is closely connected with his definition of the state. Though he customarily used the term with various meanings when speaking of domestic society, professional society, and the like, usually, when he refers to *the* society in the modern world, the term denotes the national political order and becomes almost synonymous with fatherland, nation, or even state. Durkheim was occasionally quite explicit in equating society with the fatherland. He says, for example, "It seems to me quite evident that we cannot live without a fatherland, because we cannot live outside organized society that exists."[33] "We must see in the fatherland *in abstracto* the normal and indispensable milieu of human life."[34] Although the term "society" is used as approximately equivalent to the fatherland and nation of the modern world, it is also used in about the same sense to denote a tribal unit among nonliterate peoples. By thus obscuring the differences between relatively heterogeneous and relatively homogeneous social structures, by making no distinction between structures with dif-

33. *Bulletin de la société française de philosophie,* VIII (1908), 45.
34. *Ibid.,* p. 52.

ferentiated political institutions and structures which lack such institutions, Durkheim made it difficult to develop a comparative sociology of political structures with the framework of his system; and this is especially true since he used the term "society" all too often in an honorific rather than in a factual sense—"the perpetual state of dependence is which we find ourselves vis-à-vis society inspires in us a sentiment of religious respect toward it."[35]

Durkheim's intense patriotism and his deep "religious" devotion to "society" have often been commented upon; what has perhaps not been sufficiently discussed is the curiously abstract character of his patriotism and his religion of society. Here it would seem appropriate to introduce a consideration of Durkheim's background.

It is customary to find evidence in most patriotic writings of an attachment to particular localities or regions, to particular historical or linguistic traditions. Not so with Durkheim. We encounter in his writings a highly rational, non-emotional attachment to *la patrie*. This intellectualized and abstract relation to his country may well have had its source in his social origin. When this son of a rabbi from the eastern fringes of France came to Paris to develop into one of the guiding spirits of the Third Republic, he did not feel bound to any one subgroup, class, stratum, or region. His loyalty went to France, which became for him the prototype of *the* society. His attachment was not mediated through tradition and history, but was, so to speak, abstractly intellectual.

This may explain why we find in Durkheim's work so little discussion and understanding of the loyalties that men have for different subgroups within a society, and also why Durkheim does not seem to have understood ideological loyalties that

35. "De la définition des phénomènes réligieux," *L'Année sociologique,* II (1898), 23.

cut across national allegiances. This is why he could write that "a class, even an enlarged class, is not and cannot be a fatherland; it is only a fragment of a fatherland, just as an organ is only a fragment of an organism. Because internationalism misunderstands this elementary truth, it is but too often the pure and simple negation of any organized society."[36] Here again, we come upon self-imposed limitations that explain why the investigator of such modern social movements as communism, for example, finds so little aid in Durkheim's sociology. He who tended at times to hypostatize society as the Hegelians before him had hypostatized history left us no instruments with which to understand those ideological movements of the Stalinist variety, for instance, which function, to use a phrase of Léon Blum, as "foreign national parties" within the national polity.

A related shortcoming is apparent in Durkheim's sociology of religion. Perhaps in no area of research was Durkheim so hampered by his initial conservative orientation as in his analysis of religious phenomena. Obsessed with the need to maintain and to re-create the basis for order in society, he wanted to see in religion an exclusively integrating and cohesive force. Ritual and ceremony, to quote Alpert's succinct summary, provide "disciplinary, cohesive, vitalizing, and euphoric social forces."[37] The practices of a cult strengthen "the bonds attaching the believer to his god [and] . . . at the same time strengthen the bond attaching the individual to the society of which he is a member, since the god is only a figurative expression of society."[38] Hence "religion has given birth to all that is essential in society."[39]

36. *Ibid.,* p. 52.
37. *Op. cit.,* p. 202.
38. Durkheim, *The Elementary Forms of the Religious Life,* trans. Joseph Ward Swain, New York, The Free Press, 1954, p. 226.
39. *Ibid.,* p. 419.

Durkheim was faced with the fact that religion had declined in France, that religious sanctions and religious symbols had lost much of their efficacy. Consequently, throughout his life he was preoccupied with finding a moral equivalent for religion. But this very fact indicates that to him religion appeared to be invariably productive of social cohesion.[40]

There is no reference in any of Durkheim's writings to the divisive and the dysfunctional aspects of religious practices. This seems almost incredible since Durkheim was, of course, well-read in European history and must have been quite familiar with the divisive effect that, for example, religious wars had had in the history of, say, sixteenth-century France. There is no Frenchman with even a modicum of education who does not know something about the Massacre of St. Bartholomew, the revocation of the Edict of Nantes, the destruction of the flowering culture of the Albigenses, and so on. These events are alive in the collective consciousness of the French. Yet exclusive attention to the demands of the theoretical and moral system that he attempted to build prevented Durkheim from considering any of them. This man, the son of a people that has suffered from religious persecution perhaps more than any other Western people, never allowed knowledge of these events to intrude into his thinking when he constructed his system.

It apparently never occurred to Durkheim that religion may serve as a means of legitimizing and glorifying acts that would

40. Many of the contemporary debates aroused by Durkheim's sociology of religion seemed to have involved a rather curious misunderstanding. While Durkheim's antagonists felt that he attempted to discredit religion by pointing to its elementary totemic forms, Durkheim had actually intended to show the eminently positive role of religion in the creation of social cohesion. Since social cohesion was to him supremely important—perhaps the most important factor—he thought that he had in fact contributed a thoroughgoing defense of religion. His adversaries, however, were concerned with a concrete religion, not with religion *in abstracto*.

not have been perpetrated in good conscience had such legitimation not been available. He was apparently unable to recognize a social fact that appeared so obvious to the ripe wisdom of Gilbert Murray when he wrote, "Probably throughout history the worst things ever done in the world on a large scale by decent people have been done in the name of religion."[41] Nor did Durkheim's theory take cognizance of the historical evidence that indicates that religion, although it may draw men together, may also separate them and set them against each other. To quote Murray again, "I suppose that a thoroughly orthodox member of any of the million religious bodies that exist in the world must be clear in his mind that the other million minus one are wrong, if not wickedly wrong."[42]

It has often been argued that Durkheim's neglect of the divisive function of religion may be accounted for by the fact that his theories were mainly derived from data on nonliterate societies. This seems insufficient grounds. The fact is that Durkheim, not an anthropologist by training, deliberately concentrated his attention upon nonliterate societies. There were a number of reasons for this choice. For one, the evolutionist tradition played some part: What was "most primitive and simple" might be expected to yield more essential data. In addition, the choice of relatively homogeneous groups as objects of analysis was clearly connected in Durkheim's case with a desire to study those groups in which religious dissension and the possible dysfunctions of religion were minimized. Having asserted that religion was necessarily productive of unity, solidarity, and cohesion, Durkheim turned for verification to those homogeneous societies where it would be easier to demonstrate this function of religion. Because Durkheim chose tribal society as the

41. *Five Stages of Greek Religion,* New York, Doubleday & Co., Inc. [Anchor Books], 1955, p. 8.
42. *Ibid.,* p. 7.

unit of analysis, he did not have to consider religious orientations that militate against attachment to society in the name of a religious ideal. It is difficult to analyze the rise of Islam or the Church Militant in Durkheimian terms, just as hard as it is to understand the secularized international religions of our time within the framework of his analysis. To the extent that a religion is subversive of the society in which it is practiced and divides that society, Durkheim's sociology of religion remains unable to cope with it.

Lest this paper degenerate into a wearisome catalogue of all the shortcomings of Durkheim's sociology, it may be advisable to close it with a discussion of two additional aspects of his work that seem to be of special import, since they concern areas in which conservative and liberal or radical thinkers have most often parted company: the question of "human nature" and the related question of education. Traditionally, the conservative has been given to a pessimistic interpretation of human nature and he has pitted his view against the progressivist belief in the perfectibility of man.[43] Traditionally—though there are exceptions—the conservative has asserted that a more or less authoritarian system of education is needed in order to curb the savage propensities of the young, whereas the progressive has insisted on permissive methods of education designed to lead to the spontaneous emergence of autonomous individuals through the careful cultivation of autonomous moral tendencies. Durkheim, too, was a pessimist about human nature and authoritarian in his educational views. As before, we shall explore these two areas, not to show that Durkheim was a con-

43. "Coming from the hand of the author of all things," begins Rousseau's *Emile*, "everything is good; in the hand of man, everything degenerates." Bonald answers, "We are bad by nature, good through society. The savage is not a man, he is not even a childish man, he is only a degenerate man. *Recherches philosophiques* (*Oeuvres*, III, Paris, J. P. Migne, 1864), pp. 360–61.

servative, but rather to indicate how his views influenced his research program and his findings.

Durkheim was strongly convinced that culture and civilization, the maintenance of social order, depend on the ability of society to curb the individual propensities and desires of its members. Like Freud—and the parallelism, we might note in passing, is quite startling—Durkheim believed that social progress depended on the repression of instincts. Freud claimed that "civilization is built upon renunciation of instinctual gratification,"[44] that "civilization consists in an ever increasing subjection of our instincts to repression," that "the process of progress in civilization is paid by forfeiting happiness."[45] Durkheim echoes him almost word for word:

> If society were only the natural and spontaneous development of the individual, these two parts of our selves would harmonize and adjust to each other without hurt or friction. . . . But in fact society has its proper nature and hence exigencies which are altogether different from those of individual nature. . . . We must do violence to certain of our most imperious drives. And as the social part of the total being that we are becomes ever greater as we advance in history, it is contrary to all expectations that there should ever come an era where man should be less required to resist himself and could live a less tense and more relaxed life. On the contrary, everything leads one to predict that the place of effort will ever increase with civilization.[46]

Durkheim believed—and passages in his works that confirm this are so well known we can dispense with quotations—

44. Sigmund Freud, *Civilization and Its Discontents*, London, Hogarth Press, 1946, p. 63.

45. Quoted in Ernest Jones, *The Life and Works of Sigmund Freud*, New York, Basic Books, Inc., 1957, III, 336–37, 342.

46. "Le Dualisme de la nature humaine et ses conditions sociales," *Scientia*, XV (1914), 220–21.

that society must control man's desires and appetites, which are potentially boundless and immoderate, and that a most rigorous social discipline is needed to build barriers against the flood of human passion and desires.[47] He saw man as a *homo duplex*; on the one hand, individual, body, desire, appetite; on the other, socialized personality. There is mutual contradiction and antagonism between those two components, and true moral action consists in the sacrifice of certain individual drives and desires in the service of society. An ever watchful superego is needed to keep the threatening id in check.[48] This profound pessimism had important consequences for Durkheim's sociology. Being convinced of the cultural necessity for repression, he was never led to ask himself whether there might not be different degrees of repression in different societies; that is, whether it was not conceivable that though there was an absolute bedrock of instinctual repression without which no society could exist, there were also "surplus-repressions," to use a phrase of Herbert Marcuse,[49] that far from being inevitable products of all societal arrangements, were functionally required in only some of them. Modern anthropologists have revealed the wide range in degrees of instinctual repressions that exist in nonliterate society, historians have pointed out that in Western society the level of repression of instinctual gratification has varied widely among the various strata of the population. Yet Durkheim's general pessimistic philosophical premises led him to ignore almost completely those most promis-

47. See *L'Education morale*, pp. 46–47.

48. Durkheim was wont to stress that repression of instincts redounded to the benefit not only of society but also of the individual. He apparently never entertained the idea that a repressive society might frustrate the individual, or rather he rejected such consideration as "utopian thinking."

49. *Eros and Civilization*, Boston, Beacon Press, 1955.

ing leads toward a sociology cognizant of differing degrees of repression.

The effects of Durkheim's conservative bias can be more clearly perceived in his writings on education than elsewhere in his work. Here, as Jean Piaget has skillfully pointed out, Durkheim's general conception of the need for social constraint to curb the wickedness of biological propensity led him to a view on education fundamentally at variance with most modern thinking, leaving no place for the idea of cooperation between children or between teacher and pupils.[50] Durkheim conceived of the schoolmaster as a kind of priest who acted as an intermediary between society and the child. As a result, everything depended on the schoolmaster, and moral rules were seen as a kind of revelation that the priest of society discloses to the child. The teacher must have a maximum of authority; he must be a stern disciplinarian. "Life is not all play; the child must prepare himself for pain and effort, and it would therefore be a disaster if he were allowed to think that everything can be done as a game."[51] No wonder, then, that Durkheim was fundamentally opposed to all forms of education that attempted to maximize individual interests and free initiative as well as cooperation. His view of education limits unduly the problems that a full-scale sociology of education has to deal with. Just as in his general sociology he placed such great stress on the antinomy between society and the individual that he was no longer able to perceive the importance of contending subgroups and conflicts within the social system, so his views on education precluded an understanding of the fact that, to quote Piaget, "far from limiting himself to the rules laid down by his parents and teachers, the child ties himself down to all sorts

50. *The Moral Judgment of the Child,* New York, The Free Press, 1948, Chap. IV.
51. *L'Education morale,* p. 183.

of rules in every sphere of his activity, and especially in that of play. These rules are no less social, but they rest on different types of authority."[52] Durkheim's sociology of education turns out to be a sociology of educational constraints, a sociology that is consequently unable to deal with the facts of educational co-operation, a sociology, moreover, that is unable to account for the complex network of social relations between peers. Here again, Durkheim's general conservatism seriously limited his vision.

In brief, it is impossible to maintain the claims that the Durkheimian system is the all-encompassing system of sociological theory that its founder, and, more particularly, some of his epigones believed it to be: Its meshes are much too wide to allow us to catch within it all social reality. This is not a reproach but a simple statement of fact. Only those who still pursue the will-o'-the wisp of believing that *the* sociological system can be built in our time could thus reproach Durkheim. Those who think that sociology today must set itself the more modest aim of developing theories of the middle range, "theories intermediate to the minor working hypotheses evolved . . . during the day-by-day routines of research, and the all-inclusive speculations comprising a master conceptual scheme,"[53] can rest content with the masterly theories of the middle range that Durkheim has given us and that will remain part of the permanent heritage of sociology. Yet it has seemed necessary to demonstrate why it is that Durkheim, though so superlatively successful in certain areas of investigation, has failed in others to enrich our knowledge. To make this clear, it must be stressed that

> observational discrimination is not dictated by the impartial facts. It selects and discards, and what it retains is rearranged

52. *Op. cit.*, p. 364.
53. Merton, *op. cit.*, pp. 5–6.

in a subjective order of prominence. This order of prominence in observation is in fact a distortion of the facts . . . . We have to rescue the facts in the discard, and we have to discard the subjective order of prominence which is itself a fact of observation.[54]

To the extent that Durkheim's conservative orientation led him to select some problems and discard others he attempted to impose on his successors a subjective order of prominence in sociological analysis. This order needs to be discarded. Only by rejecting it can that which is of value in the Durkheimian heritage be fully incorporated into the body of sociology as a cumulation of theoretical interpretation.

54. Whitehead, *op. cit.*, p. 159.

III

CONFLICT THEORY

AND CURRENT POLITICS

9

Prospects for the New Nations:

Totalitarianism, Authoritarianism, or Democracy?

This chapter essays an interpretation of developmental tendencies in the new nations in the light of general conflict theory.

Much sociological and political writing on the process of modernization has been marred by the twin defects of excessive empiricism and attempts to build imposing conceptual and theoretical edifices with but little grounding in concrete realities. Specialists in area studies have supplied an imposing array of descriptive studies that allow a much more sophisticated knowledge of the new nations' developmental thrust—or the lack thereof —than was available until recently. Yet, many of them are uninformed by any theoretical framework and consequently provide but too often compilations of theoretically unassimilated, unsifted, and ill-assorted facts. On the other hand, recent books such as those by Marion Levy and David Apter* dwell on a level of abstraction so high that they seem hardly capable of offering guides to either specific analysis or to an orderly coming to

* David E. Apter, *The Politics of Modernization*, Chicago, The University of Chicago Press, 1965.

Marion Levy, *Modernization and the Structure of Societies*, 2 vols. Princeton, Princeton University Press, 1966.

terms with concrete problems.* They hardly help us to focus argument upon facts.

This chapter steers a middle course. It introduces three relatively abstract models of sociopolitical development that are distilled out of the European historical experience and then attempts to analyze their applicability to the New Nations in relatively concrete terms.†

In my political analysis also I steer a middle course, disagreeing both with those who would come to terms with authoritarian regimes in the new nations and those whose wishful thinking leads them to expect democratization in the near future. I disagree with much of the current writing on the new nations in which one can find subtle, and sometimes not so subtle, justifications for the authoritarian and repressive aspects of many of these new polities. Such justifications are often coupled with some kind of witting or unwitting condescension. It is held that although democracy is indeed a prerequisite for the good life in the West, other nations cannot expect to share its benefits and so may rest content with monocratic rule or one-party states. At the same time I cannot concur with those other writers who still seem to think that is is an easy matter to introduce democratic process into structures that lack an institutional framework similar to that which gradually developed in the West over several countries.‡

I shall argue that the chances for authoritarian regimes to dominate in most of the new nations are very high indeed,

* See, however, the recent books by S. N. Eisenstadt, esp. his *The Political System of Empires,* New York, The Free Press, 1963, and by Wilbert Moore, esp. his *Social Change,* Englewood Cliffs, N.J., Prentice-Hall, 1963, for a more promising theoretical orientation.

† For another attempt at using conflict theory in the analysis of a modernizing polity see A. R. Zolberg's stimulating, *One-Party Government in the Ivory Coast,* Princeton, Princeton University Press, 1964.

‡ Cf. William McCord, *The Springtime of Freedom,* New York, Oxford University Press, 1965; and Peter Worsley, *The Third World,* Chicago, University of Chicago Press, 1965 for more balanced views.

but that possibilities for the gradual fostering of pluralistic politics are not foreclosed.

This chapter attempts, even though in a necessarily schematic and sketchy way, to indicate the political lessons that might be drawn from an emphasis on processes of group contention and group conflict in the analysis of sociopolitical structure.

THE SUDDEN EMERGENCE OF NEW NATIONS IN ASIA AND Africa poses crucial problems for our age. No longer is it sufficient to applaud the demise of imperialism. We have also to discard any previous reliance on simple ideologies of progress. And we have to recognize that some or all of the new nations will present features deeply distasteful to men of a libertarian vision. There is no guarantee that the new will be desirable or appealing. Nor can we assume that the end of colonial servitude will necessarily usher in an age of democracy. We must ask bluntly what are the chances that a democratic polity can ultimately win over authoritarian and totalitarian politics?

Owing partly to the rapidity with which they have gained independence, most of these new states are characterized by fluid and ill-defined social and political structures. Many of them have a political structure boasting the paraphernalia of the modern state while their social structure is composed of essentially tribal or semi-feudal units. In many of these new nations a thin veneer of twentieth-century ideology is superimposed on a community in which magical rather than rational modes of thought predominate. In most of them the cultural distance between the intellectual elite and the underlying population is so wide that the two strata seem to live in entirely different worlds.

None of the new nations outside of the Soviet orbit has achieved even relative social and political stability. All are in flux, open to various courses of development. This very openness poses a challenge: Is it possible to isolate at least some crucial factors that will help determine the structure of these nation-states? This essay will focus attention on a few such variables without claiming that these are the only ones needing consideration.

THREE SOCIETAL MODELS

The difficulty inherent in the fact that political systems differ in a great many ways, so that comparison seems almost an impossible task, can best be overcome by constructing theoretical models against which particular units can be measured. I shall describe three such models, the liberal, the totalitarian, and the authoritarian, and then discuss their applicability to the new nations. The forces likely to push toward one or the other model in the years immediately ahead can then be analyzed and an attempt made to assess the long-run chances for democracy.

Any society beyond the relatively undifferentiated tribal level can be broken down, for purposes of analysis, into major institutional orders of which the political, the economic, the military, the religious, and the family or kinship orders may be considered the most important.[1] These institutional orders must be integrated in some way if the society is to function. But the way integration is brought about may differ very significantly. Three "ideal typical" models of social integration, derived from a variety of concrete instances, will be outlined. No claim is made, of course, that any of them is fully embodied in any society or nation-state. The three were chosen because they have all been associated with the course of development in a variety of historical settings. The democratic-socialist model is not discussed here because, as Marx foresaw, it has been approximated only in those nations that have already gone over the hump of development.

The Liberal Model

In the classical liberal model of society, the structure is unified, yet leaves a high degree of autonomy to the various insti-

1. Cf. Hans Gerth and C. Wright Mills, *Character and Social Structure*. New York, Harcourt, Brace and Co., 1953, esp. Chapter XII.

tutional orders and minimizes the dominion of the state. Conflict and competition between the various orders, far from endangering integration, help to "sew society together."

In the liberal model, economic agents are relatively free from political interference, and so are religious organizations, which are usually not dominated by economic agents; the family also is protected from political interference. Only the military order has limited autonomy; it is firmly controlled by political agents. All orders are interrelated and influence each other, yet each maintains a high degree of autonomy.

In the nineteenth century, when the liberal model was most nearly approximated in parts of Europe and North America, non-governmental forces such as kin groups, autonomous religious organizations, owners of landed or mobile property succeeded in restricting and limiting governmental action. The political order thus never achieved a large measure of dominance over the other institutional orders; nor did it dominate the individual. Neither did any other order achieve dominance. By being pitted against each other in competition and conflict, and struggling for the loyalty and allegiance of men, they furthered individual autonomy.

To be sure, the freedom thus made possible was a negative freedom only, freedom *from* rather than freedom *to*. To the extent that the various institutional orders limited each other they allowed individuals a certain interstitial leeway. The full flowering of positive freedom was precluded in the liberal model if for no other reason than that it could function only if internalized repression among its citizens domesticated drives and energies into institutionally approved channels. The liberal society assured that, to use Erich Fromm's term, the great majority of individuals wanted to do what they had to do.

Some political compulsions did in fact face the individual in such liberal societies. The state may have been a "night-watchman" state, but it nevertheless imposed, even if hesitatingly and sparingly, compulsory military service, education, and taxation, and it held firmly to its monopoly over the legitimate exercise of the means of violence. Yet the state's recourse to its power of compulsion, that is to political means, was only thought of as a last resort; the major decisions within the society were preferably brought about through bargaining, conflict, and competition between the agents of the various institutional orders. The state claimed primacy during situations of emergency or stress, but in the ordinary course of events limited its impact on the other orders.

What has been said about the relations between the various institutional orders in liberal society applies even more strongly to relations within these orders themselves. In none of them did a single interest dominate the whole. Even where a state church existed, other organizations served to balance and limit its power in the religious sphere. The competition for souls between proselytizing religions furthered the freedom of the individual; the competitive struggle for scarce resources between a great variety of economic interests prevented the preemption of economic chances. Competition for marriage partners prevented the domination of the marriage market by kinship groups and enhanced the chances of free marital choice. Within the political realm, different political parties competed for power and thus maximized the chances for the citizen's democratic participation in the political process.

Liberal society was crisscrossed by many conflicts and antagonisms between, as well as within, institutional orders. As individuals affiliated with a multiplicity of groups and as these multiple affiliations crisscrossed each other, they welded society together. The multiple antagonistic and diversified interests that found expression within such social structures served as a balancing mechanism, preventing the cleavage of society along one line. At the same time the multiple affiliations of individuals in a variety of groups and associations served to enhance personal freedom.[2] The individual came, so to speak, to stand at a point at which many conflicting or non-conflicting groups and institutional orders intersected. Such a position in social space helps to maximize the chance of individual autonomy.[3]

The Totalitarian Model

In comparing the liberal with the totalitarian model one can apply Max Weber's distinction between individual and collective appropriation of power.[4] Individual appropriation takes place through conflict and competition among the members-at-large of those strata that have a legitimate claim to power; in collective appropriation all positions of power have been appropriated by a single ruling group that then allots shares to individuals and groups according to their status.

The totalitarian model may be considered the antithesis of the liberal model. Here integration is attained through deliberate coordination of all institutional orders and the suppression of conflict among them. The essence of totalitarian regimes is that their claims are total; i.e., that they aim at the control of all institutional spheres. In such regimes we witness an apotheosis of the political order. Political power has been appropriated by a political elite that suppresses all rival claimants. The political order has unquestioned primacy over all others; no independent organization even of an utterly non-political character is al-

2. Cf. Georg Simmel, *Conflict and the Web of Group Affiliations,* transl. by Kurt H. Wolff and Reinhard Bendix. New York, The Free Press, 1955.

3. Cf. Lewis A. Coser, *The Functions of Social Conflict,* New York, The Free Press, 1956.

4. Max Weber, *The Theory of Social and Economic Organization,* transl. by A. M. Henderson and T. Parsons. New York, Oxford University Press, 1947, pp. 139–43 and 245–50.

lowed to exist. Every social unit must be *gleichgeschaltet;* i.e., coordinated with the governing apparatus. Insofar as different institutional orders still continue to exist, activities within them are heteronomous; they do not follow laws of motion of their own but are impelled by forces emanating from the political order. Economic agents act in accord with the demands of State and Party, religious institutions become adjuncts to political institutions, and even the family is pressed into the service of political goals.[5]

Totalitarian societies destroy traditional social groups, communities, or self-conscious classes and then replace them by new units that are subject to coordination and control by State and Party. Deprived of the support of non-governmental structures, the individual faces alone the immense tutelary power of the Party and State. Though in such societies he has multiple affiliations with a great number of groups, these do not conflict with or crisscross each other; they follow the same impelling direction. Social forces, insofar as they are not driven underground, are no longer antagonistic, the various interests are no longer diversified; indeed, their pressures are mutually reinforcing. The distinction between public and private spheres, central to the liberal model, disappears in totalitarian society. Just as the totalitarian state cannot tolerate autonomous organizations, so it cannot tolerate individual withdrawal into a private—and hence uncontrolled—sphere. The engineering of souls is as essential as the engineering of the social structure. The private as well as the public man must be caught in the seamless web of control. To the totalitarian powerholder anything that is not controlled will seem a fatal flaw.

5. Cf. Hannah Arendt, *The Origins of Totalitarianism.* New York, Meridian Books, 1958; *Totalitarianism,* ed. by Carl Friedrich. Cambridge, Harvard University Press, 1954; William Kornhauser, *The Politics of Mass Society.* New York, The Free Press, 1959.

Monopolistic control of the means of violence and of the channels of communication, as well as an official ideology covering all major aspects of a man's existence, characterize totalitarian societies. No claims of family, property, or religion counter-balance or limit the actions of the State and the Party. All social life is "politicized"; society is integrated by fiat of the State.

The Authoritarian Model

The authoritarian model may be said to stand midway between the totalitarian and the liberal models. Whereas totalitarian societies suppress all forms of autonomous organization and all independent sources of information, the authoritarian regimes suppress organized opposition and public criticism. Whereas liberal society fosters the autonomy of the various institutional orders, the authoritarian society limits and confines activities within these orders but does not attempt to control them completely. Whereas totalitarian societies suppress all conflict among component parts of the social structure, the authoritarian society channels and deflects such conflicts without, however, eliminating them altogether.

In such societies the political powerholders may recognize no constitutional limitations of state power, yet in practice they do recognize *some* limitations. They may try to make the Church into a pliant instrument of their rule, yet they will not attempt to deny the religious order a measure of autonomy in regard to otherworldly concerns. They may limit the exercise of proprietary rights and channel the allocation of scarce resources, yet they will not attack the legitimation of property as such. In authoritarian societies the military order is typically somewhat independent of the political order; it may even tend to dominate it. Where totalitarian societies have "politicized armies," authoritarian societies often have a "militarized polity." Authoritarian regimes will attempt to mobilize the citizen in the pursuit of their political goals, yet they will not obliterate the distinction between the public and the private sphere—they will leave the latter relatively untouched. The political elite monopolizes political power but it shares social powers with the agents of other institutional orders.

Consequently such societies do not exclude conflicts between the various orders or within them. The Church, the army, economic agents, class interests—all may clash and limit each other. At the same time such groupings and institutions will limit the political agents and prevent them from exercising unchallenged sway. The Church, the army, the family, and property constitute distinct and not always harmonious interests; they compete, and the resultant balance of power among them leaves a deep impress on political decision-making. As distinct from liberal societies, here the non-political orders enjoy no customary immunity from the exercise of political will, but neither are they deprived of all power.

The individual in authoritarian societies does not enjoy the autonomy granted him in liberal societies. He is cribbed and confined by agents of the political order. Yet he can escape from the public scene into the relative autonomy of an uncontrolled private life. To the degree that conflicts between groups and orders mark the social life of authoritarian society—even though they may be channelled and partly directed—individuals have some chance to realize their non-political interests.

The integration of authoritarian society is achieved by a "mixed" process of authoritative imposition on the part of the political agents and spontaneous balancing among the other institutional orders. Shifts in the balance of power between the various groups will find their indirect reflection in political life. Such regimes are likely to lack the frozen rigidity of totalitarian regimes while also lacking, owing to the heavy predominance of the political order, the flexibility of the liberal model. They tend to have a somewhat unstable character. They face two dangers: the rise of liberalism through a revival of the power of temporarily suppressed groups, and the establishment of a totalitarian regime through a *Gleichschaltung* of all orders and interests.

The Consequences of Underdevelopment

By comparison with the West, all the new nations are "underdeveloped" economically. Their productivity, national product, and per capita income is low and this is reflected in low standards of nutrition, housing, education, and health. The bulk of their populations live in traditional rural communities; most of them have not yet reached the take-off stage in the process of industrialization. This underdevelopment is due to a complex of historical circumstance that can only be hinted at here. Colonial exploitation both through unilateral transfers of wealth from colonial countries to Western Europe and the seizure of peasant-occupied lands for plantation purposes, played a major part. The destruction of rural handicraft industries through the competition of cheap industrial goods from Europe and America was another significant factor. Imperialist domination hindered the development of a class of indigenous industrial entrepreneurs, though it often favored the emergence of a partly Westernized class of *comprador* traders and middle-men.

But quite apart from the impact of imperialism, the traditional cultures of Asia and Africa in themselves did not foster strong and independent middle classes—the classes that in the West were the main promoters of capital accumulation, industrial enterprise, and rational work discipline. The gradual development of a "Protestant" work ethic and a peculiar pattern of repression and self-control has been a precondition for the development of capitalist industrialism in the West. Individual autonomy, discipline, methodical application to work characterized the early entrepreneurial middle class, and this "innerwordly asceticism" was a powerful stimulant for that energetic pursuit of rational domination over the world and of industrial creativity that has characterized the West since the seventeenth century. There are few equivalents to this entrepreneurial ethos as yet discernible in the new nations. This relative absence of a work ethic and a tradition of individual self-control and autonomy accounts also for the fact that nepotism, corruption, and the like do not encounter institutional or internalized obstacles to nearly the same degree as in the West.

The underdevelopment of economic resources has significant consequences for the system of stratification. The poorer a country, the greater the differences between the rich and the poor; i.e., the steeper the stratification pyramid. Not only are the poor in underdeveloped countries poorer in absolute terms than those of the West, but they are relatively poorer within their own class system. The social and economic distance between them and their own upper class is greater than that between the poor of the West and their upper class. Not only absolute but relative deprivation characterizes the mass of the underlying population in the new nations; with the growth of modern mass communication and transportation, the poor of the underdeveloped countries increasingly have occasion to compare their lot with that of the population of the developed countries of the West.

So long as the ideology or mystique of a society continues to hold the allegiance of the masses, they will endure the grossest inequalities of wealth, status, and power. But when the traditional legitimations for the status quo break down— and they have broken down to a greater or lesser degree in all underdeveloped countries—then a new standard of judgment seeps into the consciousness of the deprived groups and leads them to compare their situations with that of other groups both within and without their own society.[6] Hence the urge to develop the country so as to reap the fruits of industrialization, raise national product, and reduce inequalities becomes well nigh irresistible in underdeveloped nations that have broken from traditional moorings.

Role of the Intelligentsia

What social stratum is likely to take the initiative in this development? Since entrepreneurial middle classes have hardly developed in these nations, and the traditionalistic leaders have a vested interest in maintaining the status quo, the partly Westernized intelligentsia is likely to take the lead. This intelligentsia first becomes aware of the backwardness of the country through more intimate contacts with Western conditions than are available to other groups. Given their trained receptiveness to new ideological currents, the Westernized intellectuals are the first to criticize the accepted scheme of things. As gatekeepers of ideas, they are strategically placed to facilitate the penetration of modern ideologies. Cut loose from traditional thought, troubled by a sense of national humiliation, intellectuals in fact have taken the lead in the movement toward independence and modernization.[7]

When the intelligentsia searched for models to guide economic development, they almost invariably discarded the liberal

6. Cf. Irving Howe and Lewis A. Coser, *The American Communist Party*, Boston, Beacon Press, 1957, pp. 513–16.

7. The process has often been described in Asia; for a fine study of similar developments in Africa cf. David E. Apter, *The Gold Coast in Transition*. Princeton, Princeton University Press, 1955. See also James S. Coleman, *Nigeria, Background to Nationalism*, Berkeley and Los Angeles, University of California, 1958. For an excellent analysis of key political factors in the new nations see Gabriel Almond and James S. Coleman, ed., *The Politics of the Developing Areas*, Princeton, Princeton University Press, 1960.

model. Lacking an independent entrepreneurial middle class and its peculiar ethic, the new nations could not rely on unaided economic development. A liberal order, moreover, requires some ideological preparation. Before a liberal politics could make its appearance in Europe a new breed of autonomous, self-governing men had first to develop. But such men are still very rare in the new nations. As Richard Lowenthal has said in an essay from which I have borrowed several seminal ideas: "If conditions were such that a liberal economy would work, the country would not have remained underdeveloped in the first place."[8] Given the absence of independent economic agents, the task of development had to fall to the powers of the state. Whereas in the West industrialization was mainly the outcome of a process of spontaneous growth in the economic order, "nourished by the enterprise of individual profit-seekers, exploiting new techniques to their own advantage,"[9] the development of the new nations required concentration of economic power in the state. The mopping up of savings to raise funds for investment, the allocation of scarce resources to the strategically most important tasks, the promotion of an intellectual climate favorable to the development of an ethos of work, the breakdown of the traditional barriers to the exercise of disciplined and rational modes of organization—none of these tasks of industrial take-off could be accomplished without public action by the agents of the political order. If the universalistic criteria that are a precondition for industrial development were to prevail, the particularism of the kinship order and the non-rational taboos of religious tradition had to be broken down. Hence the liberal model with its emphasis on the balanced in-

8. Richard Lowenthal, "The Points of the Compass," *Encounter,* London, Sept., 1960, pp. 22–28.
9. Myrdal, *Beyond the Welfare State,* New Haven, Yale University Press, 1960, p. 121.

teraction of different institutional orders found little favor in the new nations.

The appeal of the totalitarian model, in particular in its Communist form, was, on the contrary, considerably stronger. Lowenthal so ably summarizes the attractions of Communist totalitarianism for underdeveloped countries that I shall quote him at length:

> In its Stalinist form, the Communist ideology has been specifically adjusted to deal with the problems of forced modernization. It justifies a ruthless policy of forced savings. . . . It proclaims the superiority of planned investment by the state over *laissez faire*. Finally, it furnishes the militant faith needed for the cultural revolution, with its materialistic attack on traditional superstition, its glorification of dedicated, disciplined work for the community, its emphasis on production as the highroad to national power and individual liberation from misery. It invests the uprooting of traditional life, the frightening impact of social and technical change, the bitterness of years of sacrifice with a meaning. And, last but not least, it justifies all the privileges a self-appointed but dedicated elite may require.[10]

Although the totalitarian model has considerable attractions for the underdeveloped countries, it also encounters deeply seated resistances. In fact, most of the leaders of these countries are not at present prepared to accept the totalitarian and monolithic state as a precondition for the planning of development.

The adoption of the totalitarian model would necessarily mean that an underdeveloped nation would forego much of the technical know-how available in however slim a stratum of native entrepreneurs and professionals. Nor would the bulk of the native Westernized intelligentsia relish a head-on clash with the traditionalistic elites—a clash that would inevitably occur

10. Lowenthal, *op. cit.,* p. 25.

should an attempt be made to mold the state according to the totalitarian pattern. They may be committed to deep-going agrarian reform, yet shrink from wholesale collectivization on the Chinese model involving the breakup of familistic property patterns. They may hesitate before the application of terroristic means for the extraction of surplus labor from the peasantry. They may harbor resentment against the West, yet shrink from a course that would inevitably cut them off from Western economic aid, both public and private. (I need hardly stress that considerations in regard to the cold war play an important role in this context.)

Obstacles to Totalitarian Model

There is a more profound reason why the Westernized elite of most of the new nations, though willing to borrow techniques of development from the Communist arsenal, cannot easily accept the totalitarian model: large illiterate populations, strong traditional ideologies, the newness and numerical weakness of the urban population and the elite—these factors preclude the planned mobilization of the total population. Such mobilization, however, is a *sine qua non* of the totalitarian model. The localism, particularism, and traditionalism that militate against the development of democracy also act against the introduction of efficient Soviet-type totalitarian regimes. Recent developments in Touré's Guinea are instructive in this respect. Not long ago Guinea seemed on its way toward a Moscow-dominated "People's Democracy." Today it has moved in the direction of a mixed regime. Even when a determined effort is made to centralize political power, this power seems all too often to seep away through innumerable rivulets to village communities and tribal structures, to money lenders or army chieftains, to religious leaders and heads of clans. Myrdal seems correct when he says that "even if they were willing, they would not be able to exert the fanatical discipline implicit in the Soviet system."[11] We may then provisionally conclude that the totalitarian regime, short of direct military take-over by external Communist powers, is not likely to become the model for developments in the new nations, at least not before the destruction of traditional power.

There remains the authoritarian model. Though the nationalist intelligentsia reacts against the traditional culture that it holds responsible for the backwardness of the country, it is also unwilling and unable to create a cultural *tabula rasa* through the imposition of a ready-made total plan. It is typically drawn toward an eclectic program in which it strives to counterbalance traditional elements and innovating plans. Hugh Seton-Watson calls such regimes "populist," by analogy to the well-known Russian movement of the nineteenth century, insofar as they attempt like their Russian forebears to achieve some kind of synthesis between traditional culture and the need for modernization.[12] In these new nations the intelligentsia is likely to exhibit a fierce pride in the distinctiveness of native culture and must hence be extremely reluctant to rupture the continuity with tradition; yet it is also well aware that only a resolute break with major aspects of past tradition will allow a take-off in development. Hence its ambivalence. And hence the chance that, though it will attempt through programmatic planning to shorten the trials of development, it will at the same time resist the temptation of totalitarianism.

The concrete forms of regimes dominated by the intelligentsia may differ widely. In some countries, as in Egypt, Iraq, and Burma, where standing armies have been available as a source of power, a revolutionary "intelligentsia in uniform" has succeeded, through domination of the military order, in con-

11. Myrdal, *op. cit.,* p. 126.

12. Hugh Seton-Watson, *Neither War Nor Peace,* New York, Frederick A. Praeger, 1960, Chapter VI.

trolling the political order; in other instances, as in Mali, Guinea, or Tunisia, a civilian intelligentsia, skilled in methods of mass propaganda, has succeeded in appropriating the governmental apparatus and has used mass parties built around a charismatic leader as an effective counterweight to the traditional forces. There are in addition, as in Pakistan, a number of mixed modernizing regimes embodying in greater or lesser degree traditional and innovating elements as well as civilian and military power, and maintaining these elements in an uneasy balance.

Such authoritarian regimes might move against the claims of the religious order if its representatives attempted to limit the innovating actions of the state through an appeal to religious norms. Yet they will not break with the religious agents or attempt fully to control the religious sphere. They will react against the particularistic criteria emanating from the kinship order or the tribal structure and attempt to displace them with universalistic standards of judgment and performance. Yet they will not try to dissolve the traditional family loyalties. They will attempt to lay out economic plans and allocate resources according to criteria of economic development rather than in terms of profitability. Yet they will not destroy the institutions of property. They are intent upon introducing the rational techniques of the West while preserving what they consider viable in native tradition.

Traditional Interests Weakened

In practice, then, whether by design or force of circumstances, the authoritarian regimes in the new nations will not be able in the immediate future to coordinate the various institutional orders. They will rather operate in an environment marked by a high incidence of clash and conflict. Nigeria, Pakistan, even Burma and Indonesia provide excellent examples. In none of these countries have the strong centripetal tendencies of the ruling strata succeeded in breaking down the centrifugal pull of various types of traditional elites. Furthermore, in none of these countries has it been possible for the ruling elite to develop an indigenous ideology and a set of organizations strong enough to attract and hold men suddenly freed from the world of tradition. In all of them, though economic development is ardently desired, the elite encounters most serious obstacles from the traditional powers.

Yet it seems true that although the day of reckoning may be postponed for a considerable period of time, in the long run such innovating authoritarian regimes will inevitably weaken the hold of traditional interests. The very process of modernization, even though it may be cushioned in various ways, undermines traditional structures, be they tribal or feudal, particularistic family domination or religious interests.

But as the checks on power that can be exercised by traditional elements decrease, so do the chances for a drift toward totalitarian regimes increase. When individuals are freed from the dominance of traditional institutions and when they cannot be attracted by authoritarian regimes devoid of a coherent ideology, they become available for a new type of integration along the lines of totalitarian coordination. Where traditionalistic sources of power have dried up and given way to modern universalistic power structures manned by members of the rapidly swollen intelligentsia, the chances of authoritarian regimes decline. At this point the new nations will face another set of choices: totalitarianism or democracy.

The Chances of Democratization

A minimal condition for democracy is the legitimation of regular opportunities for changing governing personnel, i.e., the presence of social mechanisms—political parties, free elections, free press, and so on—permitting the underlying population to choose among contenders for political office.[13] But in addition to such mechanisms, a democratic polity requires a sufficient dispersion of power. If the community is to have the right to share in the direction of political affairs, the diffusion of power among a number of power centers is essential. Since only power can effectively check power, democracy requires the presence of secondary groups and associations that can be nodal points of power interposing themselves between the individual and the state.

Democracy has historically been highly correlated with relatively high standards of living, with urbanization, industrialization, and education. But the correlation is not automatic, for in Europe democracy grew out of the resistance of various semi-autonomous communities, strata, and religious bodies to the absolutist state that had begun the process of modernization. And in most cases, this was not a gradual growth but a series of revolutions. In feudal times, the immunities of Church and estates, of landed aristocracy or independent townships prevented the center from monopolizing power. When absolute monarchs attempted to win such a monopoly, democracy was powerfully enhanced by the struggle of new social formations, reformed churches and sects, trade unions, voluntary organizations of all sorts, and local and regional bodies, all of which sought to limit governmental power and ensure their members a voice in the affairs of state.

In the new nations, with their low living standards, their small degree of industrialization, and urbanization, their low standards of education, and their lack of a "protestant ethic," the basis of a democratic polity is not at present available. These nations are not only underdeveloped in the economic but also

13. Cf. Seymour M. Lipset, *Political Man*, Garden City, N.Y., Doubleday, 1960, p. 45 ff.

in the political sense, since in none of them is there a sufficient degree of development of those key factors that are necessary for secure democratic systems (though in some, notably the Philippines, India, and Ceylon, a number of favorable factors have allowed approximations to Western democracy). Nor have the social groups and classes that made revolutions in the West developed in the new nations. These revolutions depended on the ability of various institutional orders (e.g., the religious and the economic) to modernize themselves, and then to provide opposition cadres—as did the protestant sects in England or the Third Estate in France. But if modernization at all levels comes to depend on the state alone, if there are no local, religious, or class forces independently pushing in the same direction, then democratic revolutions become unlikely.

With gradual modernization, one can expect a gradual rise in education, living standards, and the like, and this will remove a significant barrier to democracy. But one cannot expect that the other major barrier—the concentration of power—will necessarily decrease and hence allow the expansion of chances for wider participation in political life. And yet the chances of democratization depend ultimately on the degree to which power will be dispersed or centralized.

The modernizing elites, in their efforts to create new collective symbols and a new source of legitimacy as well as a new economic and social structure, clash with traditional centers of power and prestige. They must attempt to undermine and neutralize traditional modes of behavior. They must desire to create citizens free from particularistic loyalties to village, communal groupings, family, tribal chief, or traditional aristocracy. They must attempt to legitimize secular power, even giving it a "sacral" character, so as to free the polity from control by traditional powerholders and representatives of the religious order.

Integrating Individuals

Yet once the power of the Indonesian traditional aristocracy, the Ashanti chieftains in Northern Ghana, or the emirs in Northern Nigeria has been broken, the new nations still face the problem of integrating individuals who have become freed from traditional allegiance and loyalties.[14] This integration can conceivably take place in two different ways: The energies and activities of those who have relinquished traditional positions of leadership as well as those who can be freshly recruited into leadership positions can be channeled into diversified centers of power, or they can be funneled into one center. If the ruling intelligentsia prevent the emergence of new diversified centers of power and loyalty, if they attempt to control all accumulations of newly available power, they move in a totalitarian direction. If, on the other hand, there emerges a diversity of allegiances and a many-sided integration of individuals in a variety of institutional orders, then the chances for a democratic development at a later time are increased. The liberal model has no chance of institutionalization in the underdeveloped countries, if for no other reason than that economic development will require an amount of deliberate centralized planning that is incompatible with liberalism. Yet, if the road toward later democratic developments is not to be blocked, the widest possible diffusion of power compatible with centralized planning is a prerequisite.

The claims of efficiency might appear often to militate in favor of authoritative directives and centralized government.

14. For ideas developed in the next few pages I have borrowed considerably from a seminal paper by Professor Samuel N. Eisenstadt of the University of Jerusalem, "Soziale Entwicklung und Politische Stabilitaet in Nichtwestlichen Gesellschaften," *Koelner Zeitschrift fuer Soziologie und Sozialpsychologie*, XII, 2, 1960, pp. 189–203. Cf. also Bert Hoselitz and Myron Weiner, "Economic Development and Political Stability in India," *Dissent*, VIII, 2 (Spring 1961).

The requirements of struggle against traditional elements leads to the erosion of local centers of feudal and tribal power. National allocation of scarce resources requires central planning. Yet if the population is not in the long run to become totally dependent on the tutelary power of the state, it is essential that the political elite of the center does not control the new forces set free, thus preventing the development of autonomous social and political centers of power.

The chances for greater participation of non-governmental organizations in the modernizing process will increase if under authoritarian regimes there grows up a new social structure with an autonomous life of its own: modernizing rural cooperatives under the guidance of new members of the technical intelligentsia; trade unions in the industrial centers; local and regional governing boards; autonomous educational and scientific institutions, and the like. If in addition there develops a rich associational life in the non-political orders, the national community may gradually be led to rely on the process of bargaining between groups and individuals rather than on governmental fiat. Under such conditions direct governmental intervention could be kept at a minimum and broad policies replace detailed directives. The very clash and conflict between autonomous centers of power would serve as a balancing mechanism. Whether such a development will come about will depend to a very significant degree on patterns of recruitment; i.e., on whether potential leaders will be attracted mainly by the centralizing state or at least a certain proportion of them will be available for leadership in local and regional centers of power, and in non-governmental institutions.

The Use of Talent

Given the dominant role of the state apparatus in the new nations, it is to be expected that it will attract a high proportion of all those who wish to rise on the scale of prestige and to profit from the reallocation of power. The discrepancy in living standards between the elite and the rest of the population that characterizes underdeveloped nations will be an added incentive for joining the elite. Employment in the state or party apparatus, be it in executive bodies or the bureaucracy, is likely to be regarded as the most significant channel of upward mobility and as the major means of access to scarce power, resources, and prestige. This would lead to the gradual erosion of other, non-political institutional orders, and the preponderance of the political over the economic, cultural, and educational elites. To the extent that the centralized state would assume predominance and come to constitute in the eyes of the population the major source of power, financial reward, and prestige, the local, regional, and non-governmental centers of power would be weakened. If other centers fail to attract gifted leaders, the political order will preempt the available supply of scarce talents.

If gifted members of the intelligentsia flock exclusively to the service of the government rather than, say, to teaching positions in schools or colleges, then the latter will be staffed by the mediocre and lose even more prestige. Consequently they will not be able to function as a counterweight to the powers of the political order. Similar consequences are likely to follow in the economic order, be it private or cooperative: the quality of the economic elite will steadily decline and so will its prestige if the more enterprising and ambitious members of the younger generation will be attracted by employment in the central economic administration.[15] When power and opportunity are concentrated

15. It should also be noted here that to the extent that there are tendencies toward closure in the political and bureaucratic structures; i. e., to the extent that they limit recruitment of new personnel from the outside, there is a danger of the creation of strata of disappointed office seekers. Such strata are peculiarly apt to engage in the politics of discontent; they are especially susceptible to the appeal of communism. Thus both a too exclusive recruitment of the elite into the central political order, and a closure in that order barring potential recruits from access and yet not

in the center, they act like a magnet, attracting the talented men from the whole society and gradually undermining the resistances emanating from off-center powers.

Tocqueville knew this well when he wrote, "In proportion as the duties of the central power are augmented, the number of public officials by whom that power is represented must increase also. They form a nation in each nation . . . they more and more fill up the place of an aristocracy." In the long run this would lead to an approximation of the totalitarian model. Such a trend can be effectively weakened only to the extent that participation in the non-governmental sphere will carry no less prestige and influence, and bring psychic and monetary income commensurate with that derived from employment by the state.

Hence, the strengthening of autonomous institutions, such as independent schools and universities, independent trade unions, regional and local power centers, village cooperatives, and the like, are of prime importance if the road toward democratization is not to be permanently barred. (This is why India, where such institutions function rather vigorously, seems to have the best chances fully to institutionalize democratic processes.) Not only are such centers of secondary power likely to function as effective checks to central power; they are also likely to struggle with the central power, as well as among themselves, for the allegiance of the citizens. As citizens are drawn into such conflicts they increase their own political awareness and participation. Conflicts with some produce associations with others and provide bonds between citizens, drawing them into a rich social life. Individuals otherwise isolated, mutually hostile or apathetic, are in this way brought into the field of public activities. A multiplicity of associations, a pluralism of power centers,

---

offering alluring chances in other areas, are likely to have detrimental consequences for the process of democratization.

whose diverse purposes crisscross each other, help to prevent the atomization on which totalitarianism has always thrived. For atomized and isolated individuals are ready to rely on the immense tutelary power of a state that alone, so it seems to them, is able to provide the satisfactions they crave; men tempered in the struggles and contentions of societies with rich and diversified group life, drawn toward each other in multifarious battles to realize their own goals, are less wont to rely on the tutelary power of the state.

The Furtherance of Democracy

Tocqueville considered the gravest peril for individual freedom to stem from conditions where "the performance of private persons are insignificant, those of the state immense." It follows that the furtherance of democracy requires the strengthening of "private persons" and this is possible only if such private persons can rely on protective secondary powers uncontrolled by the state. They must, in other words, become part of a network of diverse social relationships in a variety of group involvements.

Those who are moved only by considerations of efficiency and consider that only neat and orderly arrangements are likely to permit the new nations to emerge from the sloth of traditional stagnation are likely to find my suggestions rather unappealing. But they should heed the warning that the most efficient administrations are likely to be found in model prisons rather than in vital human communities. The best chances for democracy may sometimes clash with the optimum conditions for efficiency. Wherever this is the case, the democrat must be willing to sacrifice optimum efficiency.

A kind of vulgar Marxism has again become quite fashionable of late. Many commentators seem to argue for a rigid determinism according to which industrialization in the underdeveloped countries must necessarily bring in its wake predetermined "superstructures." Yet the European experience itself suggests no such easy generalizations. Consider only the immense difference in the "superstructure" of, say, nineteenth century Germany and England. This is why I cannot subscribe to the theory of an ineluctable drift toward totalitarianism that is now so often bandied about. The new nations, and those who will make the key decisions with them, face a series of crucial choices. Much will depend on their intentions and on the ideology that informs them. They can, if they so desire, deliberately create or at least permit the growth of a dispersed power structure in their countries. They can, though ruling as authoritarians, lay the foundations for a future democracy. Whether they will do so in a significant number of cases it would be rash to predict. All one can say at this stage is that this is possible, and that the road into the future of the new nations, far from being determined in advance, is still open.

10

The Myth of Peasant Revolt

Whereas the previous chapter discussed what I take to be the most likely development tendencies in the new nations in the years to come, this chapter takes up an alternative vision of the future development of these nations. It examines the revolutionary doctrine of the late Frantz Fanon, the most creative ideologist the new nations have produced so far.

I think that the work of Fanon is important not as a correct depiction of the realities of the ex-colonial nations, but rather as a most powerful mythopoeic effort, as an attempt to change history through the creation of a new energizing myth of *The Revolutionary Peasant* to be set alongside George Sorel's myth of *The General Strike*.

Fanon has fashioned an apologia for violence and its regenerative virtues that makes Sorel's efforts look positively timid and pusillanimous in comparison. In these pages I had occasion to refer repeatedly to the social functions of violence. It seemed important, therefore, to take note here of an ideologist whose myth of pan-violence ended, or so it would seem to me, in apocalyptic visions. It may be true that these visions lack hold on realities and that they are doomed to ultimate failure, but it cannot be gainsaid that they may not inspire disenfranchised and desperate peasant masses to revolt. To the extent that a myth gains a hold on the minds of men it can move them to action. "If men define situations as real they are real in their consequences."*

* For a stimulating recent discussion of the revolutionary potential of the peasantry, see Barrington Moore, *Social Origins of Dictatorship and Democracy,* Boston, Beacon Press, 1966. See also John H. Kautsky, ed., *Political Change in Underdeveloped Countries,* New York, John Wiley & Sons, 1962, especially the chapters on the politics of intellectuals.

ONLY RARELY DOES A BOOK IMMEDIATELY CONVEY A SENSE that it will rank among the influential works of the time. Frantz Fanon's *The Wretched of the Earth*[1] is just such a book. It is badly written, badly organized, and chaotic. The author's reasoning is often shoddy and obviously defective. But all this is finally unimportant. This is not a work of analysis. Its incantatory prose appeals not to the intellect but to the passions. Its author wished to create a modern myth and he must be ranked among the very few great mythopoeists of our age even by those who, like myself, think he has created an evil myth.

"Myths," wrote George Sorel, "are not descriptions of things, but expressions of a determination to act. . . . A myth cannot be refuted, since it is, at bottom, identical with the conviction of a group, being the expression of these convictions in the language of movement." "One must not try to analyze such complexes of pictures," he added, "as one would break down a thing into its elements; one must take them as a whole, as historical forces, and . . . must above all refrain from comparing actual accomplishments with the images of them that had been generally accepted before the action." It is such a myth that Frantz Fanon has created and I venture to think that it will have an enduring influence in the world of politics and ideas, perhaps more so than Sorel's own myth of the General Strike.

Frantz Fanon was born in 1925, on the island of Martinique in the French West Indies. He studied medicine in France and specialized in psychiatry. During the Algerian revolt against French domination, Fanon was assigned to an Algerian hospital and soon threw in his lot with the revolutionists to become one of their major ideological spokesmen. Out of this experience came two books, *The Year V of the Algerian Revolution* and the present volume, first published in France in 1961. Fanon

1. *The Wretched of the Earth*, by Frantz Fanon. New York, Grove Press, 1965.

died of cancer, at the age of thirty-six, soon after the book appeared.

The Wretched of the Earth could be read as yet another indictment of the evils of colonialism, but so to understand it would by-pass its real importance. Fanon wished to do a great deal more. He wished to show how the native, degraded by his conquerors, can reconquer himself. The book is, above all, an apologia for violence. The violence of the conquest, he argued, has dehumanized the native and only counter-violence can make him whole again. ". . . Violence is a cleansing force. It frees the native from his inferiority complex and from his despair and inaction; it makes him fearless and restores his self-respect. . . . For the native, life can spring up again out of the rotting corpse of the settler." Violence is the only effective individual and social therapy; it helps overcome a schism of the soul which has been caused by colonialist contempt, and it welds together a body social that had been rent by the colonial system. "Violence unifies the people."

In Sorel's hands the myth of violence had a somewhat bloodless character. Sorel was, to be sure, a man given to apocalyptic visions, yet upon inspection his heroic violence turns out to be more literary than real, more a figure of speech than a concretely envisioned event. This safely settled petty-bourgeois moralist dreamed of heroic virtues, but fantasies of a real blood bath seem to have been utterly alien to him. Matters stood very differently with Fanon. He was a marginal man, torn from his moorings, most of his adult life spent working in the world of French medical professionals without being of that world. Scarred and humiliated, stripped of his previous identity, he searched for redeeming wholeness through a cataclysmic destruction. To him, the call to violence, the belief in its redeeming quality, was no rhetorical device; he meant it. He believed in the cleansing quality of the knife, the gun, the bomb. Only these, he thought, could make colonial man whole again. During the Mau-Mau revolt, it was required, he wrote, "that each member of the group should strike a blow at the victim. Each one was thus personally responsible for the death of that victim. To work means to work for the death of the settler. This assumed responsibility for violence allows both strayed and outlawed members of the group to come back again and to find their place once more, to become integrated. Violence is thus seen as comparable to a royal pardon. The colonized man finds his freedom in and through violence. This rule of conduct enlightens the agent because it indicates to him the means and the end."

Anti-colonial violence was to Fanon the only way to bring about a total transformation in the former colonies. It leads to a comprehensive transvaluation of values. "Without any period of transition, there is a total, complete and absolute substitution." All decolonization creates a *tabula rasa* at the outset, and this is the precondition for all further advances. Decolonization does not mean the substitution of one kind of regime for another; it signifies total rebirth and it can only be the work of new men, men reborn through acts of violence.

Fanon was at his most original when he attempted to locate potential revolutionary actors within the structure of colonial societies. Here he departed most markedly from classical Marxist theory. Very little, he argued, can be expected of the embryonic working class. The workers enjoy a comparatively privileged position. They may be the most faithful followers of the nationalist parties but when the chips are down, they realize that they have much to lose when the colonial regime is overthrown. By virtue of the privileged position they hold in the colonial system, they constitute a "bourgeois" faction of the colonized people. Pampered, and sheltered from the worst slights and the worst misery, they can easily be bought off. So much for the traditional proletarian vanguard of the Marxist textbooks.

Nor is there reason to believe that the national bourgeoisie can play a role. It has none of the characteristics of its Western counterpart. It "is not engaged in production, nor in invention, nor building, nor labor; it is completely canalized into activities of the intermediary type. Its innermost vocation seems to be to keep in the running and to be part of the racket." Fanon treated this national bourgeoisie with a withering contempt that was only matched by his contempt for the assimilationist and partly Westernized intelligentsia. If the working class can be bought off and the national bourgeoisie is "good for nothing" where, then, can the true agents of total transformation be found? Here Fanon, true to an age-old millenarian tradition that, by the way, strongly informed the thought of the young Marx, answered: Only those who are totally disinherited, those who have nothing to lose in the old system can be the architects of the new. The biblical "The last shall be first and the first last" runs like a refrain through the book.

The last in colonial society are the peasants and they are hence the true agents of the revolution. ". . . The peasants alone are revolutionary, for they have nothing to lose and everything to gain. The starving peasant, outside the class system, is the first among the exploited to discover that only violence pays. For him there is no compromise, no possible coming to terms." The anti-colonial revolution must hence be a peasant revolution. Yet this revolution, in order to succeed, must of necessity spread from the countryside into the towns. A peasant *maquis* can hardly be expected to take the cities. Here the mass of ex-peasants, settled in the huts and shanty towns around the fringe of the city, assumes a major strategic role. The city *lumpen-proletariat* is the predestined ally of the rural masses. "The *lumpen-proletariat,* that horde of starving men, uprooted from their tribe and from their clan, constitutes one of the most spontaneous and the most radically revolutionary forces of colonized people." They have not yet found "a bone to gnaw in the colonial system." They are physically near the city but spiritually very far from it. Their very presence is "the sign of the irrevocable decay, the gangrene ever present at the heart of colonial domination. So the pimps, the hooligans, the unemployed and the petty criminals, urged on from behind, throw themselves into the struggle for liberation like stout working men. These classless idlers will by militant and decisive action discover the path that leads to nationhood." Truly, the last will be the first.

Fanon played many variations upon the theme of the revolt of the wretched, the eruption of colonial society, bringing to the fore the new heroic man created in and through revolutionary violence. But what after the morrow of victory? Will the heroic days of struggle not be followed by the dullness of quotidian routine? This is a persistent danger of which Fanon was acutely aware. "During the struggle for liberation the leader awakened the people and promised them a forward march, heroic and unmitigated. Today, he uses every means to put them to sleep, and three or four times a year asks them to remember the colonial period and to look back on the long way they have come since then. . . . After independence, the party sinks into an extraordinary lethargy . . . the local party leaders are given administrative posts, the party becomes an administration, and the militants disappear in the crowd and take the empty title of citizen . . ." When the revolution grows cold, its leaders tend to develop into cold and calculating monsters. Once it freezes into bureaucratic mould, it becomes but a means for the advancement of its functionaries, and the pursuit of their private pleasures replaces the heroic dedication to public revolt. But all of this, thought Fanon, although an ever present danger, is not a necessary outcome.

The revolution can be saved provided it is not halted prematurely, and provided it remains permanent. The soft life of the city must not be allowed to corrupt the new governing elites. The city, to Fanon, was always corrupting. He hated it with the traditional hatred of the peasant; it was to him the true whore of Babylon. The city represents softness and relaxation in contrast to the lean and hard energy and dedication of the countryside. Hence only geographic decentralization of power can save the revolution. Revolutionary virtue can be maintained in the village square; it will inevitably succumb to the vices of the city if power comes to be centered in the capital.

The anti-colonial revolution is primarily a revolution of the peasant people and it can maintain itself only as long as it remains rooted in that people. The party, the leaders, once arrived in power will attempt to exclude the people from participation. They will say that the people are too ignorant, that they do not understand the intricacies of political decision-making. These are self-serving lies. "Everything can be explained to the people, on the single condition that you really want them to understand . . . when the people are invited to partake in the management of the country, they do not slow the movement down but on the contrary speed it up." Hence the birth of a national bourgeoisie or of a privileged caste of bureaucrats must be vigorously opposed. The masses must be educated so that they can form the politically decisive arms of the revolution. If this is done, the nation will become a living reality to each of its citizens.

The book closes with a violent diatribe against European civilization. "Europe undertook the leadership of the world with ardor, cynicism and violence . . . Europe has declined all humility and all modesty; but she has also set her face against all solicitude and all tenderness . . . she has only shown herself parsimonious and niggardly where men are concerned; it is only men that she has killed and devoured . . . today we know with what sufferings humanity has paid for every one of their [the

Europeans'] triumphs of the mind." European civilization, Fanon argued, by its very success in taming the forces of nature, has only succeeded in dehumanizing man—colonial man in the first place, but ultimately, European man also. Hence Fanon's message, and this distinguishes him from almost all previous colonial rebels, rejects the whole heritage of Europe. He declines to accept guidance even from the West's revolutionaries. Corrupted to the core, the West can teach nothing but death of the soul. "So, comrades," says Fanon on his last page, "let us not pay tribute to Europe by creating states, institutions and societies which draw their inspiration from her." Most previous colonial revolutionaries paid tribute to the West in the very act of revolting against it. Fanon's myth involves a much more profound rejection than do the ideologies of a Ghandi or of a Nehru, a Lenin, or a Stalin. He warned the nations of the Third World that they should not create a Third or Fourth Rome, a pale imitation of a civilization, decaying at its very roots.

Spengler coined the term "historical pseudomorphosis" to "designate those cases in which an older alien culture lies so massively over the land that a young culture, born in this land, cannot get its breath and fails not only to achieve pure and specific expression-forms, but even to develop fully its own self-consciousness. All that wells up from the depth of the young soul is cast in the old moulds, young feelings stiffen in senile works, and instead of rearing itself up in its own creative power, it can only hate the distant power with a hate that grows to be monstrous." It is to prevent such a state of affairs that Fanon fashioned his myth.

If, contrary to Sorel's prescription, one compares actual accomplishments with the mythical images that Fanon set forth only a few years ago, one is brought up against the fact that the book has already dated. The Algeria of Boumedienne bears but little resemblance to the peasant democracy of which Fanon dreamed. The tough military men who now run independent Algeria presumably look at men like Fanon as ideologists whose usefulness to the regime has long been exhausted. African rulers have grown fat on resources pumped out of the countryside and they have flocked to the central cities where they build skyscrapers and airports, slavishly imitating Western models. The peasants have fallen back into the immemorial routines of traditional life styles; sometimes they are prodded into the world of modernity by tax collectors, recruiting sergeants, or party organizers. The peasants' lot differs in the various new nations, to be sure, but in none of them have they become history-making subjects as Fanon expected and hoped. Everywhere they are the subjects of historical processes over which they have, at best, only minimal control. The specific weight of the peasantry in the political life of the underdeveloped nations is low indeed and the tutelary power of the new state comes to lie as heavily on today's peasantry as European power rested upon them in the colonial past.

Fanon's picture hardly fits the reality of 1967. Yet it would be foolish to dismiss his work as a mere regressive fantasy—though it may be that, too. The myth that he has helped to create will stay alive, I believe, precisely because the reality of the new nations departs so very crucially from the image he has drawn. The peasantry does make up the great majority in these nations and this will remain so for a very long time to come. Peasant discontentment will persist as a consequence of the dislocation of traditional styles of life that the modernizing regimes attempt to institute. Fanon was quite right, of course, when he noted that the young working class and the bulk of the Westernized intelligentsia would not, as a whole, play a revolutionary role in the history of the new nations. They have tasted power or gained at least a modicum of higher standards of living, and they are most probably not willing to risk these. But it is conceivable that dissatisfied peasants may come to learn of this book in due course and make it a kind of breviary for their aspirations. Yet although the future, contrary to what Fanon believed, belongs to the city and not the countryside, the death throes of traditional peasant society will last for a very long time and may well be punctured by uprisings and revolts, a variety of peasant *jacqueries*. And even though I believe them ultimately doomed to failure, they may for a time, perhaps in alliance with disaffected city intellectuals, create large revolutionary movements. Africa may see a repeat performance of Europe's peasant revolts before it enters the new world of modernity. For quite some time to come, the new rulers of the African nations will be faced by the specter of peasant uprisings and disaffection—and Fanon's myth will haunt them, much as the Communist Manifesto and *its* myth haunted the mill owners of Victorian Europe.

In the West this book will be read for a long time and might indeed become a bible for romantic rebels and sophisticated university students in quest of primeval innocence. Jean Paul Sartre's incredibly naive Introduction gives a foretaste of what may be in store. A man who can speak in earnest about North African Arabs, of all people, "recovering their lost innocence" can believe anything—anything, that is, which feeds his anti-Western masochism.

It seems hardly necessary to say here that I consider Fanon's myth an evil and destructive vision. I find his view of violence as a healer profoundly mistaken. Violence may sometimes be necessary, but those who wield it systematically cannot help becoming brutalized by it. And this holds true for colonizer and native alike. Similarly, I think that the course Fanon charts for the new nations is not only morally dubious but politically inept and self-defeating. What I have tried here is to convey Fanon's symptomatic importance rather than engage in refutations of his views.

One must never forget while reading Fanon's book that it

was written in anguish and heartbreak, even though one might recognize in it elements of a "paranoid style" with which we have become familiar in many a sinister context. The vision that informs the book may be profoundly repellent, but we must not forget that the violence and hatred it breathes on every page is a reactive violence, a testimony to the havoc the white man has loosed upon Africa. Finally, one might hope that the myth Fanon has wrought may move some Western men to that compassion and sense of fraternity with the downtrodden of Africa that Fanon—who expected only white hatred and, at best, condescension—plainly believed impossible.

11

The Breakup of the Soviet Camp

This chapter examines changes in the relations of the Soviet
Union with its European satellites and Maoist China as they
emerged out of the social dynamics at work within these
countries. It is an attempt to illustrate that when trying to understand power relations between nations, it is not fruitful
to predict their development while assuming that internal social
conditions remain static. Rather, internal social processes,
whether or not they are a result of these external relationships, in
turn affect them in a determinate manner.

Many observers wittingly or unwittingly have assumed that
the process of domination of Russia over its satellites would
continue unchecked once set into motion. They tended
to extrapolate a trend that had become dominant in the immediate
post-war years into the indefinite future and to assume that
Russian control over its newly founded "empire" would continue
to grow. This view overlooks the fact that the very act of
domination may set new forces at work that may help undermine
it. It ignores what Pitirim A. Sorokin has called the *Principle of
Limits*. Sorokin writes: 'The causal-functional relationship between two or more variables A and B has certain definite
limits: beyond a given value of A and B it ceases to exist or
undergoes a radical change. Within certain limits the more

firmly we strike a piano key, the louder the resulting sound. Beyond this point the result will not be louder but merely a broken key board."* This seems precisely to have happened in the Soviet case. Measures of control that were adequate at earlier stages in the relations between Russia and its European satellites, proved incapable of restraining autonomist tendencies in the latter once they had achieved a certain degree of development. At a certain point, Russian attempts to continue exercising control in the old manner turned out to be counterproductive: They broke the key board.

The analysis of the relationship between Russia and China provides yet another case in point. The structure and size of a unit are interrelated so that increases in size beyond a certain limit require structural modification in its component parts if the unit is to remain viable. Russian policy-makers and Western analysts alike seem to have neglected this principle when they assumed that Russia's control over Maoist China would present no problems that were qualitatively different from those posed by the control of the European satellites. It turned out, however, that there are certain limits to the "span of control." When that span is stretched too far, and when measures leading to decentralization and devolution of powers are insufficient and inadequate, the ties of control are bound to snap—which is exactly what happened in the Sino-Soviet case.

Most analysts of the Soviet scene tended to be hampered by their imperfect grasp of the interplay between the internal dynamics of development within the satellites and their impact on the relationship with Moscow's dominant power. They tended to assume that a dominance once achieved under given conditions would continue independently of any internal change. It turned out, instead, that internal accumulations of power within the satellites led sometimes to gradual but often to quite sudden shifts in their relations with Moscow. Antagonisms that had been

* Pitirim A. Sorokin, *Society, Culture and Personality*, New York, Harper & Row, 1947, pp. 700–706.

driven underground so that, to use Dahrendorf's* terminology, only latent interests were hurt by Russian dominance, were transformed into manifest struggles of national interest once internal development within the satellites provided the basis for such a transformation. The interactive relations between Russia and the satellites was qualtitatively changed when it became obvious that it could no longer be determined by a unilateral imposition of Russia's will but only through a mutual adjustment and readjustment of their relative powers in a series of conflicts between them. Conflict now provided a balancing mechanism.

* Ralf Dahrendorf, *Class and Class Conflict in Industrial Society,* Stanford, Stanford University Press, 1959, pp. 173 ff.

THE BREAKUP OF THE COMMUNIST CAMP IN THE 1960's IS an event of world historic importance that may well rank with such crucial turning points as the break between the Western and the Eastern Church, the Reformation, or the halting of the Islamic onslaught on Western Europe in the eighth century.

Radicals and liberals tend in their analysis to focus attention upon dynamic factors, upon the change and flux of history, whereas the defenders of the *status quo* tend to think in terms of equilibria and static models. But in the face of the Soviet phenomenon, radicals and liberals, it must be admitted, have been prone till very recently to accept the static assumptions of the academic and diplomatic Establishment. This has been so with respect to internal developments within the Soviet bloc and it has been even more pronounced in regard to the relations among the nation-states of world Communism. As regards the first, many, perhaps most, commentators were influenced by the static models of totalitarianism that had been proposed by such thinkers as Hannah Arendt. They tended to think of Russia and its satellites as societies in which all major internal social forces, be they classes, associations, or communal institutions, have been eroded and undermined so that the immense tutelary power of State and Party would stand unchallenged and unchallengeable over a prostrate and atomized society. The events since the death of Stalin both within Russia and within the satellites have shattered this static model and have shown its inability to do justice to the dynamics within Soviet society. I would suggest that it is now high time that the similarly static model of the relations between the various components of world Communism be likewise consigned to the dust bin of history.

By a curious paradox both proponents and opponents of world Communism have in the past often shared a similar view of the extension of Communism on the world scene. They saw it spreading, like a huge inkblot, from the Russian heartland into wider and wider areas, and although they naturally disagreed on whether or how further expansion could be checked, neither seems to have been much concerned with locating the sources for internal contradictions and conflicts among the component elements of the Soviet bloc. Much as it had been assumed that totalitarianism once in power would put an effective stop to the play of antagonistic social forces within a society, so was it assumed that extension of the Soviet sway over previously independent nation-states would put a stop to the play of antagonistic national forces. It was somehow believed that Moscow's domination over Hungary or Rumania or China would not pose problems qualitatively different from those encountered by the Kremlin within the confines of Russia proper. This turned out to be an egregious error.

THE FORCE OF NATIONALISM

Two major reasons for the inadequacy of the static model of world Communism can be suggested: an underestimation of the forces of nationalism in the contemporary world, and neglect of problems of effective control that increasing size brings to the fore. The first error, the underestimation of nationalism, is ultimately rooted within the very foundations of Marxism. Not that Marx, and even more so Lenin, was not aware of the force of nationalism in the "transitional period" between the era of bourgeois domination and the advent of world socialism. But it would seem that Marx, in tune with Manchesterian liberal thought, felt that nationalism as an operative force in the world was bound to decline and in the long run to wither away. As the nations of the world became more securely tied to the world market, and as industrialization, even though at the price of immense sacrifices and dislocations, would create an essentially similar type of modern civilization all over the world, the forces of nationalism would gradually spend themselves. Once socialism was victorious within a number of nation-states, these states, so it was assumed, would build close fraternal bonds among themselves. The common ties wrought in the effort to build socialism would reduce national divergencies and cleavages to insignificance.

This vision, it now turns out, was utterly false. Outside the Soviet bloc, more particularly in Asia and Africa, nationalism, rather than class struggle, has assumed a central place both as an ideology and as a secular religion. The new nations in their effort to force a minimal unity out of a welter of regional, tribal, or ethnic components have seized upon nationalism as the only notion that might weld together these otherwise divergent forces within their borders. Even though, or perhaps because, modern means of transportation and communication have shrunk the globe and released tendencies that push toward global uniformities in a worldwide post-capitalist civilization, nationalism has become all over the non-Soviet world as virulent a force as it ever was in nineteenth-century Europe. And as it now turns out, the Soviet bloc is by no means exempt from this drift.

When Stalin fell heir to political power over a series of previously independent states around the rim of the Russian heartland, he evidently thought that, once Russian domination was consolidated these countries would be run from the Kremlin in a manner not qualitatively different from the way outlying provinces of Russia proper were administered. Heads of states, and top Party personnel, although nominally independent, so as not openly to depart from previous traditions on the "national question," would in fact be *Gauleiters* ultimately dependent upon and responsible to the Kremlin. Milked for resources in the first stages of reconstruction of Soviet society, they would in later stages benefit from Russia's rebuilt industrial might and gradually be brought up to the Russian level. Like other underdeveloped regions, they would be grateful for the benefits received and willing to accept the direction of the Russian Big Brother. They would bathe in the sun of their all-powerful and benevolent Moscow leaders.

This image was shattered with Tito's revolt. No irreparable harm would have come from an outright defection of Tito to the Western camp. Leninist strategy has always been flexible enough to allow for temporary setbacks. A defection to the capitalist camp by a renegade would have been comparatively easy to digest, but a heresy obstinately clinging to the major goals of Marxist-Lenin orthodoxy created permanent damage to the monolithic unity of the Soviet bloc. Tito suggested that one could be a perfectly good Communist without taking orders from Moscow. He thereby shattered the sacrosanct linkage between Communist ideology and Moscow power. He suggested that ideological dominance by the Church Fathers of the Kremlin had been used as a cloak to cover realistic power aims of the Russian state. The Kremlin was not a Third Rome, a spiritual center unifying all believers; it was in fact a hub of centralizing power that attempted to subjugate all areas it dominated to its designs. Tito, although clinging to the major orthodoxies of the faith, rejected the temporal reign of the Kremlin.

Tito could mount his assault upon the Kremlin much earlier than any of the other satellite leaders because he had come to power independently of Moscow, on the crest of a genuine national movement. In the other satellites where the Communist leadership had initially been mere satraps imposed on the population by Russian force, the process of disaffection took much longer. Yet in all of them a similar process became operative over time. As a semblance of normalcy began to return to these countries, as they gradually developed their economy and their polity, as new strata of native leaders began to replace the old

Moscow-trained personnel in Party and state, they gradually began, even though timidly at first, to develop autonomist tendencies. All these countries were, of course, run by highly authoritarian regimes in which the mass of the population was deprived of political participation. Yet even authoritarian rulers are not insensitive, it turned out, to the needs and desires of their "constituency." Once a measure of stability, and even of well-being, had been reached in these countries, once absolute misery and deprivation had given place to a condition of relative deprivation (i.e., to a situation in which the population learned to compare its lot with that of others within or beyond the Soviet bloc), it became much more difficult for the rulers to ignore the demands of the ruled. And when Khrushchev himself began to define the goals of Communism as plentiful "goulash" for the masses rather than in loftier terms, such demands for the good things of life assumed political salience. Once the Russians stressed abundance and affluence as the proximate, and perhaps ultimate, goals of a good society, it became even more difficult to ignore the insistent query of the satellite populations: "Why isn't what's good for the goose just as good for the gander?"

This is not the place for detail about the differences in the evolution of satellite politics in the fifties and early sixties. Specific historical and sociological factors account for the different speeds with which nationalist demands developed in most of them. The degree of industrialization attained, as well as the presence or formation of an indigenous stratum of intellectuals capable of articulating and formulating popular discontents, were key variables in this respect. But it seems to hold, even though there were marked discrepancies of pace between the various satellite nations, that in all of them polycentric and autonomist tendencies have now asserted themselves in a manner wholly unforeseen but a few years ago by Kremlin planners and Western commentators alike. When even as corrupt and unpopular a regime as that of Rumania dares to raise its voice in opposition to inter-bloc planning goals on the ground that they are contrary to the national interests of Rumania, a qualitative change in the relations between Moscow and the satellites has taken place.

Khrushchev tried several times to come to terms with these increasingly polycentric tendencies. Whereas Stalin had openly asserted the primacy of Soviet interests, Khrushchev soon after his accession abandoned the principle that all Communist parties be subject to the organizational discipline of the Kremlin. He urged instead that the Communist movement be reconstituted as an alliance of parties that were in principle recognized as independent equals, even though they must accept the ideological authority of Moscow. But when he stated in his report to the Twentieth Congress of the CPSU that each Communist Party must find its own road to power according to national conditions, this was not meant to apply to the Eastern European satellites. Here Khrushchev was prepared to loosen and modernize the forms of control but not to renounce its substance. Yet the crisis of Soviet authority which followed almost at once in both Poland and Hungary led the Kremlin to make further concessions. "Though unable to gain real independence," says Richard Lowenthal, "the Polish Communists won a higher degree of domestic autonomy than Khrushchev had originally been willing to grant them, and similar autonomy henceforth had to be conceded to the other satellites as well."[1]

A reversion to the earlier pattern of total Kremlin domination over the satellites seems highly unlikely. Nationalism has turned out to be an irresistible force. Monolithic ideological unity, as well as centrally-directed economic development throughout the bloc, has turned out to be a chimera. The

1. Richard Lowenthal, *World Communism, the Disintegration of a Secular Faith,* New York, Oxford University Press, 1964, p. 225.

Kremlin is now forced to let a great variety of flowers bloom within its sphere of influence. National varieties will become pronouncedly dissimilar as they adapt themselves to local climate and environment. It might not be too fanciful to expect that the drift will increasingly be toward a series of federated national states huddled together for protection under the nuclear umbrella of Russia and loosely held together by the common fear of popular revolts from within, yet otherwise following increasingly divergent paths of development. The hopes for a new Russian centralized empire bestriding Eastern, and eventually Western, Europe has turned out to be a pipedream.

THE SINO-SOVIET RIFT—THE CHINESE CASE

The European satellites strive for greater independence from Russia; the aims of the leaders of the Chinese Communist party are different. They not only wish a greater degree of autonomy, they now openly challenge the Soviets for leadership of the Communist camp.

Western commentators have in recent years been engaged in what would seem a rather Byzantine dispute on whether the Sino-Soviet rift ought to be explained by ideological factors or by claims of national interests. This seems to me a rather fruitless way of attacking the issue. Clearly national and ideological motives are intertwined in reality, even though they can be separated analytically. It is probably true that Russia's refusal to allocate as large sums of money for the industrialization of China as the Chinese seem to have initially anticipated and desired, started the divergence in the early 1950's. It is also true that the Russian's refusal to share the secrets of the atom bomb with the Chinese came to be seen by them as a symbol of the Kremlin's desire to keep them in subjection. Moreover the Russian attempt to come to a *modus vivendi* with the West raised Chinese fears of being left holding the bag. But it is also true that Sino-Soviet relations began to deteriorate rapidly when the Kremlin, after having accepted a measure of Maoist guidance in international and inter-bloc affairs during the years of upheaval of 1956–58, reverted to a policy of strict emphasis on Kremlin superiority in these matters. By 1958 the Chinese realized that they would not continue to have a major influence on the formation of international Communist policy and they also realized that their place on the Russian list of priorities was fairly low. They now began to develop a clearly distinct ideological line and to assert their claims to preponderant influence over the world Communist movement.

It is essentially correct to explain the current "left" orientation of Mao and his clash with the "right" course advocated by the Soviets in terms of differing circumstances in their respective national polities and economies. Yet one must not forget that the Chinese at times favored a relatively "liberal" line—they supported Gomulka's heresy in 1956 and veered leftward only after the Hungarian fiasco. The major differences between Communism according to Mao and the "goulash Communism" of Khrushchev and his successors can be accounted for by the different stages in the development of Communism in China and Russia respectively.

China is still in the stage of primitive accumulation. Its totalitarian rulers must squeeze from the population the last ounce of energy in order to attain the take-off stage in industrial growth as fast as possible. Hence it must foster a mentality that corresponds to the conditions within a beleaguered fortress. A fanatical purism and "puritanism" corresponds to the needs of the regime. It must again and again attempt to whip up enthusiasm and the spirit of total dedication among the party cadres and the population at large. Total devotion to the state, unquestioned loyalty to the primacy of collective purpose over individual gratification, are functional necessities of totalitarian polities in the early stages of development. And nothing can serve better to sustain total commitment to the state and unquestioned obedience to the leadership than an ideology which feeds on frenzied hatred of the surrounding capitalist world. In the Maoist canon, this world is conceived as the source of evil, sin, and corruption. Any contamination spells disaster.

This is not to say that the Chinese are necessarily at all times bent on aggression or that they are incapable of compromise when the constellation of forces seems to demand it. They have in fact shown a number of times that they are quite realistic in this respect.[2] But, somewhat like the Soviets in their early stages of development, they combine a measure of flexibility in tactical questions with rigidly held total conceptions of the world. To these puritans of the Eastern world the dichotomy between the Children of Light and the Children of Darkness is as vivid a reality as it ever was to Western puritans.

The Maoist ideology is not only peculiarly adapted to the needs of a totalitarian regime in the stage of primitive accumulation; it is also in tune with the ideological needs of many members of the intelligentsia in the underdeveloped countries. It can hence serve the Chinese penetration of the world Communist movement, especially in the underdeveloped nations. Certain intellectuals of the underdeveloped nations have come to perceive China as a have-not nation, bent, like themselves, upon industrialization in a hurry. The Chinese model can have little appeal among the working class in the industrialized nations of the West. Its insistence on fanatical devotion to the Party and the state, its puritanical bent, has little to offer to Western workers who participate or are about to participate in

2. *Vide,* for example, their acceptance of the status quo concerning the off-shore islands of Quemoy and Matsu, i.e., their giving up attempts to conquer them by force.

the benefits the affluent society has to offer. But matters are very different in the miserable circumstances in which Asian or African opposition leaders, or would-be leaders, find their countrymen eking out a meager living. Among them, the appeals of Maoism are bound to be considerable. The Chinese model suggests to many of them that through an almost superhuman act of will it may be possible to jump over a number of stages of industrial development. They have come to believe that the tantalizing slow pace of modernization that they witness in their own countries might be replaced by an immense effort in which all collective energies will be harnessed to one overriding goal: the overcoming of the sloth and backwardness of the present and the reaching of the Jerusalem of modernization and industrialization, not in an indefinite future, but on the morrow.

It stands to reason that Russia has much less to offer to these men than has China. They increasingly perceive the Russians as a *have nation.* Russia's current problems are of no relevance to them. Her preoccupations with attaining Western standards of living, with enjoying the fruits that almost fifty years of deprivation has made them long for, are far removed from their own hopes and desires. They are "out of phase" insofar as Russia is concerned.

THE RUSSIAN SIDE—SIZE, CONTROL, AND SYMPATHY

A major clue to the Sino-Soviet rift can be found in the twin notions of "relative size" and "span of control." Structure and size are interrelated. If men, for example, were to attain the size of elephants, major anatomical modifications would be required to allow them to function. It is absurd to suppose that organisms, be they social or biological, can just grow indefinitely. There always comes a point where a reorganization of the relationships of the component parts is necessary if the unit is to remain viable.

Historians are familiar with the problems of the ancient empires of the East which, be it in China or the Middle East, had always to contend with centrifugal forces undoing the work of the central power. The whole history of these empires is marked by revolts, breakoffs, and "feudal" tendencies at the periphery. Yet the lesson learned in these cases seemed, until recently, not applicable to modern empires such as that of the Soviets. Modern means of communication and transportation, it was held, provided the means of control denied the rulers of ancient empires. The problem of size could be overcome, so it seemed, in an age in which an order from the Kremlin's nerve center could be almost instantaneously transmitted to its Far Eastern dependencies. This view has now turned out to be short-sighted. Just as in the case of the earlier Wallace-Willkie vision of One World, it confused technological with political and sociological possibilities. The fact that you can now circle the globe in a day or two does not necessarily bring an Indonesian "nearer" to an American; similarly the fact that the Kremlin can now reach any party functionary in the bloc on the long distance phone does not make for greater "nearness" between Mao's party and the Soviets.

What seems involved here is the notion of the "span of control." As the executives of major American corporations know very well, once a certain size has been attained, total control from the center becomes an impossibility, and a measure of decentralization is functionally necessary. In the Russian case, although the span of control might still be stretched to include the whole of the Soviet Empire proper, it cannot be lengthened also to include a gigantic new territory such as China, which, moreover, faces problems totally different from those of Russia at the present.

What was said earlier about nationalism in Eastern Europe and its opposition to Russian domination applies *a fortiori,* to the Chinese. They are a major nation, not a relatively minor satellite, and, moreover, they came to power on their own, not by the force of Russian bayonets, as did all East European satellites except Yugoslavia. In addition, they were, when Mao won power, in a stage of economic development much lower than that attained by nearly all East European satellites. This meant that much vaster resources would have had to be mobilized by Russia were China to be brought up to the Russian level within a relatively short span of time, as the Chinese of course desired. This would have meant gigantic Russian investments in China and a corresponding slowing down in the Russian growth rate. And this, the Russians refused to do.

Fraternal aid to weaker and less developed brother nations, was, of course, a fundamental tenet of Communist philosophy. But when tested in practice it was soon found to be wanting. Here a nation related to that of "span of control" would seem to be applicable. I propose to call it "span of sympathy."

It is a familiar fact that even persons of liberal and humanitarian sentiment tend to be less affected by catastrophic events occurring far away than by those nearer home. Protestations of pan-human sympathies notwithstanding, I take it to be a common phenomenon that Americans are less affected by news of a flood in India than they are by similar news from Ohio. And it is probably true that to the Easterner a disaster in California is less "visible" and less "felt" than would be a similar disaster in New York. Distance, both geographical and cultural, affects the sense of sympathy and identification. Hence, one is more likely to make sacrifices for an afflicted neighbor than for a faceless victim in far off lands. The "span of sympathy" is even narrower than the "span of control."

I take this process to be operative in the relations between the Chinese and the Soviets. In the Russian population at large, but also among the policy-makers, Chinese problems necessarily rated lower than problems nearer home. Russia was indeed willing to contribute economic and technical help to Mao, but it was not willing to tighten the belt at home in order to assist the Chinese who were geographically and culturally very far away.

This general tendency could only be reinforced at a moment in time when Khrushchev had whetted the appetite of Soviet citizens for consumer goods, when visions of affluence began to dance before their eyes. The Russian policy-makers had proclaimed this new "goulash" vision of Communism precisely because they felt an increasing pressure from their "constituents." When they had liquidated Stalin's terroristic means of control and replaced them with more "liberal" versions, it became essential for them to deliver the goods—at least some of the goods. The Chinese claims on their scarce resources thus came at the worst possible moment. Not that they did not now have more resources than at earlier stages in their development, but that the claims upon these resources made by the Russian population at large had become so much more insistent.

Aspirations toward a better life seems to me one of the two pillars of the political conscience of the New Soviet Man. Fear of war is the other. The Chinese could only be seen as threats in regard to both. Mao made "exaggerated" claims to scarce and valued Soviet resources and at the same time suggested policies that endangered the precarious peace. The belligerent stance of the Maoists must be deeply unsettling for Russian policy-makers and population alike. Just when Russian society is discarding the messianic features that marked earlier Soviet history, just when the average Russian citizen—and also the apparatchik—sees a chance to relax a bit in a new-found Victorian comfort, the Chinese seem to be saying that atomic war is but a paper tiger. Just when the Russians are predisposed to arrive at a number of accommodations with the West, the Chinese appeal for a new crusade. No wonder that the Sino-Soviet rift has reached a stage where basic agreements, if not temporary accommodations, are no longer probable or even possible.

The Russians might now develop more understanding for the businesslike matter-of-factness of the "capitalist" world than they have for the fanatical egalitarianism and the puritanical crusading spirit of the Chinese. "Who would benefit from a new war?" a Russian recently asked a foreign correspondent. "Our cities and our new towns would be destroyed, America and Europe would be devastated. But the Chinese do not have much to lose insofar as industry is concerned, and even with immense numbers of dead and wounded, there would still be enough to inundate the world."[3]

PROSPECTS—THE WORLD COMMUNIST MOVEMENT

Were world Communism a purely ideological movement, or were it solely an association of nation-states having political and economic interests in common, one might envisage its perpetuation, though with some major modification, into an indefinite future. The fact is, however, that it is neither. An "ecumenical" coexistence of variant ideological orientations is only possible in regimes in which ideology is not directly tied to the exercise of political power. Such, however, is emphatically not the case in any of the Communist countries. They are all Caesaro-Papist regimes in which priestly (ideological) power is subordinated to worldly (political) power, but where secular authority needs the buttressing of faith in order to maintain legitimacy. The clash of national interests between Russia and China is now so intertwined with the clash of creeds that co-

3. *Daily Telegraph*, October 12, 1963.

existence within a common political or ideological framework seems practically unattainable. Temporary accommodations are possible, even probable; the underlying rift can no longer be bridged.

If the differences between the Chinese and the Kremlin prove ineradicable, as I assume and as the respective historical actors also seem now to assume, then it stands to reason that both sides will accelerate their drive toward gaining allies within the Communist parties of the Third World and the West. I have already stated that the Chinese are likely to be relatively successful in mobilizing allies in the underdeveloped nations. They are likely to be relatively unsuccessful, however, in the industrialized and developed areas of the Western world. Here they will find support only among marginal groups of disaffected students and intellectuals or among especially alienated sectors of uprooted working-class or middle-class groups still susceptible to messianic appeals. The bulk of the working class, however, being by now not only within but also, though to different degrees, of society, will not provide fertile ground for them.

Nor will the Western Communist parties continue to be passive instruments of the Kremlin. The partial emancipation of the Eastern European satellites has had an impact on the West European Communist leaders. They too now feel that they must adjust if they are not to lose their "constituency" to the new forces operating in the "post-capitalist" modernized welfare states of the West. Chiliastic dreams do not appeal to a working-class youth bent on hedonistic pleasures, but neither do the old slogans with which Stalin's Kremlin nourished the imagination of earlier generations of European Communists. Since the death of Stalin and Khrushchev's revelations, since the Hungarian events and the Sino-Soviet split, the Western Communist parties have become orphans in an alien world. They are now engaged in the painful process of mapping the new territory into which they have suddenly been propelled by forces they only imperfectly understand.

It seems likely that the Western Communist parties, slowly shedding their dependence on Moscow directives, will now attempt to reintegrate themselves into the constellation of political forces within their own nation-states. To the new generation of Communist leaders of the West, Peking has little appeal but Moscow can no longer be the Third Rome either. There remains only the hope to play a more significant role within the national polity. We can expect in the years to come efforts on the part of the Communist parties of Italy, France, and of other Western nations to adopt a more flexible policy. Even at the present time, the Italian Communist party is groping toward an autonomist course, relatively free from Moscow guidance, and with its ears cocked to the internal developments of Italy rather than to the winds of doctrine blowing from Moscow. Belgian trends are similar. The French party is more rigid, but one notices the gradual emergence of parallel tendencies within its ranks.

This increasing "national" development of the various Western Communist parties will in the long run force other leftists to assess anew their relation to them. Léon Blum was quite correct when he asserted before World War II that the Communists were not oriented toward the left but toward the East, but this characterization is not likely to be applicable fully in the future. As the revolutionary potential in the West will further diminish, as the leaders of the Communist parties in the West come to feel that continued reliance on Moscow, continued acceptance of Kremlin tutelage, must fatally decrease their effectiveness at home, it is likely that they will try to become part of the legitimized and institutionalized political dialogue at home. It would seem futile and self-defeating for the non-Communist Left to then refuse such a dialogue with them. The time might come, though it will not be tomorrow, when the orphans of Western Communism might have to be welcomed back to the house of Western democratic socialism.

It is, of course, obvious that for something like this to happen, these Communist parties will have to undergo a fundamental self-transformation. Not only will they have to reject publicly their previous unconditional subordination to Soviet authority, not only will they have to convince their adherents and potential partners alike that their goals are from now on to be carried out within the framework of democratic rules, but they will also have to change the very structure of their organizations. The centralistic and totalitarian form of organization that marked these parties in the past was originally justified by the need to forge an instrument for the revolutionary road to power and to ensure disciplined obedience to the Kremlin's orders. Once the Communist parties give up these goals they will have to restructure their organizational means. And it is only when they have done so that they can be acceptable as partners by other political forces on the left. "We must expect resistance against organizational change to be tougher than on any other issue," writes Richard Lowenthal. "Here, not only the vested interests of the party machines are at stake, but ultimately the distinctive character of the Communist parties itself—their 'being' as distinct from their 'consciousness.' "[4] This is why it would be foolish to expect them to change *in toto* at once. The process is likely to be painful and long drawn out. Yet it would still seem likely that in the long run the Western Communist parties will abandon the Bolshevik organizational structure. They will then come to resemble militant left socialist parties having organizational forms adapted to a non-revolutionary

4. Richard Lowenthal, "The Prospects for Pluralistic Communism," *Dissent,* Winter 1965.

situation in which their only hope can be to win a share of power as partners of other left forces within the framework of national democratic politics.

Two parallel Communist movements will from now on exist in the world. The Chinese-oriented movement is likely to have considerable appeal among the underdeveloped nations, though the Russians will not surrender, without a struggle, ideological and political influence within these countries. In the developed nations, on the other hand, Peking's chances of attracting more than relatively unimportant strata of alienated intellectuals and marginal elements are slim. Here the previously Moscow-oriented parties will maintain themselves against their Chinese competitor, but it is likely that they will succeed in doing so only at the price of further emancipation from Moscow directives and of basic ideological and organizational changes. The ground for messianic and chiliastic visions or for reliance on a Third Rome no longer exists in the West. To the degree that the Western Communist Parties reenter the political dialogue within their nation-states they will be pushed further from dependency on Moscow or Peking.

The days when many on the Left might harbor apocalyptic visions of the Coming Victory of World Communism are definitely gone. World Communism is now irredeemably split into two antagonistic camps. In the West, moreover, the Communist parties are definitely caught by the drift toward a desacralization of politics. True Believers, messianic and chiliastic prophets, will no doubt continue to peddle their wares, but the bulk of the Western working class has lost its appetite for the Second Coming, even as its appetite for worldly goods has increased.

There is now a chance for the Socialist left, about to be relieved from the Communist incubus that fatally hampered its movements for two generations, to embark anew on its effort to build a more democratic and fraternal society upon the foundations the welfare state has provided. Will it be able to take advantage of this second chance? It is hard to know. One thing seems certain: As the heavy mortgage of Communism is about to be lifted, new failures can no longer be attributed to the impact of world Communism. As the promised World Empire has fallen heir to the clash and contentions among warring kingdoms, the forces of radical democracy and socialism have won a breathing spell—it will depend on them whether they make use of it.

12

The Dysfunctions of Military Secrecy

This final chapter differs from the rest in that it does not limit itself to analysis but moves on to make recommendations for policy.*

I have endeavored in the past to distinguish clearly between my scholarly and my political writings, even though I may not always have been successful in this respect. I believe that Max Weber was essentially correct when he urged with a great deal of vigor that science as a vocation and politics as a vocation referred to different types of calling—even though one person, like Weber himself, might be strongly drawn to both. The value neutrality that Weber advocated may never be fully realized in practice; it would seem, rather, that he described what mathematicians call an asymptote, that is, a curve that can be continually approached though never reached. But the attempt to implement value neutrality, even if it is bound not to be fully successful, seems to me a moral imperative imbedded in the very ethos of science.

There exist, nevertheless, instances in which it would seem

* An earlier version of this paper was presented to the *International Arms Control Symposium* held at the University of Michigan, December 17–20, 1962. I wish to thank my colleague Robert S. Weiss, of Brandeis University, who read the earlier version and made a number of helpful suggestions which I have incorporated in this paper.

legitimate to deal at one and the same time with the realm of the "is" and that of the "ought." There are situations so extreme that they seem to warrant at least momentary relaxation of self-imposed restraints. I believe that the current dangers of an atomic holocaust have created such an extreme situation. Hence I have deliberately employed in this chapter both the rhetoric of analysis and the rhetoric of advocacy.

The concrete policy proposal suggested in the following pages, the abandonment of a policy of secrecy on the part of the major powers and its replacement by a policy of disclosure of all national secrets, is likely to be viewed as utterly utopian by most hard-headed policy-makers. My answer here again would follow Max Weber's lead when he wrote: "Certainly all political experience confirms the truth—that man would not have attained the possible unless time and again he had reached out for the impossible."

ONE OF THE MOST STARTLING PARADOXES ADVANCED BY that master of the sociological paradox, Georg Simmel, runs as follows: "The most effective prerequisite for preventing struggle, the exact knowledge of the comparative strength of the two parties, is very often attainable only by the actual fighting out of the conflict."[1] In other words, the most effective deterrent to violent conflict is the revelation of comparative strength; however, relative strength can often be ascertained only through such conflict.

This paradox arises from the fact that in contentions for national or international power, as distinct from, say, economic competition, no clearcut index of strength is readily available. In economic transactions, money functions as a measure of available resources; in contrast, for power contentions "no medium of exchange could be devised which would bear the same relation to estimates of fighting power as monetary metals [bear] to estimates of economic value."[2] Money can serve as a common denominator to express many dimensions of economic values such as quality, quantity, scarcity. But military strength is multidimensional. Military power consists not only of the number of men in the armed forces and those who can be devoted to war indirectly; it is also dependent on military equipment presently available as well as on the potentialities for future production of such equipment. It depends on the totality of economic resources that can be mobilized. Furthermore, the relative strength of the contenders can hardly be measured by such objective factors alone: The number of military personnel and the quantity of military hardware is given value only by the willingness to

1. Georg Simmel, "The Sociology of Conflict," transl. by Albion W. Small, *American Journal of Sociology,* 9 (January, 1904), p. 501. Cf. the discussion of this in Lewis A. Coser, *The Functions of Social Conflict,* New York, The Free Press, 1956, pp. 133–137.

2. Harold D. Lasswell, "Compromise," in *Encyclopedia of the Social Sciences,* New York, The Macmillan Company, 1930, Vol. IV, p. 148.

fight and the willingness to utilize resources. Finally, strength may well depend on the issues at hand. Just as in many species animals will fight harder to defend the bit of land they are using as a base than to invade another animal's land, so nations may fight harder, or mobilize more effectively, in relation to vital issues than in relation to peripheral ones. And, of course, there will be a hierarchy to the extent to which a vital issue is truly seen as a life-or-death matter.

Thus, not only do we deal here with multidimensional factors, but with motivations and attitudes that are difficult to assess before they have been converted into actions. Under such conditions the contenders may be strongly tempted to engage in violent conflict to test their respective strength. In other words, relations in which unambiguous measures of relative strength are not available contain a higher probability of the use of violent trial through battle than of the use of other mechanisms of conflict resolution. This fact seems independent of the causes and conditions that define the substance of the conflict, such as contentions for power or resources, or ideological dispute. The manifest issues over which conflict arises can in principle be resolved by a variety of means ranging from violence to mediation or bargaining. I wish to claim, however, that no matter what the specific causes of the conflict, indeterminacy in the assessment of the strength of opponents increases the likelihood that violence rather than other means of resolution will be resorted to by the opponents.

Of course, a state is unlikely to go to war if it perceives its power to be obviously smaller than that of its enemy. Even though power cannot be accurately assessed, very large discrepancies of power can be readily perceived. This is why the chances of attack of the United States by, say, Mexico in the twentieth century are exceedingly small. But when contenders feel that their power is more or less evenly matched, then, given their common inability to gauge their relative strength more precisely, the temptation is strong to engage in trial through battle.

When antagonists make estimates of their respective power, it is the perceived power, not the actual power, that is important in shaping their policy. Therefore, misperceptions of the power of the other side may seriously contribute to faulty policy decisions. One may *overestimate* the adversary's powers. S. F. Huntington has noted, for example, that: "in 1914, for instance, the Germans estimated the French army to have 121,000 more men than the German army, the French estimated the German army to have 134,000 more men than the French army, but both parties agreed in their estimates of the military forces of third powers."[3] The recent clamor about an alleged "missile gap" between Russia and the United States provides another example in point. But one may also *underestimate* the power of the antagonist, as did Hitler with respect to Russia and England. In such cases the lack of accurate knowledge, the discrepancy between perceived and real power, has profoundly destabilizing effects on the relationship and leads to disastrous policy decisions. In most of these cases, the actual power of the contenders in relation to each other became clear only during and after the fight.

A high measure of pluralistic ignorance is built into any conflict situation in which there do not exist single indices of strength, such as monetary values. Although such indeterminacy spurs the readiness to engage in violent conflict, the reverse must be considered also. If it is felt that only violent conflict can resolve the indeterminacy, each party in the preparation for the

3. S. F. Huntington, "Arms Races," in *Public Policy, Yearbook of the Graduate School of Public Administration, Harvard University, 1958*. Edited by Carl Friedrich and Seymour Harris, Cambridge, Harvard University Press, 1958, p. 54.

conflict will tend to maximize secrecy about its own strength, thus further increasing the indeterminacy and making the outbreak of violent conflict even more likely. Thus, built-in ignorance of the strength of the antagonist is not the only factor to be considered; the adversaries also deliberately *increase* the ignorance of their antagonists.

The withholding of information about one's power and capability is one of the most frequent and effective defenses available to powerholders. To the extent that the outsider can be prevented from gaining full knowledge of one's real strength, to that extent one maximizes one's power over him. Secrecy has been traditionally one of the major instruments of the men of power. "Everywhere," says Max Weber, "that the power interests of the domination structure toward *the outside* are at stake, whether it is an economic competitor of a private enterprise, or a foreign, potentially hostile, polity, we find secrecy."[4]

Furthermore, secrecy has often an asymmetrical significance. It may be of greatest importance to the potentially weaker party. Hitler hid the extent of his weakness when he was weak in 1936, but used as much publicity as he could to communicate how strong he was in 1939. In fact, secrecy becomes an element in the manipulation of one's image as an adversary. One leaks out what one wants to leak out and keeps under wraps what one doesn't want the adversary to know.

The fact of having secrets may not in itself be as destabilizing as the fact that *if* one has secrets the enemy does not know whether to believe or not to believe one's pronouncements, and finds it difficult to evaluate the probable outcome of a clash.

Secrecy protects from observation, it shields the powerholder, and this ability to keep the adversary guessing is a major weapon in his armory. But this very secrecy also contributes to

4. *From Max Weber*, Transl. by H. H. Gerth and C. Wright Mills, New York, Oxford University Press, 1947, p. 233.

lack of stability in as far as it makes relative appraisal of power more hazardous.

There seems to be no way out from the impasse. In order to avoid violent action it is necessary that the parties to the conflict have at their disposal adequate information about their relative strength; yet the very lack of adequate indices for measurement of such strength, as well as the tendency of the contenders to use secrecy as a weapon, seem to make it impossible for them to resolve the conflict in a peaceful way. If there is to be bargaining, the cards must be on the table. But in the situation that I have sketched, both sides always have some of the cards up their sleeves.

But let us imagine that both contenders have become aware of the fact that any conceivable outcome of a violent conflict between them will without doubt redound to their mutual disadvantage. In such a case, in a situation in which it has become impossible to achieve national objectives through armed clash, the dysfunctions of secrecy become especially salient. This is particularly so if the *avoidance* of armed conflict should become itself an aim of national policy. Arguments against the maintenance of secrecy then acquire a weight that they may not necessarily have under other circumstances.

Suppose that both are aware that their struggle, far from being a zero-sum game in which one wins what the other loses, is in fact one in which there is no payoff at all for either party. In such struggles the very notion of winning and losing is no longer applicable. In all previous wars the situation was essentially the same as that in the Westerns we can see on TV screens every night. The "equalizer" of the Old West made it possible for *either* man to kill the other; it did not assure that *both* would be killed.[5] But this is precisely the outcome that both

5. This example is borrowed from Thomas C. Schelling, *The Strategy of Conflict*, Cambridge, Harvard University Press, 1960, p. 232.

adversaries have to envisage now. If any result of the conflict can only be a situation in which the survivors envy the dead, strategies that applied to other types of conflict have ceased to be applicable.

In situations in which the most probable outcome of violent conflict is destructive of the very values and aims of *both* contenders, rational and prudent strategy would seem to require that both turn toward the search for solutions that maximize their common chances of survival. In such situations both have a common interest in the avoidance of violent conflict and such avoidance becomes a problem to be solved by each of them. Their common interest in avoiding the struggle must lead them to search for means of falsifying Simmel's prediction. They are mutually dependent in the very pursuit of their otherwise antagonistic goals.

This situation seems to have something in common with a condition discussed by economists in which the optimum output of a pair of competitors can only be reached if both parties, instead of simply attempting to maximize their own utilities, cooperate in developing a set of norms specifying that the utility of one is to some extent dependent on the utility of the other. Maximum joint utility in such situations can only be reached if both develop an ethic in which the concern for self and for other are of equal weight.[6] This is approximately the case in a

6. Cf. Anatol Rapoport, *Fights, Games, and Debates,* Ann Arbor, The University of Michigan Press, 1960, pp. 71 ff. Prof. Rapoport also provides a discussion of what among game theorists has come to be known as the Prisoners' Dilemma. It may be useful to spell this out here.

The situation, simply, is that two men are arrested for a crime and not allowed to communicate with each other. The same proposition is made to each: (a) if neither confesses they will be judged guilty of a minor offense and get three years; (b) if both confess they will be judged guilty of a major offense and get ten years; (c) if one confesses but the other does not, then the one who confesses will get off scot free and the other will have the book thrown at him and will get twenty years. In this

situation in which both contenders are aware that the outcome of a struggle between them will be disastrous for both of them. Hence the joint utility of searching for means of refraining from struggle must, in this case, take primacy over the pursuit of individual utilities that are unattainable.

In situations in which the respective parties conduct a conflict to maximize their individual utilities, they have a powerful incentive to hide their capabilities from potential adversaries. But the problem is very different if the joint utility of avoiding violent action is to be pursued. Since the probability is high that indeterminacy of power relations will lead to a trial through battle, only the overcoming of this indeterminacy can insure against the outbreak of violent conflict. Therefore both sides must be concerned with keeping the potential adversary fully informed of their respective strength so that the indeterminacy of the system is reduced as far as possible. If both sides want to avoid violent action, they must both be strongly motivated to replace the strategy of secrecy by a strategy of disclosure. Their common interest now leads them to accept rules allowing them to assess their relative strength without engaging in violent struggle. Their joint interests require that their power positions be communicated unequivocally so that trial through battle is no longer necessary. Full disclosure of one's own strength

---

situation we may reproduce the thought processes of prisoner *A:* "I do not know what *B* will do, but let me examine the possibilities. If he does not confess and I do not confess, then I will receive three years. But if he does not confess and I *do* confess, I will go scot free. So, if he does not confess, then I am better off if I do confess. Now let me consider what will happen if he does confess. If he confesses and I do not confess I will receive twenty years. If he confesses and I do confess, as well, I will receive ten years. Therefore, if he confesses then I am better off if I also confess. Then either way, I am better off if I confess." However, Prisoner *B* must also go through this thought process, if he is a good game strategist, and so it must happen that both prisoners confess and receive ten years. They cannot maximize their joint utility without agreement *and* trust.

allows the adversary better to assess relative strength, and hence increases the chances that adjustments can be made through bargaining rather than through violence. It might still be objected that if A is informed of an Achilles' heel in the position of B, this will be an incentive for A to strike. My counter-argument would be that if both are convinced that violent conflict is a joint disutility to be avoided, then if B knows that A knows his weakness, this will be an incentive for B to come to a peaceful settlement which corresponds to their relative strength of the moment. In such a situation B will consider it most rational to concede a point to the adversary while proceeding to prepare for elimination of the present Achilles' heel in order to be in a better situation in future bargaining. Furthermore, though secrecy may indeed afford some protection to the weaker party, it also may work against that party. To the extent that one party is prevented from assessing the relative strength of the other it may engage in a policy of "insurance buying," that is, it might build up a measure of armed might which would be superfluous had it an adequate knowledge of the other side's capabilities. In this way secrecy may indeed increase the vulnerability of the initially weaker party and make the power differential between the two greater rather than smaller.[7] This is what seems to have happened in the American-Russian case in the last few years.

The assessment of relative power is not complete when the adversaries are provided with certified knowledge of their respective military strength. They also need to know under what circumstances the adversary is willing to fight. They need to know which types of events have a symbolic value that would induce the other party to transform his war-making potentialities into warlike action. The signposts for violent action are

7. Amrom Katz "Secrecy and the Dilemma of Inspection" paper read at the International Arms Control Symposium, the University of Michigan, Dec. 1962, makes this point.

likely to differ according to the social structure of the antagonistic camps. Whereas in one social system the crossing of a
particular line of demarcation or the erection of a missile base
near its borders may be sufficient to activate a warlike response,
in another system very different sets of circumstances, say an
attack against the political system of an allied nation, may set
off the will-to-fight. If this is so, it stands to reason that both
parties must engage in a cooperative effort to disclose to the
other as fully as possible those events that would move them to
violent action. Disclosure of *intents* must accompany disclosure
of strength. Here again the main problem is to make the statements as credible as possible. Both sides must bend their efforts
to persuade the other that they are not merely bluffing. How can
this be attained?

It would seem that disclosure to the potential enemy of
variant plans of action that decision-makers habitually prepare
for various contingencies would constitute the best means of
conveying to the adversary the extent of the commitment to
risk a war. If in the Cuban events the Russians had had access
to the advance plans of America with respect to Russian missile
bases in Cuba, if they had known that such missile bases were
not acceptable to American decision-makers, be it because of
their real or their symbolic value, there would have been no
need to go to the brink of war through drastic demonstrations
of our will-to-fight. In this area also, just as in the cases discussed earlier, full disclosure will help decrease the uncertain-
ties that might lead antagonists to attempt a trial through battle.

NEW STRUCTURES OF COMMUNICATION

A strategy of disclosure involves more than a different way
of doing things: It involves a different structure of communications. If we are to find means that serve to relay information to
an adversary in reliable fashion, we must maximize the chances

that the messages he receives will be taken by him to be credible. Statements made by A about his strength and capability must be communicated to B in such a way that they are believed.

The need for a measure of disclosure is, of course, by no means a new problem that arises only out of the present atomic stalemate. Really secret arms can by definition never be of use as a deterrent. Hence military men have always advocated a balance between disclosure and secrecy. They have thought it necessary to divulge certain types of armaments so as to deter potential adversaries, while keeping others secret so as to keep them guessing. Thus maneuvers or air shows to which foreign military observers are invited are meant to inform them of one's armed strength. And often a kind of tacit cooperation between powers allows each to gather at least a certain amount of information otherwise unavailable. One might surmise that Russian acquiescence in American monitoring of Russian launchings and tests, at least from the outside, falls into this category.[8]

Yet the strategy of disclosure that is envisaged here goes beyond such limited measures. It depends on a much wider opening of channels of information, a full unblocking of lines of communication between the antagonists. If such a policy is adopted, it is of central importance to devise special means of relaying information about one's full strength, means that are so convincing to the receiver that he will not fail to act upon them. Suppose that each side has indeed arrived at a decision to abandon its previous strategy of secrecy and to engage instead in a strategy of disclosure. There would still remain the problem of making this credible to the other side.

A few years ago, Leo Szilard suggested that "in a state of virtually complete disarmament, neither the United States nor the Soviet Union would have any military secrets. In these circumstances America and the Soviet Union might choose to per-

8. Cf. Katz, *Ibid.*

mit each other to employ plainclothes inspectors, whose identities are not known, as the simplest way to convince each other that there are no evasions."[9] This suggestion to transform the traditional spy system into a mutually accepted reciprocal intelligence network has considerable merit even before complete disarmament has been reached.

The employment of spies to pierce the cover of secrecy with which the adversary surrounded himself has been an age-old tactic in the strategy of warfare. However, the credibility of the messages received through such spy systems has been a perennial problem for intelligence officers. As any reader of spy stories knows, many of the messages transmitted by spies, though they contained most valuable information, had little if any effect because they were simply not believed by the receiving party. A person receives a message in a predisposed state of mind, with sets of beliefs based on prior experience. If the message clashes sharply with this prior state of belief it is very likely that it will be disregarded and will hence fail to influence future courses of action. Only those messages that seem credible to the receiver have meaningful consequences. In other words, the receiver will rank-order incoming messages and act only upon those which seem to him to contain a high degree of probability.[10] In the world of spies and counterspies, with conflicting messages crisscrossing each other, much that is objectively correct information will nevertheless be discarded as improbable. Spy systems, then, have a relatively low capacity to communicate information that can be acted upon. Roberta Wohlstetter's fine history of *Pearl Harbor*[11] provides a host of pertinent examples. Even though

9. Leo Szilard, "Disarmament and the Problem of Peace," *Bulletin of the Atomic Scientists, 11* (October, 1955), p. 302.

10. Cf. Colin Cherry, *On Human Communication*, New York, John Wiley and Sons, 1957, pp. 245–250.

11. Roberta Wohlstetter, *Pearl Harbor, Warning and Decision*, Stanford, Stanford University Press, 1962.

we had broken Japan's secret codes, Washington still proved unable to forestall the Japanese attack on Pearl Harbor. The gap between knowledge and action was never closed.

Following Szilard it may now be suggested that in the new situation which has been sketched, the adversary's inspector should be highly welcome to his antagonist and the information he conveys should therefore carry much higher credibility. To again quote Szilard:

> Today an American agent operating in Russia is a spy who serves the interest of America as well as his own interest; he does not serve the interest of Russia. But when the proper agreement has been concluded, the plainclothes inspector operating on behalf of America on Russian territory serves the interest of Russia, as well as of America, for he is but the means chosen by Russia to convince America that it is indeed disclosing all its capability.[12]

Karl Deutsch recently suggested a related measure in a somewhat different context when he urged an agreement for the mutual or international registration of all scientific and technical personnel. He wrote:

> Professional inspectors might then be able to make sure . . . of the whereabouts and the accessibility of scientific personnel. The agreement might then explicitly protect the scientist's freedom to travel and gossip—two propensities which have long been the despair of security officers—and any attempt on the part of any country to conceal the whereabouts of its scientists, to keep them inaccessible to inspectors, or to interfere with their freedom of travel and communication, might serve as prima facie evidence of bad faith. . . .[13]

12. Szilard, *op. cit.*
13. Karl W. Deutsch, "Communications, Arms Inspection, and National Security," in *Preventing World War III, Some Proposals,* ed. by Quincy Wright, William M. Evan, and Morton Deutsch, New York, Simon and Schuster, 1962, p. 68. Cf. also T. C. Schelling, "Arms Con-

The more freely the scientists talk and gossip the more credible the contention of their government that no valuable information is being withheld.

An invitation to representatives from the opposing camp to participate in key meetings of military and political decision-makers would be another means conducive to making knowledge about one's intentions credible. Military attachés of the opposing power should be given full access to hitherto "top secret" files so as to facilitate to the utmost their ability to gauge correctly the other side's intentions. When the uncertain and contradictory knowledge hitherto gathered through spy systems and by military attachés is replaced by certified knowledge and a strategy of full disclosure, one moves from a highly unstable system of interaction to one in which the antagonists, to be sure, are still hostile to each other, but are disposed to engage in bargaining rather than in trial through battle in order to achieve their differing goals.

This is not the place to enumerate in detail the great varieties of proposals for the reduction of pluralistic ignorance between potential enemies that have been advanced in recent years. These range from the monitoring of troop movements or suspicious explosions to systems of inspection by specialized personnel or by ordinary people. My concern here is only to stress that any and all of such measures, to the extent that they serve to make available credible information to the antagonists, will serve to reduce the area of uncertainty in their dealings with each other and will allow accumulation of reliable information about relative strength—which is the precondition for rational bargaining.

Before such bargaining is discussed in some detail, two pertinent matters need still briefly be alluded to. 1) When I refer

trol: Proposal for a Special Surveillance Force, *World Politics,* 13 (October, 1960), pp. 1–18.

to a strategy of disclosure I am under no illusion that *everything* pertinent to an adversary's strength will ever be disclosed. This is so for the simple reason that the adversary himself will never be in possession of all the relevant knowledge about his *own* strength. What is not fully known cannot be fully communicated. When I hence speak about full disclosure this has to be taken in a relative rather than an absolute sense. It refers to a maximum of disclosure rather than to exhaustive information. 2) Several studies, such as Wohlstetter's book on Pearl Harbor and a series of studies now being conducted under the direction of Prof. Robert C. North at Stanford,[14] indicate that in a number of historical cases foreknowledge of military inferiority proved no effective deterrent to attack. "With all the necessary economic and military data to predict their own defeat, the Japanese never seriously considered restraint in the pursuit of territorial expansion, with which they identified 'national honor.' "[15] These are cases, then, in which the nonrational elements lead to decisions that would have been eschewed had purely rational considerations prevailed. There is at present no warranty that rationality will indeed be the sole or even the major criterion influencing future decision-makers when they choose between war and peace. All that can be claimed is that the very awesomeness of such choice in our age will maximize the chances that reason prevails, and that reduction of secrecy will in itself lead to a powerful enhancement of rational as against irrational decision-making.

During the Agadir crisis of 1911, the French premier, Caillaux, called in his chief of staff, Joffre, and said: "General, it is said that Napoleon only gave battle when he thought that he had at least a 60 per cent chance of victory. Have we a 70 per

---

14. Cf. the special issue, "Case Studies in Conflict," *The Journal of Conflict Resolution,* 6 (September, 1962), ed. by Robert C. North.

15. Wohlstetter, *op. cit.,* p. 357.

cent chance of victory if the situation drives us into war?" Joffre replied: "No, I do not think we have it." Thereupon Caillaux said: "That's good. We shall then negotiate."[16] This attitude exemplifies the uses of rationality in decision-making. The reduction of secrecy and the policy of disclosure advocated in these pages attempts to maximize the chances for such rational action.

BARGAINING UNDER CONDITIONS OF MAXIMUM DISCLOSURE

Let us assume that both parties approach a condition of maximum knowledge about their respective power. Perceived power then approximates actual power. The cards are on the table. This does not resolve the conflict between the two sides —they are still contending for realistic issues, power, territory, influence, or ideas—but it provides a setting in which the conflict is divested of the collective anxiety that arises in both camps from guessing—instead of knowing—about the relative balance of power. This is the point at which nonrealistic conflict tends to give way to realistic conflict. The distinction between realistic and nonrealistic conflicts involves a distinction between conflicts as ends and conflicts as means.[17] Conflicts which arise from frustration of specific demands and from estimates of gains of the participants can be called realistic conflicts, insofar as they are means toward attaining a specific result. Nonrealistic conflicts, on the other hand, are primarily occasioned not by the rival ends of the antagonists, but by the need for tension release of at least one of them. Since nonrealistic conflict is occasioned by the need for release of tension and affords relief through the acting out in the conflict, it

16. *Mémoires de Joffre*, I, 15f. as quoted by Alfred Vagts, *A History of Militarism*, New York, Meridian Books, 1959, p. 335.
17. Cf. Coser, *op. cit.*, pp. 48–55.

admits of no functional alternative. The conflict *is* the goal. In realistic conflict the situation is different: here there exist functional alternatives as to means. Means other than violent conflict, depending on assessments of their efficacy, are always potentially available to the participants.

In realistic conflicts, the weighing of the cost of alternative means of action is a major component of the decision-making process. If disclosure of the adversary's capabilities reveals that the costs of engaging in violent action are likely to be prohibitive, such means will be abandoned and replaced by other means of conflict resolution. Furthermore, if it is realized that there can be *no* payoff for *any* of the participants in an outbreak of violence, there is all the more reason to seek for functional equivalents to war. If this is the case, the atomic age may paradoxically present a most hopeful feature. In no other age was it likely that *both* parties would under *all* circumstances feel that going to war would maximize disutilities for *both* of them. The atomic age maximizes the chances that bargaining rather than violent conflict will be the mode of adjustment engaged in by both adversaries.

In collective bargaining, the common interest of both parties leads them to accept rules that enhance their mutual dependence in the very pursuit of their antagonistic goals.[18] Collective bargaining requires that *some* agreement be reached between the parties. Hence, no party is independent of the other since it cannot attain its goals without the other. Each side is dependent for the achievement of its own goals upon the maintenance of a working relationship with the other. A student of the bargaining process in labor-management relations, Neil W. Chamberlain, describes this process in terms which seem applicable here and bear quoting:

18. Cf. "The Termination of Conflict," in this volume.

The coming together of union and management . . . arises not because of any sympathetic regard for the other, or because of a voluntary choice of the other as a partner; it arises from the absolute requirement that some agreement—*any* agreement—be reached, so that the operations on which both are dependent and which give to both their functional significance may proceed. This represents the striking of a working relationship in which both agree, explicitly or impliedly, to provide certain requisite services, to recognize certain seats of authority, and to accept certain responsibilities toward the other. Without such an agreement there could be no operation.[19]

In the bargaining relation both attempt to maximize their own interests and each party secures its interest in the measure of its bargaining power. Each party wrests from the other the maximum advantage possible by using all legitimate means at its disposal yet both parties have an overarching interest in maintaining the relation and in coming to *some* agreement.

Compromise is the very stuff of bargaining relations. In a compromise, each party agrees to scale down some of its initial demands and modifies its initial perceptions of what would constitute "victory" or "defeat" in terms of what it can attain within the bargaining relationship.[20] Bargaining and compromise may never in themselves permanently settle the terms of the relationship. Whenever there is a change in the relative power position of either contender, they will have to enter into new bargains to settle their accounts. Bargaining, in other words, is a resolution mechanism, but it can only help to solve problems as they appear within the constellation of forces given at any particular moment. Yet it may be suggested that a

19. Neil W. Chamberlain, *Collective Bargaining,* New York, McGraw-Hill Co., 1951, pp. 445–446.

20. Cf. "The Termination of Conflict,"; Lasswell, *op. cit.;* and Robert C. North *et al.,* "The Integrative Functions of Conflict," *The Journal of Conflict Resolution,* 4 (September, 1960), pp. 355–374.

continued bargaining relation is likely to broaden in the long run the area of common values and common sentiments. The more habitual the recourse to bargaining and compromise, the higher the chances that both parties slowly move toward a measure of integration. In integration, "new alternatives 'are accepted of such a kind as to render it extremely difficult to discern the balance between concessions made and concessions received."[21] The true integration of two desires—in contrast to their compromise—signifies "that a solution has been found in which both desires have found a place, that neither side has had to sacrifice anything."[22] The world powers are very far indeed from such a condition, yet we can dimly discern it in the future providing they follow the road of bargaining and compromise in the settlement of disputes.

21. Lasswell, *op. cit.*
22. Mary Follett quoted in North, *op. cit.,* p. 371.

Index